NEO-AFRICAN
LITERATURE

NEO-AFRICAN LITERATURE

A History of Black Writing

by Janheinz Jahn

translated from the German by
Oliver Coburn and Ursula Lehrburger

Grove Press, Inc., New York

To the memory of
LANGSTON HUGHES

CONTENTS

9

NOTE

Each chapter is followed by a bibliography showing the primary literature and the most important secondary literature. The literary works listed in my *Bibliography of Neo-African Literature* (André Deutsch, London and Frederick Praeger, New York, 1965, see p. 284) are here given only by their numbers in that bibliography, where all bibliographical details can be found. Works not appearing in that Bibliography are listed here with their bibliographical details.

The statements of sources refer to the section of bibliography which follows each chapter. Where there are several works by the same writer, the year of publication or the title is added.

The abbreviations in the bibliographical parts of this book agree with those used in my *Bibliography of Neo-African Literature*: A = autobiography; Anth = anthology; B = biography; Es = essays; Lyr = poetry; Nar = narration or tale; Nars = narrations or tales; Ro = novel.

PART ONE

Introductory

Chapter 1

DEFINITIONS

1. 'From the Rubbish-Heap'

Some time in the first half of the sixteenth century there was a Franciscan monk in a Lisbon monastery, who wrote racy dramatizations of legends about the saints, under the name of Chiado–the Portuguese called such pieces '*autos*'. Having run away from his monastery, he led so dissolute a life that he was eventually arrested, to await punishment from his Superior. He wrote some verses pleading for mercy, but received a scathing answer from the Superior's lay secretary, also a literary man, a certain Afonso Álvares: Álvares called him a 'Friar Rottenshell, a cask of Bacchus' ('*frei mexilhão . . . feito vasilha de Baccho*'). In his fury Chiado responded from his cell by hammering out savage five-liners against his fellow man-of-letters, castigating him as 'a mulatto sprung from the rubbish-heap', i.e. a bastard.

This Afonso Álvares was born and bred in the palace of Don Afonso of Portugal, the Bishop of Évora. He was married to a saddler's daughter, had children, and acted as occasional secretary and schoolteacher; he earned his main income, however, by turning out 'autos' on commission from the Franciscans. Three of these, which appeared in print between 1613 and 1639, are still extant; but they do not show any of the rich humour of his model, Gil Vicente, nor even the bold characterization in the 'autos' of his enemy Chiado.[1] Nothing in the style or content points to his African mother, and it is only from the quarrel with Chiado that we know of his origins. He is the first author of African descent I have discovered who wrote literary works in a European language. Does this make him the first author of 'Neo-African Literature'?

To answer that question, I must begin by explaining what the term 'Neo-African Literature' is intended to convey and why I have had to introduce it.

15

2. World Literature and National Literatures

The end of colonialism does not mean merely redrawing the political maps of Asia and Africa. The independence of the countries outside Europe which were formerly colonies is far from being only a political phenomenon; it tends to find expression in all spheres of life, especially the cultural sphere. If a true partnership is to be reached, the values hitherto centred on Europe need to be re-appraised. For each member of a partnership should try to under-stand every other member on the basis of the fellow-partner's values – instead of taking his own standards as universally appli-cable.

Literature is no exception. Even today it is still taught classified by languages, a handy method of classification which was justifiable enough until the beginning of this century. Literature was national literature, the nation from a literary point of view was identical with the area where the language was used. Switzerland's literature in German was considered part of a national German literature, long before the idea came up of a unified German state. On the other hand Rousseau the Swiss belonged to French literature; while Conrad the Pole was one of the lights of English literature. The language in which an author wrote, in fact, showed his spiritual home and his sphere of action. The only works to be regarded as 'world literature' were those which acquired importance outside their language areas – getting translated into other languages.

The term 'world literature', therefore, by no means included all the world's literature, in the way that national literature included all literary works in a national language. To say that a work belonged to world literature was to say that it had somehow made its mark in the literatures of other countries; and the only works in the world's literature which ranked as 'world literature' were those which became known outside their own language areas. European nations, however, had close contact with each other, so that many works crossed the linguistic frontiers, gained a reputation in neighbouring countries, and were in due course promoted to the rank of 'world literature'. To achieve the same distinction, an important work written in a non-European language depended on three factors: first, a European to discover it; second, a European who knew the language well enough to translate it; and third, the luck to find favour with the prevailing taste in Europe.

This meant the exclusion from 'world literature' of Indian epics which were translated into the languages of Tibet, China, Japan, Burma, Malacca and Java, unless they were noticed by one of the few European scholars in these languages; of masterpieces in Arabic which were admired in the Sudan, East Africa, India and Indonesia, simply because they were beyond European translators; and of Chinese 'social novels', simply because their realism was considered lascivious by the European taste of the time. Admittedly in the basic conception of 'world literature', all national literatures, even those still unknown, were to be equally considered: Goethe, who originated the term, saw 'world literature' as a 'great fugue', in which 'the voices of different peoples gradually make themselves heard'. But Europe felt she was the conductor, entitled to decide on key and beat, and also to exclude from the choir those who sang in exotic tones outside her comprehension.

A good German encyclopaedia published around 1900 shows how far the idea of 'world literature' was concentrated on Europe. In a survey of 'world literature' it listed 1,100 names, of which only fifty-seven (not counting the Biblical prophets) were non-Europeans: three Turks, twelve Persians, twenty-two Arabs, fifteen Indians, five Chinese. No work of ancient Egyptian literature was included, nothing from the early civilizations of the rest of the Near East – although the Book of the Dead had been published in Europe as early as 1848, and the cuneiform scripts had been deciphered since early in the nineteenth century. The authors listed were neatly divided according to national literatures: under the heading of 'England' the only North Americans we find are four humorists, one of them Mark Twain. Melville and Walt Whitman are missing, although the latter is mentioned in the article on American literature; but he was not in the 'world literature' league! The only American poet named is the romantic poet Gonçalves Dias from Brazil.

So the European 'educated' public around 1900 saw 'world literature' as confined to Europe, save for a few works from the Near and Far East emerging mysteriously from the past like golden pagodas, and a little laughter from America ringing out across the Atlantic. The rest of the world contained 'folk poetry' – a literary desert, in fact, with extremely modest blooms.

Admittedly in 1778–9 Johann Gottfried Herder, the German poet and critic, had published his *Stimmen der Völker in Liedern* (the People's Voices in Song), expressing his view that poetry had been given to all the world, and was not 'the private heritage of refined and educated men'. But since then the universalism of the early romantics had been generally discarded, and Herder's ideas on the subject were no longer accorded any importance.

Meanwhile Europe had extended her political power over the countries of the 'primitives' in their literary desert. Sometimes she unwittingly destroyed the continuity of their oral poetry, and did not recognize the damage inflicted until decades later, when it was often too late to pick up the pieces. Europe had also taught literacy, carried her languages and her models into distant countries, and created the basis for a new written literature which could later on become a medium for collecting indigenous traditions.

The first break in the principle of classifying literature by language occurred with English, as North American literature began going its own way. At the beginning of the nineteenth century this was only considered a valuable part of English literature where it gained attention and approval from the British public. But after the Civil War of 1860–5 some authors sought their literary roots not in Europe but in the oral story-telling of the pioneers and frontiersmen, who used everyday speech and expressed America's changing consciousness; such authors were looked on as a fringe phenomenon of debatable value. The Americans themselves, for all the popularity of their native authors, continued for a long time to defer to European judgement. Decades later, in the twentieth century, they gradually discovered that their literature had a tradition of its own. When an overseas literature breaks away from Europe, it gains its independence through finding such a tradition, whether based on specific experiences in history or on a non-European spiritual heritage; and it will still be independent even if it goes on using a European language.

North American literature, then Latin American, then other literatures too broke away, to be distinguished no longer by their language but by their specific traditions. In the view of some writers and literary critics, however, the growth of modern movements in Europe which have transcended linguistic frontiers (naturalism, expressionism, surrealism etc.), combined with the spread of European languages in other continents, has worked, and will increasingly work, against the development of independent literatures in those continents: indeed these people tend to regard all locally tinged literature as inferior and 'provincial'.

Marxists, for instance, and those influenced by Marxism, believe that the means of economic production determine literary style, and that with the growth of technology in Africa, European styles like surrealism are bound to be adopted there too. French existentialists, starting from different premises, have the same sort of idea; while the English version, still held by some missionaries and others, is that with education, Christianity, etc., the style of ex-'savages' will become 'civilized', i.e. a copy of each European pattern.

But these strange and rather arrogant views assume that industrialization and technology, or Christianity and 'civilization', will level out all cultural life and do away with all separate traditions of style and thought. Although a common European nightmare about industrial civilization, such an assumption is refuted by the continued existence of creative writers in an industrialized society. For, even if sometimes unwittingly, creative writers are defending a wealth of historic common traditions: e.g. originality and individuality of expression, experiments with form, commitment to particular causes, and the right to private dreams.

All these are traditions central to European civilization. Real poets will never devalue their art by writing 'poetry off the peg'. In non-European cultures as well, the more industry expands, the more creative writers – who are civilized in the true sense of the word – will resist alike the temptations to produce cheap, stereotyped work and the domination of a literary 'establishment' from Europe or anywhere else. And as these creative writers have to defend traditions and values which are different from those of the West, their poetry too will continue to be distinguishable from Western poetry.

3. The Cultures of Africa

Africa is a geographical, not a cultural term. There are two different cultural areas, with different histories and traditions: on the one hand North Africa, and on the other what is variously called 'Negro Africa', 'Black Africa', 'non-Islamic Africa' and 'Africa south of the Sahara'. The peoples in these two areas have had all sorts of relations with each other over thousands of years, yet the differences between them have remained. North Africa today is part of the Islamic cultural area, which has spread into the Sudan, an area of a different culture – where the two together have produced a variety of hybrid forms.

The other area has no satisfactory name. 'Black' or 'Negro' Africa is an expression of racial geography, which one can only use with reluctance, since it implies the idea of identity between culture and race. Besides, 'Negro African' culture and 'Negro Africa' have for some centuries ceased to be identical. On the northern borders of 'Negro Africa' there are many Negro Africans who are now part of

Islamic culture; and for another thing, it is 'Negro African' culture, not 'Negro Africa', which has spread to the New World. 'Non-Islamic Africa' is equally inexact, for north of Islam's southern borders there are many peoples only partly Islamic or not Islamic at all. 'Africa south of the Sahara', a clumsy periphrasis at the best of times, avoids racial connotations, but is not exact either: the frontier between the two dove-tailed cultures does not coincide with the Sahara (in the Sahara itself there are non-Islamic groups among the Bideyat and Zaghawa). One is also in difficulties for an adjective–'sub-Saharan African culture' sounds still more ungainly.

Everyone knows, however, what is meant by these unsatisfactory phrases: the area or culture of the peoples living partly in the Sahara but mostly south of it. They form one of the main races of mankind, they have had a separate history since ancient times, they have developed specific cultures in their comparative isolation, their values largely coincide, they speak languages which according to the latest research all belong to the Congo-Kordofanian family (Greenberg), and they inhabit the land-mass extending in ancient times south of Libya into the unknown. On his map of the world Ptolemy, the Egyptian astronomer and geographer, gave this land-mass the name 'Agisymba'.

No one has yet been able to discover the origin or meaning of this name: it is presumed to have meant either the Highlands of Tibesti or the Lake Chad region or the countries south of the Equator. In Ptolemy's time Africa meant only the coastal strip on the Syrtis Minor (Gulf of Khabs), i.e. the modern Tunisia. To the west of that were Nubia and Mauritania, to the east Cyrenaica, Libya and Egypt. South of these countries, already in the desert, were Gaetulia, Phazania (Fezzan), Ethiopia and Numidia. All the unknown area farther south was Agisymba–and no doubt Ptolemy had good reasons for calling it that.

I should like to follow him, but appreciate that British and American readers would be unhappy with the world 'Agisymba' and its adjective 'Agisymbic', so these terms will not be used in the English-language editions of this book. I hope, however, that they may one day become acceptable. Meanwhile, as a *pis-aller*, one can make do with 'Africa south of the Sahara' and 'sub-Saharan', or in many contexts 'Africa' and 'African' for the same complex. Readers will know what I mean, and will remember that I should have preferred to use 'Agisymba', 'Agisymbic' and–for the people living there–'Agisymbians', as I have done in the German and French editions.

4. The Literatures of Africa

Africa's traditional literature is oral. But since Africans began coming into contact with Arabic and Western cultures, they have produced written literary works; at first only a few did so, but afterwards a great many. Former slaves who somehow ended up in Europe or America were writing in European languages as early as the sixteenth and eighteenth centuries. With the establishment of mission schools in Africa, written literary works have been produced there too, in both European and African languages, since the beginning of this century (for figures see Appendix).

As I said above, literature today can no longer be classified by language, since European languages and Arabic have spread beyond their traditional areas. But literatures cannot be classified geographically either, for geography does not provide literary categories. An African literature which, geographically speaking, would include in one group North Africa, sub-Saharan Africa and the Boers of South Africa, would be bringing together more contrasts than similarities, and would ignore the close relations between Africa and the Caribbean, between North Africa and the Near East. Such a classification pays no regard to culture, history or style, and so has nothing to do with literature.

Nor, finally, can literature be classified by the authors' complexions or birth-places, which are also categories outside literature. For years I have been fighting against phrases like 'Negro literature', '*littérature noire*', '*littérature des noirs*'; for those who use such terms are expressing a conviction, perhaps unconsciously, that the colour of an author's skin is enough to decide the literary family he belongs to. This would mean that the works of a black-skinned author, who happened to be born in Portugal, who grew up in a purely Portuguese environment, lived there most of his life and wrote Portuguese plays—must belong not to Portuguese but to something called 'Negro' literature. In the works of Afonso Álvares, however, there is nothing to suggest a style or pattern of literary expression different from the Portuguese styles and patterns of his age. Without the quarrel with Chiado nobody would know he came from Africa, nor would anyone think of connecting him with anything but Portuguese literature. He may or may not be the first Negro author in Europe; for the literary works he produced it made no difference.

Literatures can only be classified by style and by the attitudes revealed: more precisely, by studying the individual works, analysing their styles and attitudes and grouping them accordingly, then fitting them into a tradition of similar styles and attitudes. You cannot hope to place literary works in their right 'families' without investigating these features; nor, without analysing a particular work, can you find out which literature it belongs to.

Africa's written literature originated in the 'overlap' area of three cultures, the African, the Islamic-Arabic and the Western. The literature from the area where the African and Islamic cultures overlap, I shall call Afro-Arab; the literature from the area where the African and Western cultures overlap, I shall call neo-African.

Neo-African literature, then, is the heir of two traditions: traditional African literature and Western literature. A work which shows no European influences, including not being written down, belongs to traditional African literature, not neo-African. The boundary between the two is easy to draw: it is the boundary between oral and written literature. Conversely, a work which reveals no African stylistic features or patterns of expression belongs to Western, not neo-African literature, even if written by an African. Although theoretically simple, the distinction is hard to make in practice, for it assumes that the styles, patterns of expression and attitudes produced by Africa's traditions are well known. But they are not—for scholars have neglected this field (see Chapter 4).

In my book *Muntu* I sketched some of the stylistic features, patterns and attitudes which spring to the eye in the poetry of 'Negritude'. African authors and poets, for instance, use magical, incantational images, pay more attention to rhythmic than to dramatic structure, and 'speak in imperatives' (see Chapter 15). Some critics have imagined that I regarded such points as the only African stylistic features, etc. that there were, and made them the sole and indispensable criteria for including a work in neo-African literature—as if I were setting myself up as a literary high priest or commissar, who insisted on a particular style from Africa's writers and would excommunicate them from neo-African literature should they be guilty of heretical or 'deviationist' work.

But a writer must always be free to write as his inspiration bids him. Historians of literature cannot hold him to a set of rules, and no one should expect them to do this. They will naturally analyse afterwards the style that authors have used, and describe those writers' work accordingly. In 1957, when I was writing *Muntu*, the Negritude school dominated modern neo-African literature, and those criteria applied to that school. Critics today who accuse me of generalizing, can refer to other works, especially those of the Nigerian school, some of which contain different attitudes and stylistic features; but in 1957 none of those works had appeared. When considering a living literature like the neo-African, historians of literature must expect to be deepening and widening their observations all the time.

They must find out the ingredients of the 'Africanism' which prompts us, when referring to most of Africa's modern works, to talk not of English, French or Portuguese literature in Africa, but of African literature in English, French or Portuguese. So we have to investigate which ideas and stylistic features come from particular African traditions, and which do not. We must examine the work, say, of a Yoruba author writing in English, not only for the modern ideas it contains and the influences of English models, but also for the stylistic features and patterns of expression which come from oral Yoruba literature in the Yoruba language.

It will not do, for instance, to consider Tutuola's *The Palm-Wine Drinkard* as merely a fantastic tale, and trace back its symbolism to psychological and mythological archetypes, through parallels with Dante, Gilgamesh, Orpheus, Yggdrasill, etc. (Moore),[1] which the author himself had certainly not had in mind. Tutuola's source, everyone agrees, is the oral Yoruba tradition, and he is closer to it than the author Fagunwa, who wrote in the Yoruba language and influenced him. So Tutuola's symbolism must be examined also in the light of the Yoruba tradition.

But oral literature has not yet been subjected to literary analysis, which makes such investigations much more difficult. Still, we do not need to ask about *all* the 'bush spirits' and their meaning, but only such a question as: in what connection does Tutuola's bush spirit 'Red Lady' appear in traditional poetry, and what function does it have there? And if we find a particular rhythm, we must ask: does this rhythm occur in the tradition, and what function does it have there? So we do not need to know the whole rhythmic system of oral poetry, desirable as that might be. This method, however, may well be the best first step towards understanding the literary forms of the oral tradition.

With an African writer writing in a European language, it would be superficial to assign him to Western literature simply because his works show no 'Africanisms' which can be recognized as such at first sight. To decide where writers should be placed, the investigations referred to above are indispensable—I would gladly have undertaken them myself, but have not had the means at my disposal. Until they are completed, many African and Afro-American authors are only 'under suspicion', as it were, of possibly belonging to neo-African literature. So there are many writers mentioned in this book who are under that 'suspicion'.

An introduction to neo-African literature, in fact, is neither a complete history of this literature nor a conclusive study of its styles; a great deal of further research is needed before works of that sort can be carried out. The purpose of the present book is to point out the problems and classify provisionally the material to be analysed: I shall try to classify this material according to its content and some of its recognizable stylistic features and patterns of literary expression.

REFERENCES AND BIBLIOGRAPHIES

1. 'From the Rubbish-Heap'

[1] cf. Sayers pp. 22–4.

ÁLVARES, Afonso: Auto de San Antonio feito a pedimento dos mui honrados e virtuosos conegos de S. Vicente: mui contemplativo em partes e mui gracioso, tirado de sua mesma vida. Lisboa: Por Vicente Álvares 1613.–Evora: Por Francisco Simões 1615–. Lisboa: Por Antonio Alvares 1639.–Lisboa: Por Domingos Carneiro 1659.–Lisboa: Na Officina de Bernardo da Costa 1719.– Lisboa: Na Officina Ferreiriana 1723.– Porto: Na Typ. de Revista 1859.
–Auto de Santa Barbara Virgem e Martyr. Lisboa: Por Vicente Alvares 1613.–Evora: Por Francisco Simões 1615.–Lisboa 1719.– Lisboa 1786.–Lisboa: Por Francisco de Sousa 1790.–Porto: Typ. de Revista 1859
–Auto de S. Thiago Apostolo. Lisboa: Por Antonio Álvares 1639
(RIBEIRO, Antonio): Obras do poeta CHIADO [pseud.], colligidas, annotadas e prefaciadas por Alberto Pimentel. Lisboa 1889
SAYERS, Raymond S. The Negro in Brazilian literature. New York 1956 (O negro na literatura brasileira. Rio de Janeiro 1958.)

2. World Literature and National Literatures

HERDER, Johann Gottfried: Herders Sämmtliche Werke. Ed. by Bernhard Suphan. Vol. 25. Berlin 1885 (Stimmen der Völker in Liedern)

3. The Cultures of Africa

GREENBERG, Joseph H.: The languages of Africa. The Hague, 1963
LEITHÄUSER, Joachim G.: Mappae Mundi. Berlin 1958
SCHNABEL, P.: Text und Karten des Ptolemäus. Leipzig 1933

4. The Literatures of Africa

[1] Moore, pp. 46 ff.

IDOWU, Emmanuel Bọlaji: Olódùmarè. God in Yoruba belief. London
1962
JAHN, Janheinz: Muntu. An outline of neo-African culture. London
1961; Muntu. The new African culture. New York 1961
–African literature. Article in 'Présence Africaine', English edition,
vol. 20, Paris 1963 (originally published in the French edition of
No. XLVIII, 1963); Extract in: African literature and the universities, ed. by Gerald Moore. Ibadan 1965
MOORE, Gerald: Seven African writers. London 1962
TUTUOLA, Amos: The palm-wine drinkard. London 1952 (Nos. 599–
605)

Chapter 2

EARLY WRITERS OF AFRICAN DESCENT

1. Pre-Islamic and Early Islamic Romances

Although we do not know for certain, there were probably Africans who wrote in hieroglyphics, and some also, presumably, who wrote in Phoenician and Greek script. The first African writers, however, whose works have come down to us, used the Arabic script.

The relations of the Arabs to Africa are older than those of the West: the knowledge of Arabic script spread over North Africa with the triumph of Islam, afterwards penetrating into the Sudan and the countries on the East African coast. Two African languages, influenced by Arabic, Hausa and Swahili, became written languages, eventually producing a written literature. Moreover, Arabic was used by all Afro-Arab authors later on (when they, like the Afro-American authors, had lost their mother-tongues), and by a number of the authors writing in the areas of Islamic influence. For religious and historic texts Arabic played a similar role to that of Latin in medieval Europe.

Not much is known about the Afro-Arab writers, and hardly anything about the Afro-Iranian and Afro-Indian ones. Here, I think, is a wide and unexplored field for research. Cedric Dover is probably right when he refers to the 'tremendous influence' of the Africans in India, and goes on: 'Modern "African Studies" will never flourish until they are linked with "Oriental Studies". And this means gaining perspective by pursuing the considerable story of the Negro in Arabic and Persian. The time has come for Negro learning to look more to "the East" than to "the West".'[1]

At any rate Afro-Arab literature begins with a poet whose place in Arabic literature is like Homer's in the West. The oldest extant anthology of Arabic poetry are the seven *Mo'allaqât* (Golden Odes), the poems 'raised to a place of honour because of their exquisiteness': those already acknowledged as masterpieces in pre-Islamic times and as such suspended in the Kaaba at Mecca. One of the poets of the *Mo'allaqât* is 'Antar Ibn Shaddad al 'Absi, often known in English as

Antar, of whom the Orientalist Brockelmann writes: 'He was the son of a black female slave called Zabība. This blemish in his birth, however, he redeemed by his personal courage. He fell in a battle against the Taiyi' tribe. His memory as the most popular Arab hero still lives on today through the *Antar Romance* and in many place-names. Although his art, which we know chiefly from his *moʻallaqâ*, is that of a typical Bedouin poet, it already shows some modern features.'[2]

According to Wilfrid Scawen Blunt, the English traveller and poet, of the seven 'Golden Odes' the one which Antar wrote is 'perhaps superior to any of its rivals', for 'of all the pre-Islamic poets Antara... has gained the widest celebrity.'[3] In his *moʻallaqâ*, which has been translated into many European languages (four times into English alone), the poet sings his own praises, as was customary at the time.

After the conventional introduction (nasīb) he describes the charms of his beloved, his life as knight and his heroic deeds. His beloved, as appears from verses 6–8, belongs to a hostile tribe:

'Among my foes, like lions wild, I came to her abode.
To thee, beloved, Makhrem's child, I had no easy road.
When first we met, I found thee fair, though I thy kindred slew.
Now by thy father's life, I swear, my love for thee is true.
My heart is thine own dwelling now, that heart thou hast
    possessed

And in it, never doubt me, thou shalt stay its dearest guest.'[4]

In verses 13–17 he expatiates on his beloved's mouth:

'Thy heart, Antara, she did tear, those lips so sweet and chaste,
So ravishing a kiss they bear, so honey-sweet the taste.
When on thy lips I plant a kiss, O lovely damosel,
Thy mouth exudes a fragrant bliss like sweet musk perfume's
    smell.

Or like some pleasant garden's scent, with air of pure serene,
A peaceful place that few frequent and gentle rains keep green.
The morning clouds with showers abound, but frostless and
    benign,
That small round puddles in the ground like coins of silver shine.
Such copious rain the skies bestow, and every eve anew
The stream with nought to check its flow comes gushing swiftly
    through.'[5]

In verses 34–6 he portrays his own character:

'Thy veil thou droppest in my sight, yet, Abla, I can tell
Of many a fully armoured knight who captive to me fell.
Thou shouldst bestow on me the praise which fairly may be paid,
For mild and gentle are my ways when none my rights invade.
But if with injury I'm faced, then is my grievance strong,
Bitter as colocynth the taste to them that do me wrong.'[6]

Then he praises his virtues, his generosity and hospitality towards friends, his heroic courage and the terror he inspires in his enemies. The poem ends with the wish that he may succeed in killing the sons of his enemy Demdem as well as their sire:

'One fear with me doth still remain, that I should die before
Demdem's two sons are overta'en by adverse stroke of war.
Men who had slandered my good name, though I'd done them
   no ill,
And though from me no quarrel came, had vowed my blood to
   spill.
Ah yes, they injured me indeed, but I their sire did slay,
A carcass left for lions' feed and aged eagles' prey.'[7]

Antar died in A.D. 615. He is thus the first author of African descent we know who wrote in verse. But besides his famous Ode he wrote many of the thousand and more poems which are spread over the *Antar Romance*. Here is a translation of one of them:

'Before the spearmen's deadly thrust she tried to rouse my fears,
As if I were defenceless and unarmed against their spears.
I answered her, "Now surely death is no more than a pool,
And some day I must drain the cup dipped in its waters cool.
So fare thee well, care for thy young, and tell thyself once more
That I'm a man who's either making love or making war.
Privation many nights and days I easily can bear,
Knowing that in the end I'll gain of noble food my share." '[8]

The *Antar Romance* has Antar himself as its subject. His deeds, his fame, his chivalry, made such an impression on his contemporaries that a great many tales of adventure soon became attached to his person. Narrators of his life story created a style of their own and were so specialized in their subject that they were called 'Antarists' ('Anātira; singular 'Antarīyya). So in the course of time an immense work grew up in verse and prose, which was finally written down by the famous philologist, Asma'i (740–830), who brought up the second son of Haroun al-Rashid. In fact Hammer-Purgstall, the Viennese orientalist, and Cedric Dover have concluded on psychological grounds that Asma'i put the collection in writing on the order of this son, Haroun al-Rashid's successor, Abdallah al-Ma'moun, who was a great patron of Greek philosophy and science, and whose own mother was a coloured slave.

Some of Antar's verse, and many poems in the *Romance* which are probably his, contain allusions to his African origin. 'Antara,' writes Dover, 'could not escape, in a genealogically-minded society, the triple stigma of being black, illegitimate and once enslaved'.[9] The *Antar Romance* is thus 'the first classical work concerned with colour prejudice'.[10]

Asma'i's record has not survived. The oldest manuscript of the *Romance*, which has presumably been expanded again, comes from Abu Muwajjid Muhammad ibn al-Mujalla al-'Antari, a name which means that this man, a doctor who practised in a town on the river Tigris in the first half of the twelfth century, assumed the epithet of 'most important Antarist'. The *Romance* appeared in print from 1865 to 1877 in Beirut in sixteen volumes, from 1866 to 1870 in Bulak (in Arabia) in thirty-two volumes.

Hammer-Purgstall wrote of it: 'This is the work, and not, as is generally supposed, the *Thousand and One Nights*, which is the source of the stories which fill the tents and cottages in Arabia and Egypt.'[11] He put an abstract of the work into French, while Terrick Hamilton translated the whole Syrian edition into English. Dover says that this translation must have extended to 'twelve unreadable volumes',[12] although the *Monthly Review* in 1820 said that Hamilton 'executed his translation with spirit and elegance'.[13] Whatever its merits or otherwise, only four volumes were actually published.

Hammer-Purgstall also wrote an article in English referring to the work's social and cultural importance: 'Without a knowledge of Arabian chivalry that of the European would be imperfectly comprehended. For the former is the root, from which the chivalrous spirit of the Middle Ages in Europe grew up into a wide spreading tree ... the very spirit and the substance of chivalry, and its romantic stories, migrated with the Arabians from the East, through Spain to Europe.'[14] The British Orientalist Clouston remarked in 1881: 'It is far from improbable that the famous *Arabian Romance* of Antar furnished the model for the earliest of the regular romances of chivalry which were current in Europe during the Middle Ages'.[15] In 1903 his compatriot Blunt said that *Sirat Antarah* was 'the most important of the oriental originals on which some of our own Christian romances of the Middle Ages were founded'.[16]

Antar was the first but by no means the only Arabic poet of African descent. I will name only two more. One is Abū Dulāma Ibn al-Djaun, who as a poet in Baghdad was received at court by the Caliphs al-Mansur and al-Mahdi, and died in 777. Brockelmann calls him 'buffoon' and 'court jester', and writes that he was 'a bad Muslim', but his verse was 'very witty'.[17] The other poet is Ziryāb (Abū 'l-Hasan Ibn 'Ali Ibn Nāfi), who became known as 'Black Nightingale', was banished owing to the jealousy of his Baghdad master, Haroun al-Rashid, and after many adventures came to Spain in 822, to the court of Caliph 'Abd al-Rahman II. There he introduced the latest refinements of the East, such as a new hairstyle with a fringe, eating asparagus, and the use of cut-glass table-ware; he died in 852. The American Arabist Nykl writes of him: 'It would require a whole volume to describe Ziryab's enormous contribution to the evolution of Andalusian music and the art of singing. His work was continued by several of his children.'[18]

2. Juan Latino, a Renaissance 'African'

We do not know whether Africans in ancient times used the Roman alphabet, but it is possible. The first dark-skinned creative writer we know by name who did so is Afonso Álvares, the 'mulatto from the rubbish-heap', who lived in Lisbon in the first half of the sixteenth century. But he was a Portuguese citizen born in Evora, whose life shows that at that period there was no racial prejudice: his illegitimate birth was the point Chiado used in order to score off him.

Admittedly the slave trade from Africa to America became official in 1517 with Charles V's concession to Flemish merchants; but slaves were not yet dishonoured merely by their status–it was a fate which might befall Christian and heathen, European and non-European. The idea in particular that people with dark skins were predestined to slavery was still new at the time; if anything, there was a tendency to believe the opposite. For 781 years the Moors had ruled over Spain, with nobles who were sometimes very dark-skinned, with centres of classical learning much finer than any in the West; the brilliance of their rule had not yet faded in Europe's memory, and had made Europeans imagine 'Moors' as mostly rich, chivalrous and extremely cultivated. We are still reminded of this today by the representations of St. Maurice and King Balthazar in the paintings of that era and by characters like Othello. In the eyes of his Spanish contemporaries, the really splendid thing about Juan Latino's career was that after the *Reconquista* they could vaunt among themselves, and to the finally vanquished Moors, the example of a 'home-made', Christian, Moor.

Probably born in Guinea in 1516, Juan Latino came to Spain in 1528 at the age of twelve. Ocete in his treatise published in 1925 asserts that Juan must have been born in Spain, because an uneducated slave could not have acquired so much education; but we may believe Juan and his contemporaries when he writes: '. . . hic scriptor nec fuit orbe satus, Aethiopum terris venit . . .'[1] (this author was not born in the region, he came from the country of the Ethiopians).* His mother and he were slaves in the household of Doña Elvira, daughter of Gonzalo Fernández of Cordoba, one of Spain's most famous generals, the 'gran Capitán'. In 1530 Doña Elvira moved with her household from Baena to Granada; Juan was then fourteen. In Baena he had had to fetch the first school-books for the third Duke of Sessa, Don Gonzalo Fernández, son of Doña Elvira, who was eight years his junior. He not only fetched the books; he read them, joined in the lessons, and, being much more talented, became his young master's tutor, learning Latin and Greek with him at the Cathedral School and later at the newly founded University of Granada.

Juan was so outstanding at Latin that he renounced his slave-name Juan de Sessa and called himself Juan Latino. In 1546 he became Bachelor of Arts. Soon he was known throughout the city for his scholarship, but also for his quick wit, pranks and fine voice. He played the organ, lute, guitar 'and other strange things' (*y otras cosas curiosas*),[2] perhaps African ones. The doors of the most elegant *salons* were open to him, including that of the duke's estate manager, Don Carlobal, who was a university 'licentiate', a councillor and a judge. There the scene occurred which made Juan famous; it was later mentioned by Lope de Vega, and inspired Jiménez de Enciso to write a comedy about it. Juan gave Latin lessons to Don Carlobal's daughter, Doña Ana, and during the conjugation of 'amo, amas, amat' they fell in love with each other. Doña Ana bore him a child, which was christened in 1549 with the name Juana. Juan and Ana

---

* 'Ethiopians' at that time meant 'Black Africans' (the term is still sometimes used with this meaning in the United States even now); whereas white, brown and black Africans were called 'Moors' without distinction of colour. Ethiopia in those days was only known as a legendary country.

got married and had a happy union which produced three other children (in 1552, 1556 and 1559).

His academic career was no less successful; in 1556 he graduated at Granada University, and in 1557 became professor there; in 1565 he received the highest honour the University could bestow on him—his Latin address (which unfortunately has not come down to us) opened the academic year. In 1569 Don John of Austria came to Granada, the subsequent victor of the great battle of Lepanto, son of the Emperor Charles V. He played cards with Juan Latino and Juan's boyhood friend and former master, the Duke of Sessa. It was a cheerful time; and two years later, when Don John won his brilliant victory over the Turks, inspiring the whole of Europe with enthusiasm, Juan Latino wrote his main work, the *Austrias*, which, though written in scholarly form, is like a long African 'praise song' for the victor of Lepanto. Works of Juan's appeared in 1573, 1576 and 1585. In 1586, when he was seventy, he gave up his professorial chair on health grounds. He probably died in 1606; a contemporary author, who saw the tombstone but probably read the date wrong, gives 1633—when Juan would have been a hundred and seventeen!

His Latin verses show the erudite academic style of the period, the zealous Spanish Catholicism and patriotism, interspersed with countless classical allusions, whereby the ancient gods are transformed into Spaniards:

> Qui pelagi Dominus Neptunus visus adesse,
> Hispanisque Deus manibus cui fuscina Sceptrum . . .[3]

> 'Neptune, Lord of the Sea, in him seems now resurrected,
> Deity with Spanish hands who wieldeth the three-prongéd
> sceptre . . .'

This is one of the things he says about Don John; and as is only to be expected, he is ardently on the side of the Catholic missionaries:

> Obvius Aethiopem Christum docet ore Philippus . . .
> Ne Aethiopi justa haec forte Philippe neges. . . .[4]

> 'If Philip Ethiops meets, on Christ he will give them instruction . . .
> Let not the Ethiops' rights, Philip, by thee be denied. . . .'

Nevertheless, he shows in some verses how much he insisted on racial equality:

> Quod si nostra tuis facies Rex nigra ministris
> Displicet, Aethiopum non placet alba viris.[5]

'If our black face, O King, seems to your ministers odious,
  Ethiops find your white faces no more to their taste.'

Of course in his everyday life Juan expressed himself less bluntly. For instance, the story is told of him that one morning when he was feeling indisposed, he was visited by a high noble, who evidently thought he looked very black lying between the white sheets; Juan laughed and called out: 'Why are you so surprised, sire? I am like a fly in the milk.'

'The Negro Juan Latino' was for Cervantes the typical representative of an over-refined, erudite style full of linguistic sophistries—and as such he gave Juan a memorial in *Don Quijote*.[6] Yet in many verses we cannot help feeling there is perhaps a faint undercurrent of African memories—of ancestor worship, fertility rites, queen mothers, and the style of the African 'praise-songs':

> Princeps nunc fato regnis concessus avitis ...
> Principis ipsa tui mater, conjuxque Philippi
>   Regina Hispanis vixeris alma diu.
> Tu regem facias hunc pulchra prole parentem
>   Natorum natos Regina mater alas.[7]

'Lo, now a prince is granted by fate to the kindom ancestral ...
Mother is she of thy new-born prince, and the wife of King
    Philip;
  Hail to thee, fertile Queen, long may you live for our Spain.
May you now make this king the father of glorious offspring,
    May there be sons of your sons, nurtured, Queen Mother,
    from thee.'

Juan Latino was born in the year when the Emperor Charles V ascended the throne, and he retired two years before the Armada was destroyed: his life, in fact, spanned the greatest period in Spain's history, and he was a shining light of the Spanish renaissance. He was buried in a family grave next to his wife Doña Ana de Carlobal; it is probably the date of her death which is given on the tombstone. He had himself composed their epitaph:

Del
Maestro Juan Latino
Catedratico de Granada
y Doña Ana de Carlobal
Su Muger
y Herederos MDLXXIII

Garnatae doctus, clarae doctorque juventae,
Oratorque pius doctrina et moribus unus
Filius Aethiopum,* prolesque nigerrima patrum,
Infans illaesus cepit praecepta salutis
Augusti Austridae cecinit qui gesta Latinus
Conditur hic cippo: surget cum conjuge fida.[8]

'To
Master Juan Latino
Professor of Granada
and Doña Ana de Carlobal
his wife
and his heirs MDLXXIII

Scholar of famous Granada and teacher of brilliant young
    students,
Orator pious in speech, outstanding in doctrine and morals,
Offspring and son deep black with black Ethiopian forebears,
He learnt as an innocent child the precepts that lead to salvation.
He sang in the fair Latin tongue the illustrious Austrian's
    glories,
Under this pillar he lies; he will rise with his wife well-beloved.'

3. Black 'Guinea-Pigs' in the Age of Enlightenment

Two hundred years later, in the 'Age of Enlightenment', more or less
enlightened people could seriously discuss the question: is a Negro a
human being or not? The slave trade flourished, and the quality
appreciated in Africans was the strength of their muscles, not their
intellect. But the spirit of the age can be given credit for the fact that
nevertheless black writers did emerge in the eighteenth century. For
Rousseau had declared all men equal, and there were people in high
places who tried to prove the point by giving selected 'Negroes' the
best education to see what the 'Negroes' thus educated could do.

One of these 'guinea-pigs' was Francis Williams, born in Jamaica
in 1700 to free parents of African descent. He was 'picked to be the
subject of an experiment, which, it is said, the Duke of Montagu
was curious to make, in order to discover, whether, by proper cultivation and a proper tuition at school and the university, a Negro might
not be found as capable of literature as a white person'.[1] Williams
attended English schools, then went to Cambridge University. When
Holdane became Governor of Jamaica, Williams celebrated the

* See footnote on p. 31.

appointment in his Latin panegyric, '*Integerrimo et fortissimo viro, Georgio Holdano*' (to George Holdane, a man of the greatest honour and courage).[2]

Another protégé of the Duke of Montagu was Ignatius Sancho, born in 1729 on board a slave ship between Africa and South America; he died in 1780. Having served the Duke's family as butler for over twenty years, he then wrote his *Letters*, which were published posthumously in 1782, 'a work not equalled perhaps in charm and literary merit by any other butler, white or black, before Sancho's days and since'.[3] It was quite usual for high-born folk to have decorative Negroes in their households, serving the chocolate and handing round the snuff-boxes; some might be tried out for experiments in education.

There are several other examples of these experiments proving successful. Ibrahim Petrovich Hannibal, educated by Peter the Great, was eventually made a Lieutenant-General of Artillery; he married a Russian noblewoman, and one of their great-grandchildren was Alexander Pushkin. Anton Wilhelm Amo, from what is now Ghana, achieved a professorship at Wittenberg University through the help of benevolent patrons; and James Eliza John Capitein, carried off from West Africa to Amsterdam, where he was educated by a rich merchant, became so thoroughly imbued with the ideas of his mentors that he defended the slave trade in a Latin treatise on slavery (*Dissertatio de servitute*). In 1742 he published this in Dutch as well, *A Politico-Theological Investigation of Slavery as not Incompatible with Christian Liberty* (*Staatkundig-Godgeleerd Onderzoekschrift over de Slavernij, als niet strijdig tegen de Christelijke Vrijheid*).

In the same year, after the publication of his 'Rousing Sermons' (*Uitgewrogte Predikatien*), he returned to West Africa–he was now twenty-five–as headmaster of a Calvinist mission school at Elmina, and translated some extracts from the Bible, including the Ten Commandments, into his mother-tongue. He put the Dutch Company in the place of God–'I am Jan Company who brought you out of the land of Egypt . . .'[4]–which the traders found quite unexceptionable. They were less pleased, however, when the rumour went round that Capitein had 'reverted to idolatrous habits'.[5] He died in 1747.

In his first published work, an elegy in Latin verse on the death of the preacher Manger in The Hague, the following passage occurs– I give it in the translation of a contemporary:

'His dear wife beats her breast and weeps bitter tears over the coffin of her beloved. Her despair is like Naomi's, condemned to sad widowhood by Elimelech's death.'[6]

And it ends with a piece of flattery:

'Let ancient times praise Nestor's eloquence; Manger was greater than Nestor himself.'[7]

In the same group of authors we may include the 'infant prodigy' Phillis Wheatley, a girl born on the banks of the river Senegal, who in 1761, when about seven, came as a slave into the possession of the Boston tailor John Wheatley. To his amazement she learnt English in sixteen months and 'was able to read the most difficult passages in the Holy Scriptures, to the great astonishment of all who listened'.[8] Her first poem appeared when she was seventeen, an elegy on the death of the preacher George Whitefield. At the age of twenty she accompanied the son of her master to England, where she stayed with the Countess of Huntingdon and was to have been presented to King George III, but had to return to Boston on account of ill-health.

Her poems, published in London in 1773, attracted great attention —till the twentieth century her little book was considered the first literary work of an Afro-American—but her fame did not help her much. When her patron died and his household broke up, she was given her freedom; the Wheatley family had lost interest in the subject of their father's successful experiment. To find a new home, she married the first comer, bore him three children, and died at the age of thirty-one as a maid at an inn.

She wrote neo-classical poems for special occasions in the style of Alexander Pope, neatly turned verse without any warmth or spontaneity, loaded with hyperbolic allusions to ancient deities and Biblical figures. Her elegy on the death of Pastor Pitkin's wife begins:

> Where Contemplation finds her sacred Spring;
> Where heav'nly Music makes the Centre ring;
> Where Virtue reigns unsullied, and divine,
> Where Wisdom thron'd, and all the Graces shine;
> There sits thy Spouse, amid the glitt'ring Throng;
> There central Beauty feasts the ravish'd Tongue;
> With recent Powers, with recent Glories crown'd,
> The choirs angelic shout her welcome round.[9]

The tone is the same as in a long poem about the power of imagination:

> *Fancy* might now her silken pinions try
> To rise from earth, and sweep th' expanse on high;
> From *Tithon*'s bed now might *Aurora* rise,
> Her cheeks all glowing with celestial dyes,
> While a pure stream of light o'erflows the skies.
> The monarch of the day I might behold,
> And all the mountains tipt with radiant gold,
> But I reluctant leave the pleasing views,
> Which *Fancy* dresses to delight the *Muse*. . . .[10]

An ode to General Washington ends:

> Proceed, great chief, with virtue on thy side,
> Thy ev'ry action let the goddess guide.
> A crown, a mansion, and a throne that shine
> With gold unfading, Washington! be thine.[11]

She composed such odes to famous men, also consolatory verses on the deaths of wives and children of people she knew, and sometimes a poem of thanks to her patrons. We learn of her attitude to slavery and her religious ideas, which reflect the influence of the Methodists, from her only personal poem, 'On Being Brought from Africa':

> 'Twas mercy brought me from my *Pagan* land,
> Taught my benighted soul to understand
> That there's a God, that there's a *Saviour* too:
> Once I redemption neither sought nor knew.
> Some view our sable race with scornful eye,
> 'Their colour is a diabolic die.'
> Remember, *Christians*, *Negros*, black as *Cain*,
> May be refin'd, and join th' angelic train.[12]

All such writers as Phillis Wheatley were torn so early from their original cultural environment that they retained no memory of it, were brought up according to their patrons' educational ideals, and eventually fulfilled the task expected of them: to write tracts, letters or poems in impeccable Latin, English or Dutch, which could just as well have been produced by any white-skinned scholar of equal intelligence and education.

The butler Sancho, however, who luckily for him had no debt to discharge for his education, at least kept a sense of humour. In one of his *Letters* he writes: 'My respect and kind enquiry to your old horse. Tell him I wish him better—and I am a real friend to the honest brutes–some I could almost envy.'[13] From the backroom of his green-grocery, which he ran with his West Indian wife in order to bring up his numerous offspring, he exchanged letters with many people, including Sterne and the Duchess of Kent; unfortunately only a few of his correspondents are named in the *Letters*. As he was now independent, he could be quite outspoken, and in his wry humour we often catch glimpses of social criticism:

> 'Madam Fortune, who by the way is a bunter (and such I love not) has been particularly cross to me since you left us–they say she is fond of fools–'tis false and scandalous–she hates me–and I have the vanity to say and believe–that if folly, sheer folly, had any charms–I should stand as fair in her esteem–as A.B. C.D. E.F.–or any of Folly's family through the whole alphabet.'[14]

Anton Wilhelm Amo, referred to above, was the only writer in this group of any consequence, though more as a philosopher than an author.* He was born about 1703 near Axim in what is today Ghana, came to Amsterdam in 1707, and was then given to Duke Anton Ulrich of Brunswick-Wolfenbüttel, who handed him over to his son August Wilhelm. In 1708 Amo was christened with the names Anton Wilhelm after his patrons. In 1721 he was confirmed, in 1727 he went to Halle University, where in 1729 he graduated in law with his Disputation *De jure Maurorum in Europa*, which unfortunately has not yet been traced. In 1730 he went to Wittenberg University and there in the same year gained a degree as Doctor of Philosophy. In 1733, on the visit of Augustus the Strong, Elector of Saxony and King of Poland, Dr. Amo led the students' procession in the monarch's honour. In 1734, after having his Disputation published, he was made Professor of Philosophy. In 1736 he returned to Halle as lecturer and there taught psychology, 'natural law' and the decimal system–a universality which was then customary.

The only poem of his which has come down to us is from that period. It was written in German as a tribute to the doctor Moses Abraham Wolff, and the English translation given below should convey something of the style, similar to that of Phillis Wheatley:

> Dein aufgeweckter Geist im klugen meditiren,
> Und unermüdter Fleiß im gründlichen Studiren,
> Hoch Edler, macht daß Du in der Gelehrten Orden
> Ein Stern, ein heller Stern der ersten Größe worden,

---

* An evaluation of his position in German 'Enlightenment' philosophy is given in the German edition, pp. 40–2.

Der immer heller wird in neuer Ehren Schein.
So einen großen Lohn giebt Weißheit ihren Söhnen.
Genug. Vom Himmel muß die Lust, die ungemeyn,
Dich und die Deinigen in Lauter Segen kröhnen!
  Glückwünschend hinzu
  Anton Wilhelm Amo
  Von Guinea in Africa, der Philosophie
  und Freyen künste Magister legens.

'Thy brilliant spir't, Sire, in skilful meditation,
And never-tyring paynes in thorough lucubration,
Have made thee in the fyrmament of scholars learnéd
A new effulgent star of magnitude discernéd,
Which ever brighter grows, in latest honours shyning.
To all her sons so great reward hath Wisdom given.
Enough. 'Tis Providence for sure by rare designing
Hath crownéd thee and thine with blessing rich from Heaven!
  Felycitations too
  From Anton Wilhelm Amo,
  From Guinea in Africa,
  Magister Legens of Philosophy
  And the Liberal Arts.'[15]

In 1738 Amo's *Tractatus de arte sobrie et accurate philosophandi* (Treatise on the Art of Philosophizing Soberly and Accurately) was published in Halle; he himself had become quite a bright star in the firmament of Halle's early Enlightenment.* The following year he moved to Jena University, where he gave his inaugural lecture on 'The Frontiers of Psychology', and no doubt stayed there till May 1740. The two sons of Duke Anton Ulrich had died in 1731 and 1735 respectively; Johann Peter von Ludewig, Chancellor of Halle University, died in 1742; and Amo probably found no other patron in Germany. At any rate we hear no more of him until 1753, when he was back home in Axim, venerated apparently as a sort of witch doctor. We do not know when he died.

The results of these experiments in the Age of Enlightenment show that, if you start early enough, you can completely transplant a person from one culture to another. This proves that cultural elements are not inherent in a race, and refutes all theories of a 'racial soul'. So much at least the experiments achieved.

---

* See footnote on p. 38.

4. Slaves and Grand Seigneurs

The remaining African and Afro-American writers of the eighteenth century need not detain us long. Two of them were born in Africa, almost at the same time, about 1745: Olaudah Equiano in Essaka near Benin in present-day Nigeria, and Ottobah Cugoano in Ajumako near Winneba in the present-day Ghana. Both were kidnapped as children–Equiano was eleven or twelve–and sold into slavery. Both found benevolent masters in the New World, eventually obtained their freedom and settled down in England, where Cugoano married an Englishwoman. The writings of both are autobiographical and written in English. Equiano told the story of his very varied life, and his is the first report we have by an African on his country of origin. It is well known and easily accessible, so I do not need to quote from it here. Cugoano worked even more zealously than Equiano for the abolition of slavery, whose horrors he graphically describes. Both have a vivid style which grips the reader.

In 1747 a slave called Briton Hammon boarded a ship from Plymouth, Massachusetts, with his master's consent. He tells the story of his strange adventures: how he was captured by the Indians, snatched from them by the Spaniards, from whom he escaped to England; and how when he returned to Massachusetts in 1760 he happened to meet his master on the ship.

John Marrant was born in 1755 in New York, and his story too is full of marvels, mostly connected with the number three. After a preacher had prayed three times, he was seized by the Spirit of God; his family in Charlestown, West Virginia, thought he was mad; he fled into the wilderness, and fell into the hands of the Cherokees, who wanted to kill him. But the fourteen-year-old boy converted three people, first the executioner, then the Indian chief's daughter, and finally the chief himself, after praying three times to Jesus. When he returned home after a few months, sisters, brothers and even his mother failed to recognize him. Only his youngest sister recognized him and had to call out his name three times before she convinced the others. Later on, when he went to sea after his military service, three was again his lucky number:

'Some time after this I was cruising about in the American seas, and cannot help mentioning a singular deliverance I had from the most imminent danger, and the use the Lord made of it to me. We were overtaken by a violent storm; I was washed overboard, and thrown on again; dashed into the sea a second time, and tossed upon deck again. I now fastened a rope around my middle, as a security against being thrown into the sea again; but, alas! forgot to fasten it to any part of the ship; being carried away the third time by the fury of the waves, when in the sea, I found the rope both useless and an encumbrance. I was in the sea the third time about eight minutes, and the sharks came round me in great numbers; one of an enormous size, that could easily have taken me into his mouth at once, passed and rubbed against my side. I then cried more earnestly to the Lord than I had done for some time; and He who heard Jonah's prayer did not shut out mine, for I was thrown aboard again; these were the means the Lord used to revive me, and I began now to set out afresh.'[1]

Prince Hall (1748–1807), born in Barbados, founded in Cambridge, Massachusetts, the first Freemasons' Lodge for coloured people, recognized by the Masons in 1787. An extant sermon of his is reminiscent, according to Loggins,[2] of the tone of the spiritual and the jubilee.

Jupiter Hammon, born between 1720 and 1730 at Long Island, New York, was the first Afro-American lyric poet of the United States apart from Lucy Terry, who wrote a single poem about 1746. Brawley finds it necessary to excuse Hammon's shortcoming: ' . . . he was a slave working without the advantage of formal education . . . Only thus can allowance be made for the faulty syntax, the forced rhymes, and the strained metrical effects . . .'[3] Personally, however, I find his naïve but sincerely felt verse more lively than the artificial elaboration of Phillis Wheatley; and if you imagine his poem 'An Evening Thought' sung polyrhythmically as a sort of spiritual, it would not sound at all laboured. Jupiter Hammon could do without metre; there is a rhythm swinging through his verse, no doubt a strongly African rhythm.

We now come to two poets who both turned into *grands seigneurs*. Manoel Ignacio da Silva Alvarenga was born in 1749 in Vila Rica in the state of Minas Gerais in Brazil, the illegitimate son of a poor musician. From 1773 to 1776 he studied at Coimbra University in Portugal, then returned with his doctor's degree to Brazil, where he played a distinguished part in literary and public life. But in his works he had completely disowned his African origins. The beloved Glaura of his poems is neither a dark-skinned nor a light-skinned lady; but a nymph. The poems are facile pastorals like the following madrigal:

Madrigal XLVI

Ó garça voadora,
Se alem do golfo inclinas os teus giros,
    Ah! leva os meus suspiros
À mais gentil Pastora desses montes.
Não temo que te enganes; prados, fontes,
    Tudo se ri com ela;
    Não é, não é tão bela,
Quando surge no Céu purpúrea Aurora;
    Ó garça voadora,
Se alem do golfo inclinas os teus giros,
Ah! leva por piedade os meus suspiros.

'O heron, wingéd soarer,
Beyond the gulf in lofty spirals turning,
    Ah, bear my sighs of yearning
To her, my gentle shepherdess o' the mountains.
You cannot miss your way, when meadows, fountains,
    All Nature's smiles are blended
    With hers; no scene so splendid
When skyward climbs the crimson of Aurora.
    O heron, wingéd soarer,
Beyond the gulf in lofty spirals turning,
O bear in pity all my sighs of yearning'[4]

Domingos Caldas Barbosa is the most important of these eighteenth-
century poets, and presumably the first great neo-African lyric poet.
He was born on a slave ship between Angola and Brazil in 1738 or
1740; his father was a Portuguese merchant, whose name is not
known. Educated at the Jesuit College in Rio, he wrote lampoons on
the Viceroy Bobadella and was consequently sent for military service
to the distant province of Sacramento. When the province fell into
Spanish hands he went from there to Lisbon, where in 1775 he published his first poems. He was 'secular priest' at the *Casa da Suppli-
cação* (the Petitions Court)–there were no civil courts in Portugal
then, so certain priests were appointed for judicial duties. His songs,
poems and plays were very successful in Lisbon, and with some Portuguese fellow-poets he founded the Academy of Fine Arts, becoming
its President; it was afterwards called Nova Arcádia. Many of his
poems follow the fashionable taste of the period; but his *modinhas*
and *lundús* 'caught on' with the people. He died in Lisbon on 19th
November 1800.

Life at the Portuguese court of the time was described by Lord Beckford, son of the very wealthy Jamaican slave-owner and sugar-planter who was Lord Mayor of London: 'It is the high ton [sic] at present in this court to be surrounded by African implings, the more hideous the more prized, and to bedizen them in the most expensive manner. The Queen has set the example and the royal family vie with each other in spoiling and caressing Donna Rosa, her Majesty's black-skinned, blubber-lipped, flat-nosed, favourite.'[5]

Of the *modinhas* Beckford writes as follows:

'Those who have never heard this original sort of music, must and will remain ignorant of the most bewitching melodies that ever existed since the days of the Sybarites. They consist of languid interrupted measures, as if the breath was gone with excess of rapture, and the soul panting to meet the kindred soul of some beloved object. With a childish carelessness they steal into the heart, before it has time to arm itself against their enervating influence; you fancy you are swallowing milk, and are admitting the poison of voluptuousness into the closest recesses of your existence.'[6]

Where the African influence is so clear in the music, it may be evident in the words as well; although Bastide has informed me in a letter that according to Mário de Andrade the *modinha* was a song 'generally played at the piano in the *salons* of the bourgeoisie . . . But towards 1850 it passed downwards to the people.'[7] Perhaps, how-ever, it was still 'on its way up' a century before, in the time of Caldas Barbosa; this is anyhow the inference to be drawn from Lord Beck-ford's fascinated and cautionary remarks.

Besides *modinhas*, as has been said, Caldas wrote *lundús*; and the *lundú* is 'indisputably of African or more precisely Bantu, origin—it is an erotic dance which with its *umbligada*,[8] "bumping the navel", more or less resembles the *batuque* and *samba*.' The *lundú*, writes Oneyda Alvarenga, 'was the first form of negro music accepted by Brazilian society, and it is responsible for some important character-istics in our music. . . . To accept the *lundú* completely, the colonial Brazilian society turned it into a song, freeing it from a choreography which was indeed scandalous for people who considered themselves white.'[10] Alvarenga gives a musical example with the words:

> Iaiá você quer morrer
>> Quando morrer morramos juntos.
> Que eu quero ver como cabem
>> Numa cova dois defuntos?

Isto é bom, isto é bom,
Isto é bom que doi.
Isto é bom, isto é bom,
Isto é bom que doi.[11]

'If now you're for dying,
    Together we'd have died.
But how shall we two dead get into
    Graves that aren't too wide?

Chorus: 'It's good, it's good,
It's good if it hurts;
It's good, it's good,
It's good if it hurts.'

If with these words we imagine the 'scandalous' choreography which shows in pantomime how the dead live on and love on in their graves, we shall find in the *lundús* of Domingos Caldas Barbosa the secularized reflection of African ideas – with African stylistic methods toned down but still clearly recognizable.

REFERENCES AND BIBLIOGRAPHIES

1. Pre-Islamic and Early Islamic Romances

[1] Dover, p. 188.

[2] Brockelmann, pp. 13 f.

[3] Blunt, quoted from Dover, p. 88.

[4] Arabic text: Ahlwardt, p. 45; German version: Rückert, p. 145.

[5] Arabic text: ibid., German version: Rückert, p. 146.

[6] Arabic text: Alhwardt, p. 46; German version: Rückert, p. 147.

[7] Arabic text: Ahlwardt, p. 49; German version, Rückert, p. 150.

[8] p. 151. English version after Rückert, p. 151.

[9] Dover, p. 42.

[10] ibid., p. 179.

[11] Hammer-Purgstall, quoted from Hamilton, vol. 2, p. xviii.

[12] Dover, p. 53.

[13] quoted from Dover, p. 54.

[14] ibid., p. 49.

[15] ibid.

[16] ibid.

[17] Brockelmann, pp. 72 f.

[18] Nykl, p. 27.

AHLWARDT, Wilhelm (ed.): The divans of the six ancient Arabic poets . . . London 1870

BLUNT, A. and W. S.: The seven Golden Odes of pagan Arabia. London 1903

BROCKELMANN, Carl: Geschichte der arabischen Literatur. Vol. 1, 2nd ed. Leiden 1943

CLOUSTON, W. A.: Arabian poetry for English readers. Glasgow 1881

DEVIC, L. M.: Les aventures d'Antar, fils de Cheddad. Roman arabe des temps anté-islamiques. Paris 1864. 2nd ed. 1878

– Antar: poème heroïque arabe des temps anté-islamiques. Paris 1898

DOVER, Cedric: The black knight. In: Phylon, vol. XV, Nos. 1/2, Atlanta, Ga. 1954

HAMILTON, Terrick (translator): Antar, a bedoueen romance. 4 vols. London 1819–20

HAMMER-PURGSTALL, Joseph Freiherr von: On Arabian poetry, especially the romance of Antar. In: New Monthly Magazine, vol. 13, 1820

–(translator): Aventures d'Antar, roman arabe. Paris 1868

NYKL, A. R.: Hispano-Arabic poetry and its relations with the old Provençal troubadours. Baltimore 1946

RÜCKERT, Friedrich: Hamâsa oder Die ältesten arabischen Volkslieder. Part 2. Stuttgart 1846

THORBECKE, Heinrich: Antarah, ein vorislamischer Dichter. Leipzig 1867

–Antarah. Des vorislamischen Dichters Leben. Heidelberg 1868

2. Juan Latino, a Renaissance 'African'

[1] Latino: Fernandi principis navitate, p. 10, left.*
[2] Salazar, p. 483.
[3] Latino: Austrias I, p. 5, left.
[4] Latino: Fernandi principis navitate, p. 10, right.*
[5] ibid.
[6] Cervantes, p. 12.
[7] Latino: Fernandi principis navitate, p. 14, left.*
[8] Spratlin, pp. 21 f.

ÁLVARES, Afonso, see p. 24

ARCO, Angel: Estudio sobre Juan Latino. In: Boletín Arqueológico de Tarragona, March/April/ May/June 1901

* Here pagination is by page-openings, each number referring to both right- and left-hand pages.

CERVANTES SAAVEDRA, Miguel de: Don Quijote de la Mancha. Vol. 1. Halle 1925

GONZÁLES GARBÍN, Antonio: Glorias de la Universidad Granadina: el Negro Juan Latino. In: Boletín del Centro Artístico, Granada, Oct. 1886

GUTIÉRREZ, Miguel: Juan Latino. In: Los Lunes del Imparcial, 28. Sept. 1896

JIMÉNEZ DE ENCISCO, Diego: Comedia famosa de Juan Latino. In Part 2 of: Comedias escogidas de las mejores de España. Madrid 1652

LATINUS, Ioannes: Fernandi principis navitate . . . Austrias . . . Granada 1573 (No. 357)

OCETE, Antonio Marín: El negro Juan Latino. Granada 1925

SALAZAR, Ambrosio de: Espejo general de gramática. Rouen 1615

SPRATLIN, Valaurez B.: Juan Latino, slave and humanist. New York 1938

VEGA, Lope de: La Dama Boba, Act II, scene 21

3. Black 'Guinea-Pigs' in the Age of Enlightenment

[1] Long, vol. ii, p. 475.
[2] Long, vol. ii, pp. 475–80.
[3] Loggins, p. 7.
[4] Schulte-Nordholt 1958, p. 17.
[5] Grégoire, p. 224.
[6] ibid., p. 227.
[7] ibid., p. 229.
[8] Wheatley 1773, p. 6.
[9] Loggins, pp. 22 f.
[10] Wheatley 1773, pp. 67 f.
[11] Hughes, p. 7.
[12] Wheatley 1773, p. 18.
[13] Sancho, vol. I, p. 153.
[14] ibid., p. 156.
[15] Lochner, p. 24.

AMO, Antonius Guilielmus: Dissertatio . . . Wittenberg 1734 (No.119)

–Disputatio philosophica . . . Wittenberg 1734 (No. 120)

–Tractatus de arte sobrie . . . Halle 1738 (No. 121)

CAPITEIN, Jacobus Elisa Ioannes: Dissertatio . . . de servitute . . . Amsterdam 1742 (Nos. 178–9)

–Uitgewrogte predikatiën ... Amsterdam 1742 (No. 180)

DATHORNE, Oscar Ronald: African writers of the eighteenth century. In: Black Orpheus, No. 18, Ikeja, Nigeria, Oct. 1965

EEKHOF, A.: De negerpredikant Jacobus Elisa Joannes Capitein 1717–47. 's-Gravenhage 1917

GRÉGOIRE, Henri: De la littérature des nègres. Paris 1808

HUGHES, Langston: The poetry of the Negro, 1746–1949. Garden City, N.Y. 1949 (No. 1189)

JEKYLL, Joseph: The life of Ignatius Sancho. In: Sancho, Letters ..., London 1782, vol. 1

LOCHNER, Norbert: Anton Wilhelm Amo. Ein Gelehrter aus Ghana im Deutschland des 18. Jh. In: Überseerundschau, 10th year, No. 1. Hamburg 1958

LOGGINS, Vernon: The Negro author; his development in America. New York 1931 and Port Washington, N.Y. 1964 (reprint)

LONG, Edward: The history of Jamaica. 3 vols, London 1774

SANCHO, Ignatius: Letters ... London 1782 (No. 541)

SCHULTE NORDHOLT, J. W.: Het volk dat in duisternis wandelt. Arnhem 1956 and 1960 (Das Volk das im Finstern wandelt. Bremen 1958)

SUCHIER, Wolfram: A. W. Amo. Ein Mohr als Student und Privat-dozent der Philosophie in Halle, Wittenberg und Jena, 1727/40. In: Akademische Rundschau, 4th year, No. 9/10, Leipzig 1916

WHEATLEY, Phillis: An elegiac poem ... Boston 1770 (No. 620)

–Poems on various subjects ... Boston 1773 (No. 621)

WILLIAMS, Francis: Integerrimo et fortissimo viro Georgio Holdano ... In: Long, History of Jamaica

4. Slaves and Grand Seigneurs

[1] Marrant 1785, pp. 35 f.
[2] Loggins, p. 84.
[3] Brawley, p. 22.
[4] Silva Alvarenga 1943, p. 239.
[5] Beckford, vol. ii, p. 108.
[6] ibid., pp. 31 f.
[7] Bastide, letter dated 15th April, 1965.
[8] cf. Jahn, p. 82.
[9] Bastide, letter dated 15th April, 1965.
[10] Alvarenga, p. 129.
[11] ibid., p. 132.

ALVARENGA, Oneyda: Música popular brasileña. México 1947

BECKFORD, William: Italy, Spain, and Portugal. New York 1845

BRAWLEY, Benjamin: Early Negro American writers . . . Chapel Hill, N.C. 1935 (No. 2167)

CALDAS BARBOSA, Domingos: Collecção de poesias feitas . . . Lisboa 1775 (No. 2034)

-Epithalamio . . . Lisboa 1777 (No. 2035)

-A doença . . . Lisboa 1777 (No. 2036)

-Os viajantes ditosos . . . Lisboa 1790 (No. 2037)

-Recopilação dos principaes successos da historia sagrada. Porto: Na Offic. de Pedro Ribeira França 1792. 32 p. p.-2.ª ed. Lisboa 1819.-4.ª ed. Rio de Janeiro 1865. Lyr

-A saloia namorada, ou O remedio e casar . . . Lisboa 1793 (No. 2038)

-A escola dos ciosos . . . Lisboa 1795 (No. 2040)

-Viola de Lereno. 2 vols. Lisboa 1798 + 1826; Rio de Janeiro 1944 (No. 2041)

-Poema mariano . . . Vitória, Brasil 1854 (No. 2042)

CUGOANO, Ottobah: Thoughts and sentiments . . . London 1787 (Nos. 1428-9)

EQUIANO, Olaudah: The interesting narrative . . . London 1789. 2 vols.; abridged: London 1966 (Nos. 278-82)

HALL, Prince: A charge delivered to the African lodge, June 24, 1797 . . . no place, no date (No. 1567)

HAMMON, Briton: A narrative of the uncommon sufferings . . . Boston 1760 (No. 2637)

HAMMON, Jupiter: An evening thought . . . 1760 (No. 2638)

-An address to Miss Phillis Wheatly (!) . . . Hartford, Conn. 1778 (No. 2639)

-A winter piece . . . Hartford, Conn. 1782? (No. 2640)

-An address to the Negroes . . . New York 1787 (No. 2641) Also in: The Magazine of History, Extra Number, No. 114 (Vol. 29, No. 2), Tarrytown, N.Y. 1925

-An evening's improvement . . . Hartford, Conn. 1790? (No. 2642)

-Jupiter Hammon-American Negro poet. Selections from his writings and a bibliography, by Oscar Wegelin. New York 1915 (No. 2643)

JAHN, Janheinz: Muntu. London/New York 1961

LOGGINS, Vernon: The Negro author. New York 1931. Reprint: Port Washington, N.Y. 1964

MARRANT, John: A narrative of the Lord's wonderful dealings ...
London 1785 (Nos. 2999–3001)
–A sermon ... Boston 1789; New York 192–? (No. 3002)
–Journal ... London 1790 (No. 3003)
PORTER, Dorothy B.: Padre Domingos Caldas Barbosa –Afro-
Brazilian poet. In: Phylon, vol. XII, Atlanta, Ga. 1951
SAYERS, Raymond S.: The Negro in Brazilian literature. New York
1956
SILVA ALVARENGA, Manoel Ignacio da: Obras poeticas. Rio de
Janeiro 1864. 2 vols. (No. 2147)
–Glaura; poemas eróticos. Rio de Janeiro 1943 (No. 2153)

TABLE 1

African Writers of Sixteenth and Eighteenth Centuries

Languages: D Dutch
E English
L Latin
P Portuguese

Type of work: A autobiography
L letters
Py poetry
Pl plays
Tr treatise
S sermons

(writers born on slave ships in *italics*, writers born in Europe underlined)

Sixteenth Century

P	Álvares	: San Antonio Pl
P	Álvares	: Santa Barbara Pl
P	Álvares	: San Thiago Pl
1573	L Latino	: Austrias Py
1576	L Latino	: Translatione Py

Eighteenth Century

MAIN WORKS BY
AFRICANS

AFRO-AMERICANS FROM

BRAZIL   WEST INDIES   U.S.A.

1734 L Amo: Dissertatio Tr
1734 L Amo: Disputatio Tr
1738 L Amo: Tractatus Tr
1742 L Capitein: Dissertatio Tr
1742 D Capitein: Predikatien S

1746 E Terry: Flight Py
1760 E Hammon: Sufferings A
1760 E Hammon: Thought Py

1785 E Marrant: Narrative A

1789 E Marrant: Journal A
        Sermon S

JAMAICA
1774 L Williams: Holdano Py

BARBADOS
1797 E Hall: Charge

1770 E Wheatley: Elegiac Poem Py
1773 E Wheatley: Poems Py

1782 E Sancho: Letters L

1787 E Cugoano: Thoughts A
1787 E Cugoano: Thoughts A

1774 P Silva: Desertor Py
1775 P Caldas: Poesias Py
1775 P Silva: Neptuno Py

1790 P Caldas: Viajantes Pl
1793 P Caldas: Saloia Pl

1798 P Caldas: Viola Py
     P Silva: Glaura Py

PART TWO

The African Scene

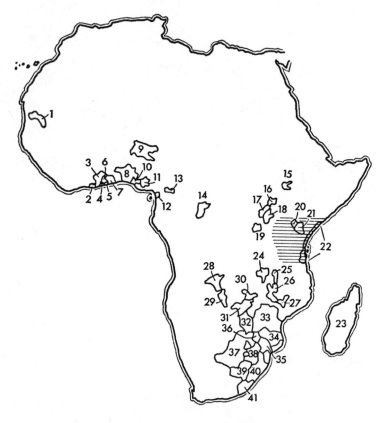

African Written Languages in Sub-Saharan Africa

1 Tukulor	12 Duala	22 Swahili	32 Ndebele
2 Nzema	13 Chaha	23 Malagasy	33 Shona
3 Twi	14 Ngala	24 Bemba	34 Tswa
4 Fanti	15 Chaha	25 Tumbuka	35 Tsonga
5 Ga	16 Acholi	26 Chewa	36 Venda
6 Akuapem	17 Nyoro-Toro	27 Nyanja	37 Tswana
7 Ewe	18 Ganda	28 Luvale	38 Pedi
8 Yoruba	19 Rwanda	29 Lozi	39 Sotho
9 Hausa	20 Kikuyu	30 Lenje	40 Zulu
10 Edo	21 Kamba	31 Tonga	41 Xhosa
11 Ibo			

Chapter 3

AFRICAN ORAL LITERATURE

1. What is Oral Literature?

African oral literature has been collected for over a century, but research on it is still at a very early stage. Consequently every new publication of proverbs, fairy-tales, songs, short stories or novels from Africa is treated as something very novel and surprising. Such publications are usually greeted by the critics as taking the reader into a 'completely unknown world', although there is disagreement over whether that world is 'utterly strange' or 'strangely familiar'.

Fifty years ago, for instance, Meinhof remarked on the surprise people felt that 'the African, whom we hardly credit with any deep feelings, is infinitely rich in fairy-tales'[1] and that 'these are so like our own fairy-tales'.[2] On the other hand, when Leo Frobenius's twelve-volume anthology *Atlantis* appeared in the 'twenties, European reviewers pointed out the basic differences and called African oral literature a complete surprise, revealing 'worlds undreamed of'. It is not a matter of taste having changed, nor is it because one anthology stresses familiar things, another the exotic. On the contrary, the same book is likely to produce quite opposite reactions from European readers and critics.

A complicating factor may be the slight unease the average European still feels on hearing that the 'black man' has a literature at all; fears of the 'savage' have not yet been fully overcome. Little has changed, indeed, since the first great anthology of African oral literature in 1896, with a foreword by August Seidel: 'A wild African! A black beast! Fancy him actually thinking and feeling, his imagination proving creative! More than that even, fancy him having a sense and appreciation of poetic form, of rhythm and rhyme! It sounds quite incredible, yet it is true. Missionaries should have the credit of first outlining a correct picture of Negroes' natural talents. Philologists, with a more accurate knowledge of native languages, were able to amend this outline. And everyone was amazed to find that the Negro thinks and feels as we ourselves think and feel.'[3]

The scholars, however, must bear some responsibility for the public's continuing amazement; and Seidel's picture of the 'amending' philologists needs some amendment itself. He and Meinhof saw Africa's oral literature as a new and rich field of activity for literary historians–as indeed it could and should have been. For if philologists had explained the common humanity and common feelings as a background, against which to point out the style– that factor determined by specific civilizations–they would certainly have reduced the amazement at this literature and gained it wider appreciation. In 1911 Meinhof suggested what needed doing:

'The poetry flows on in irregular lines, of course without rhyme. So far as I can see, the rhythms are different from prose rhythms. At any rate I could register a special poetic rhythm with the Venda. But little research has been done on this, and it presents great difficulty for the European. I have, it is true, found out the rules of stress for some of the African languages and have shown that two different kinds of stress occur side by side in the same language. This in itself is something new for the European ear. Moreover, the pitch plays a very important part. So it will be some time before we establish the rules of poetic sound. Then again, the connections with music in these poems, which resemble lyrics, is obvious; but African music, despite the efforts of many years, is still far from being so familiar to us that we can learn anything from that about the poetic stresses. We only know that incredibly complex and varied rhythms occur. So we cannot hope to make much progress until all the material has been more thoroughly examined.'[4]

Meinhof's remarks could have provided a programme for research, but they were not acted on. Like many other sciences African Studies not only developed their special esoteric lore, they also lost their impetus and independence, and were reduced to being merely subsidiary to other disciplines. Scholars continued to collect African poetry, but did not investigate it as poetry, looking for its stylistic rules. They let it be used as handy materials for ethnology, anthropology, linguistics, theology, psychology, etc. It has remained a treasure trove of manners and customs, a storehouse of vocabulary, a reservoir of archetypes, an inexhaustible source for the historian, a training-ground for the phonetician, a quarry for the anthropologist, a paradise for myth-collectors. But as literature, as poetry, it has remained unexplored territory.

The question arises, of course: how far are the oral texts collected for linguistic, ethnological and missionary purposes to be considered as literature? What exactly *is* literature? And how is oral literature to be distinguished from mere speech? If we do extend the term 'literature' to oral matter, is any text literature that gets handed down and preserved? Whiteley has discussed the problem in the introduction to his anthology: do we or do we not consider an elder's verdict after a trial as literature, or the formulas used by initiants at an initiation ceremony? As starting-point in the discussion Whiteley uses Laurence Lerner's rather 'functional' definition of literature as any texts which impart knowledge, express emotion and/or arouse emotion in the reader or listener. Since Lerner makes this a general definition, not simply a statement about a particular unwritten literature, Whiteley applies it to Africa and writes:

'All Lerner's criteria presuppose the existence of an individual author/reciter, and whereas this presents no problem where authorship can be ascertained, the status of the individual in African society, as transmitter and exponent of the oral tradition, is by no means clear. Is traditional material *ipso facto* literature, in which case one can conveniently ignore the individual, or is it the task of the individual to create literature from a mass of traditional material? If one accepts, for example, Pfeffer's evidence that the Ful'be narrator's constant aim was to reproduce the material in the strictest traditional way, then in what light is one to regard such historical traditions? They certainly impart knowledge, and may well both express and arouse emotion, with the individual contribution at a minimum. There will undoubtedly be those who will admit such a material to be literature, but I prefer to take the view that if the expression and arousing of emotion is due, not to the individual reciter, but to the material itself, then one still has not got literature but only the stuff from which literature is created.'[5]

Here I must beg to differ. Whiteley makes the narrator's creative role the only criterion for literature. But is a text only literature if the narrator (reciter) gives it his personal stamp? If an actor recites a text according to a fixed tradition, this surely presupposes a 'literary' basis. The borderline between raw material and art may, but need not, depend on the 'instrument of transmission'. If it always did, music played on a tape-recorder would be just a noise, not music. When the Fulani story-teller recites his 'material', which as such is not yet literature, 'in the strictest traditional way', he is repeating a particular sort of delivery, following a particular tradition of story-telling, a style, and transmitting a text already moulded—in fact literature.

Whiteley has gone astray, I believe, in his statement of the whole problem. For Lerner's criteria are wrong in the first place. They are the criteria of a sociologist trying to define literature by its social functions. Now literature, art and music no doubt *have* social functions, but they are not themselves social functions. They are something more than that.

Art is never formless, never without structure. Thus music is structured sound, and visual art has to be constructed out of a raw material. In the same way literature is 'made' from language, regardless of its function, regardless of any particular period of time, regardless also of whether the author happens to be identifiable or not. The form and the medium depend on convention. This convention, in turn, will differ from one society to another. Unless there is an aesthetic element and a principle of form, there can be neither art nor literature. Lerner seems to have overlooked this vital point.

Every text must, at some time or other, have received the formal approval of a group. This applies not only to the *form* of a literary work, but even more to the method by which it is produced or performed. There are many examples in Africa which prove that what we may call 'procedure' was considered to be even more important than the final result. Sometimes the narrator was not allowed to vary his procedure in any way at all. The fact that there was a laid-down procedure is highly important where a spoken text is concerned, because this point may enable us to decide whether a particular work should be classed as literature or not.

A proverb can be literature, not because it may impart a piece of wisdom, but because it expresses something, whether wisdom, triviality or nonsense, in an imaginative, pithy, witty or euphonious way. The feelings of the person quoting the proverb are as irrelevant to its literary value as are the feelings of the listener or the information it contains. 'A glance at the literary form of aphorisms in any [Bantu] language,' writes Doke, 'makes it abundantly clear that they are different from ordinary prose utterances. This difference is not entirely due to the pithiness of the sayings, but also to a tendency towards the rhythmic, a tendency which at times borders on the poetical.'[1]

He gives many examples of products constructed on very formal patterns, in various Bantu languages, alluding among other things to parallelism in syntax, doubling of words, alliteration and rhymes. In the Swahili proverbs '*Haba nahaba kujaza kibaba*' (equivalent to the Scots 'Many a mickle mak's a muckle') and '*Haraka, haraka, haina baraka*' (haste and pressing have no blessing),[7] rhythm, rhyme and alliteration turn the saying into poetry.

The plot of a fairy-tale is, of course, raw material. Through his delivery, which shapes this material, the good story-teller turns it into literature. But when an ethnologist draws someone out about a particular myth, that myth is not literature – though it can become literature if the ethnologist is a good author and writes it down in a good form, only then it is no longer African literature. Conversely, a good African story-teller may have passed on excellent literature to an ethnologist, who will write it down and perhaps produce merely raw material for mythologists.

2. The Material

So we ought to examine all the collected material for traces of the oral forms of 'procedure' discernible in the written form. Such research would have to be based on a comprehensive annotated bibliography, which included not only the anthologies and local collections of proverbs, stories, myths, sagas, fairy-tales, epics and songs, but also most of the ethnological monographs, grammars, travellers' accounts, and the vast numbers of special articles in ethnological journals. For oral literature is widely dispersed, and the most authentic texts are often to be found in the most insignificant publications.

Such a bibliography, however, would be outside the scope of this book. I shall confine myself to giving two lists, both in chronological order, to provide the reader with a sort of survey of discovery: in section 2 of the bibliography for this chapter, a list of the popular anthologies which are widely known; and a table naming special collections from particular areas, classified according to the main subjects of the collections – proverbs, stories and lyric poetry.

Where the compilers are Africans, I have put their names in italics, saving space by not quoting the titles (often long) and not listing the first names or initials of the editors; these, however, the reader can find in the index. If interested, he can find the works even without knowing their title, since I have also given date and place of publication, and the names of the people or territory from which each of these traditional texts is drawn. It is also important, of course, to know in which collections the texts may be found in the vernacular languages: where this is the case, the name of the people, language or region appears in capitals. For the years before 1870 (but only for them) I have included works which are neither books nor special collections–especially grammars and articles from journals which contain some 'literature', mainly proverbs–so that it can be seen where and when oral literature first received attention.

It has been asserted that the first collectors were all Europeans. But after the studies of the Tswana language made by Eugène Casalis in 1841, which contain fifty-six proverbs in French translation, the first book in which proverbs appeared in their original language was a Yoruba grammar of 1843 produced by Samuel Adjai Crowther of Oshogbo in Nigeria. Crowther was a former slave, emancipated by the British, who was trained as a missionary in Sierra Leone, and became bishop in his native country.

Except for the famous British traveller and explorer, Sir Richard Francis Burton, and the Berlin philologist, Wilhelm Heinrich Immanuel Bleek, 'the father of Bantu studies', who worked as a librarian in Capetown, almost all the pre-1870 scholars were missionaries: Hans Nikolaus Rijs, J. B. Schlegel, Karl Hugo Hahn, Thomas J. Bowen, Christian Friedrich Schlenker, Jakob Friedrich Schön, H. Callaway, Gottlieb Christaller and Sigismund Wilhelm Kölle–to mention only the most important. Christaller produced the first big collection of proverbs, giving 3,600 of them in the Twi language. Kölle, who produced (in 1854) the first collection of fables and stories, from the Kanuri by Lake Chad, had not actually been staying in the Kanuri area; he did his research from Sierra Leone, where freed slaves from many parts of Africa, including some from Bornu, had been settled.

The early collections were strictly functional: their purpose was the study and learning of languages, and proverbs offered easily assimilable material for learning. In 1893 the station of the Paris Evangelical Mission at Morija in Basutoland, which was soon to become a centre of early neo-African literature in African languages, published the first collection by an African which contains traditional texts: *Buka ea pokello ea mokhoa ea Ba-Sotho* (Collection of Sotho Customs) by Azariele Sekese (1849–1931).

By the end of the nineteenth century stories had been collected from many peoples and poems from a few; fragments had been published here and there in grammars. In 1896 August Seidel was able to compile the first anthological survey *Geschichten und Lieder der Afrikaner* (Stories and Songs of the Africans). The actual poetry was given closer attention only where the culture of the Arabic script had penetrated into sub-Saharan Africa: Rudolf Prietze had translated Hausa epics; Carl Velten, Swahili songs.

The next big anthology was published by Leo Frobenius under the provocative title of *Der Schwarze Dekameron* (The Black Decameron), with a foreword addressed to Boccaccio; it had the success expected. Meinhof's collection of *Afrikanische Märchen* (African Fairy-tales), published in 1917, also became extremely popular, and Frobenius was encouraged to start in 1921 on the collection *Atlantis*, which appeared in twelve volumes up till 1927. With its 4,128 pages it contains many hundreds of stories, myths, sagas, fables, fairy-tales and traditional texts. It is an inexhaustible treasure-trove.

The famous *Anthologie Nègre*, by Blaise Cendrars, which for the first time introduced the West European public to the wealth of African tradition, is unfortunately also the worst. All earlier anthologists were men who knew and studied Africa; whereas Cendrars, sailor, juggler, foreign legionary, journalist and poet, picked some of the plums out of their collections and translated them into French, mixing the traditions of various peoples with a view of the world and nature of his own design. He selected the texts, too, in such an arbitrary way that the general impression left is thoroughly misleading.*

Since his work was eventually translated into English and Spanish, it contains pieces which in the end are translations at fourth or fifth hand. Thus a Nupe story was told in English to Frobenius by a Yoruba who knew the Nupe language. The second translation was put into German by Frobenius. Cendrars turned in into French, and his translator, Margery Bianco, finally turned it into English. Naturally only the barest skeleton of the original is left. Such methods could be considered justifiable only because interest was centred on content, and not on literature at all.

The later anthologies rely on the earlier ones. Whiteley's collection in 1964 was the first to bring a new perspective, since the selection he made was based on literary considerations.

My list of collections divided by place is neither representative nor complete, and my classification by groups is not to be taken as exact. Stories, proverbs and songs are often to be found in the same volume, which I have then not listed several times but simply allotted to the dominant group. I have not included the many small volumes of under fifty pages, mostly published by Africans. The list makes it

* The first sentence of his introduction is copied from Seidel's foreword, including the misprint this contained, turning the name of the scholar McCall Theal into Mc. All Theal. Cendrars also speaks of Heli Chatelain as having studied the 'Ambantou' language, which does not exist. The language is in fact 'Kimbundu', and Seidel, who always gives the name of the tribe, gave that correctly as 'Ambundu'.

clear, however, that African collectors first became prominent between the two world wars, and played a leading part after the second
war.

Still, the bulk of oral literature, and the most important clues for
its investigation, have been published in the international ethnological
journals of the last hundred years. This is a mass of material which
literary scholars have so far barely considered. It provides most valuable material for stylistic analysis, which has been further expanded
by the tape-recordings of the last decade. Stylistic research could
start with these tape-recordings, if they have a phonetic transcription,
a literal and a freer translation into a European language, and a description of the cultural background. There should also be notes on the
locality, function and other relevant factors, The fact that hardly any
of this research has been carried out increases the difficulty of exami-
ning neo-African literature; since (as stated above) it is only through
oral literature that one can show where African stylistic elements
have been retained and where exactly there have been changes.

3. Some Stylistic Forms of the 'Praise Song'

African oral literature is not the subject of this book. I must confine
myself to pointing out some of its principles which are also important
for neo-African poetry.

In the introduction to his collection *Yoruba Poetry* Beier writes:

'Most translations of African literature are in fact collections of
myths, legends and fables. Thus the false impression is sometimes
created that African literature consists of nothing but tales about the
tortoise and spider. In reality poetry is more common in African life
than prose.

'In traditional Yoruba life (as in most illiterate societies) nothing
at all is done without poetry. No state or religious ceremony can take
place without the professional bards singing the praises of the king
or the gods, while at the same time they improvise on current events
and comment with considerable licence on the deeds and character
of the chiefs. Each religious cult has its own kind of poetry with a
special technique of recitation. The hunters invent poems about the
animals and plants of the forest: even the Ifa oracle is pronounced in
poetic form. Nor is poetry reserved for special or festive occasions. It
is part of everyday life. The woman selling cassava may sing the
praise names of cassava. The appearance of a person from an important compound will provoke some old person to sing the history of

his family. Any individual has, in fact, a body of poetry attached to his name.

'Names are very important in Yoruba life. In Europe we often use names without being conscious of their actual meaning. We are not always aware that Emmanuel means "God is with us" or John means "the beloved of God". In Yoruba country the name has greater significance, and children will be named "Joy enters the house", "I have someone to pet", "The God of iron sent you to console me", "The God of the river has visited this house". But in addition to these names given at the naming ceremonies, there are others with which the child is born and which relate in fact to circumstances of birth. Names indicate that a child is the first-born of twins, or born face downwards, or with the umbilical cord round his neck, or born on a Friday and so on. Most important, however, is the third group of names, the *oriki*, of which a person may acquire more and more during the course of his life.

'The *oriki* are descriptive phrases referring to the character or deeds of a person. They may be invented by relatives or neighbours or—most frequently–by the drummers, and they remain with the person, and everybody in his surroundings will know them by heart. A collection of *oriki* is like a very loosely constructed poem having as its subject a single individual or a chief, a town or even a god.'[1]

The larger poetic form, the poem, is made up, then, of separate 'praise names', of compressed aphorisms alluding to events, stories and myths which are the common possession of the neighbourhood or the group, and which only need to be hinted at, because everyone knows them. The smaller and more isolated a stylistic group, the bigger the proportion of such 'inside knowledge'. The larger the group, such as a state (the area subject to a king) the more widely the praise songs of his bards will be understood. But in both cases we recognize throughout sub-Saharan Africa the same structure in the praise song, which has spread everywhere: it is put together from a series of aphoristic parts, which in their turn consist of praise names, allusions, proverbs and picturesque incantations. Here are a few examples:

(a) Extract from a Yoruba *oriki* on the *Ogoga* (King) of Ikerre:

'However small the needle, the hen cannot swallow it.
The toad jumps about happily in the face of the cook.
Two hundred needles do not equal a hoe, two hundred stars do
    not make a moon.

The white hair of an albino cannot be dyed,
A good rider will not be thrown off his horse.'[2]

(b) From a Zulu praise song (*izibongo*) to King Shaka:

> 'The nations he hath all destroyed,
> Whither shall he now attack?
> He! Whither shall he now attack?
> He defeated kings,
> Whither shall he now attack?
> The nations he hath all destroyed,
> Whither shall he now attack?
> He! He! He! Whither shall he now attack?'[3]

(c) Some verses (*enkome*) from a Hima boasting song (*ekyevugo*):

'I Who Stand Firm in Battle defeated them utterly and so did
  The One Who Needs No Protection.
I Who Am Clear Headed faced the spears together with The
  Ceaseless Fighter.
I Who Am Eager For Battle, with The One Who Seeks No
  Help, captured a slave girl.'[4]

Each section of such a poem is a complete poem in itself. The
beginning and end are, so to speak, 'open'. The thing which formally
joins the parts is the rhythm, for they are recited to percussion instruments or sung according to an established rhythmic style. Lasebikan,
in his investigation of the structure of Yoruba poetry–one of the very
few investigations of style which have been made–has referred to
tonal structures and a sort of tonal rhythm. And Morris writes of the
Hima praise song: 'The high tones are the same in number, are similarly spaced and fall on comparable syllables in each line. It may be
that we are dealing here with tonal rhyme which is characteristic of
Luganda poetry.'[5] The significance of the style is made clear by the
fact that composition (among the Yoruba) is classified, as Beier
writes, 'not so much by the contents or the structure but by the group
of people to which the reciter belongs and the technique of recitation
he employs.'[6]

 In the case of Example (a), each verse looks as if it had no connection with the others, as if needle, toad, moon, albino and rider were
images strung together at random. But they all refer to the subject of
the praise song, the King of Ikerre: the enemy can overcome him no
more than the hen can overcome the needle or the cook the toad; as

two hundred needles do not equal a hoe, and two hundred stars do not make a moon, two hundred men and warriors are no match for the King of Ikerre; and it is just as impossible to depose him as to give colour to an albino or make a horse throw a good rider. The common reference is to the mighty life-force, the *magara* (see p. 161–2) of the subject of the praise song. We shall find this 'referential' technique again in the North American 'Blues' (Chapter 10). This, it seems to me, is no coincidence. Lasebikan quotes a poem for the talking-drum, which has a typical Blues structure:

> 'Dancing with irregular steps you are heading for the marsh,
> Dancing with irregular steps you are heading for the marsh.
> If you always dance with irregular steps, you will never be a
>   good dancer.'[7]

In translation the Blues form may be less obvious; especially as the terse Yoruba phrase 'Jo-báta-batá' has turned into the clumsy 'dancing with irregular steps'. So I give the original as well:

> 'Jó báta-batá o gb'ônà àbàtà
> Jó báta-batá o gb'ônà àbàtà
> Ojó báta-báta
> Ojó báta-báta
> Opa b'ó ti mo jó lailai.'[8]

The structure of Example (b) also recurs in a Blues form in North America. All these examples are improvised poetry, and Morris has this to say of the way the boasting songs represented by Example (c) got handed down:

'. . . a poem would attain a peculiar popularity while the event was still fresh in people's minds, but would not survive its composer. Since every well-brought-up Muhima* was expected to be capable of composing, he would not have the slightest inclination to learn or preserve the poems of another. By good fortune, however, Bairu servants who worked in the kraals of Bahima would often hear and learn by heart these recitations and pass them on to their descendants though usually in a fragmentary form.'[9]

The art of poetic improvisation within the framework of the historical style has also been preserved up to modern times. In the bars of big African towns a praise song is improvised for any prominent guest,† and even specialized forms like the Hima vaunting-songs have

---

* *Muhima* is the singular of Bahima (generically Hima).
† An example of this style is given on pp. 177–8.

neo-African successors, some written down, like these verses from a modern *ekyevugo* by Patrick Kirindi:

'He Who Fails Not To Overthrow The Foe and He Who Is
Slow To Show Fear made the cannons roar . . .
The letters were sent out by The Disperser of Warriors,
The typing was done by Mashunju . . .
The letters went through the printing-press,
They passed through the linotype . . .'[10]

I have restricted myself here to a few stylistic forms of a single type, the praise song; though I should like to have gone into other forms such as those of the hunting songs, the oracular verses and the dirges. There is, however, only one detailed study of such forms, and this is by Kwabena Nketia, on the burial songs of the Akan. It is unique in quality and the best work I know yet published on African oral literature. But until similar works appear from other areas, stylistic rules of general validity cannot be formulated. My purpose in this section has been merely to make suggestions for research and to show the possibilities by a few examples.

REFERENCES AND BIBLIOGRAPHIES

1. What is Oral Literature?

[1] Meinhof, p. 9.
[2] ibid., p. 10.
[3] Seidel, pp. 1–3.
[4] Meinhof, p. 64.
[5] Whiteley, p. 6.
[6] Doke, p. 105.
[7] ibid., p. 110.

DOKE, Clement Martyn: Bantu wisdom lore. In: African Studies, vol. 6, No. 3, Johannesburg 1947
MEINHOF, Carl: Die Dichtung der Afrikaner. Berlin 1911
SEIDEL, August: Geschichten und Lieder der Afrikaner. Berlin 1896
WHITELEY, W. H.: A selection of African prose. I.: Traditional and oral texts. Oxford 1964

2. The Material

A large bibliography is given at the end of William Bascom's article, Folklore research in Africa, in 'Journal of American Folklore', vol. 77, No. 303, Richmond, Va., January/March 1964, pp. 21–31

1896: SEIDEL, August: Geschichten und Lieder der Afrikaner. Berlin

1906: STAFFORD, Alphonso Orenzo: Animal fables from the Dark Continent. New York

1910: FROBENIUS, Leo: Der schwarze Dekameron. Berlin

1917: MEINHOF, Carl: Afrikanische Märchen. Jena

1921–8: FROBENIUS, Leo: Atlantis. Jena. 12 vols.

1921: CENDRARS, Blaise: Anthologie nègre. Paris
(– The African saga. New York 1927)
(– Antología negra. Madrid 1930)

1925: EINSTEIN, Carl: Afrikanische Legenden. Berlin

1944: OSÓRIO DE OLIVEIRA, José: Literatura africana. Lisbon

1950: FINBERT, Elian-J.: Le livre de la sagesse nègre. Paris

1952: RADIN, Paul: African folktales and sculpture. New York

1958: RUTHERFOORD, Peggy: Darkness and light. London (Nos. 44–5)

1960: HUGHES, Langston: An African treasury. New York (Nos. 25–7)

1962: COURLANDER, Harold: The king's drum, and other African stories. New York

1962: JAHN, Janheinz: Die Welt ist Wind. Afrikanische Pointen. München

1963: FELDMAN, Susan: African myths and tales. New York

1964: WHITELEY, W. H.: A selection of African prose. Oxford

1966: BEIER, Ulli: African poetry. Cambridge
–The origin of life and death. London

3. Some Stylistic Forms of the 'Praise Song'

[1] Gbadamosi/Beier, p. 6.
[2] ibid., p. 23.
[3] Nyembezi, p. 114.
[4] Morris, pp. 54–6.
[5] ibid., p. 39.
[6] Gbadamosi/Beier, p. 9.
[7] Lasebikan, p. 48.
[8] ibid.
[9] Morris, p. 13.
[10] ibid., p. 92.

BABALOLA, S. A.: The content and form of Yoruba ijálá. London 1966

GBADAMOSI, Bakare *and* BEIER, Ulli: Yoruba poetry. Ibadan 1959

GUMA, Samson Mbizo: The forms, contents and techniques of traditional literature in Southern Sotho. Unpublished thesis, University of South Africa, Pretoria 1964

KUNENE, Raymond: An analytical survey of Zulu poetry both traditional and modern. Unpublished thesis, University of Natal, Durban, no date.

LASEBIKAN, Ebenezer Latunde: The tonal structure of Yoruba poetry. In: Présence Africaine, new series, Nos. 8–10, Paris 1956

MORRIS, Henry F.: The heroic recitations of the Bahima of Ankole. Oxford 1964

NKETIA, Joseph Hanson Kwabena: Funeral dirges of the Akan people. Achimota 1955

NYEMBEZI, Cyril Lincoln Sibusiso: The historical background to the Izibongo of the Zulu military age. In: African Studies, vol. 7, Johannesburg 1948

TABLE 2

Collections of African Oral Literature

CAPITALS : original African text is given
Italics : Collector is an African
(Brackets) : in journal, grammar, monograph etc.
[Square brackets] : Afro-Arabic written literature

Collections of Proverbs	Fairy-tales, Stories	Songs, Epics, Poems
(1841 Casalis (Sotho) Paris)		
(1843 *Crowther* (YORUBA) London)		
(1843 Schön (HAUSA) London)		
(1853 Rijs (TWI, AKWAPIM) Basel)	1854 Kölle (KANURI) London	
(1857 Schlegel (EWE) Stuttgart)		
(1857 Hahn (HERERO) Berlin)		
(1858 Boilat (WOLOF) Paris)	1861 Schlenker (TEMNE) London	
(1858 Bowen (YORUBA) Washington)	1862 Hahn (HERERO) Gütersloh	
(1858 Zimmermann (GA) Stuttgart)	1864 Bleek (Hottentot) London	
1865 Burton (WEST AFRICA) London	1866 Callaway (ZULU) London	
(1867 Mitterrutzner (BARI) Brixen)		
(1867 Steinthal (VAI) Berlin)		

Collections of Proverbs	Fairy-tales, Stories	Songs, Epics, Poems
	1870 Steere (SWAHILI) London	
	1882 Theal (Xhosa) Cape Town	
	1885 Schön (HAUSA) London	
	1889 E. Meinhof (Cameroon) Straßburg	
1897 Christaller (TWI) Basel		
1891 Cordeira (KIMBUNDU) Lisboa		
1891 Taylor (SWAHILI) London		
	1893 *Sekese* (SOTHO) Morija	
	[1894 Büttner (SWAHILI) Berlin]	
	1894 Chatelain KIMBUNDU) Boston	
	1894 Woodward (BONDEI) London	
	1895 Jacottet (Sotho) Paris	
		1897 Junod (Ronga) Lausanne
	1898 Junod (RONGA) Neuchâtel	
	1898 Velten (SWAHILI) Stuttgart	
1901 Cook (GANDA) London	1901 Jacottet (SUBIA), LUYI) Paris	
		[1904 Prietze (HAUSA) Kirchhain]
1907 *Sekese* (SOTHO) Morija	1907 Rattray (NYANJA) London	[1907 Velten (SWAHILI) Berlin]
	1908 Jacottet (SOTHO) London	
	1909 Schönhärl (EWE) Dresden	
	1909 Landeroin & Tilho (HAUSA) Paris	
	1910 Fuchs (Masai) Jena	
	1910 Thomas (EDO) London	
	1911 Bleek (BUSHMAN) London	
	1913 Equilbecq (West Africa) Paris	
	1913 Rattray (HAUSA) Oxford	
	1913 Thomas (IBO) London	
	1913 Westermann (PÖL) Berlin	
	1913 Zeltner (Senegal, Niger) Paris	
1914 Thomas (IBO) London		
1915 Bürgi (EWE) Braunschweig		
1916 *Lakeru* (YORUBA) Abeokuta		
1916 *Plaatje* (TSWANA) London		

1916	*Rattray* (TWI) Oxford
1931	*Gaden* (PÖL, TUKULOR) Paris
1934	Lindblom (KAMBA) Uppsala
1936	*Junod* (TSONGA) Cleveland, Tr.
1953	*Kagame* (RWANDA) Kabgayi
1954	*Nyembezi* (ZULU) Johannesburg
1955	*Betoté* (FANG) Paris
1955	*Sissoko* (Malinke) Paris
1957	*Nkongori* (RWANDA) Tervuren

1917	Barker (Ghana) London
1920	*Ndawo* (XHOSA) Mariannhill
1921	Tessmann (Fang) Berlin
1921	Ruskin (MONGO) Bongandanga
1922	Hurel (RWANDA) Bruxelles
1923	*Travelé* (BAMBARA) Paris
1927	Trautmann (Popo, Nago, Fon) Paris
1927	Doke (LAMBA) New York
1928–35	Lindblom (KAMBA) Uppsala
1929	Mischlich (HAUSA) Leipzig
1930	Rattray (ASHANTI) Oxford
1931	Cardinall (Togo/Ghana) London
1935	*Dube* (ZULU) London
1936	Struyf (BAKONGO) Brussels
1949	*Nketia* (TWI) London
1950	*Kani* (TWI) London
1950	Coyssi (Dahomey) Paris
1951	*Desewu* (Ewe) London
1951	Himmelheber (Baule) Eisenach
1952	Kayombo (Tanzania) London
1953	*Itayemi* + Gurrey (West Africa) London
1954	Ekwensi (Ibo) London
1954	Anim (TWI) Accra
1956	Kohl-Larsen (Tindiga) Kassel

1921	*Mangoaela* (SOTHO) Morija
1926	Patterson (KANURI) Lagos
1935	*Phala* (PEDI) Pretoria
1938	Jaques (TSONGA) Johannesburg
1949	Boelaert (NKUNDO) Antwerpen
1949	*Nketia* (TWI) Accra
1949	*Kagame* (Rwanda) Kabgayi
1949	Tracey (ZULU) Roodepoort
1951	*Ahamba* (IBO) Aba
1951	*Kagame* (RWANDA) Bruxelles
1952	*Manisi* (XHOSA) Lovedale
1955	*Nketia* (AKAN) Achimota

Collections of Proverbs

1958 Farsi (SWAHILI) Dar es Salaam
1958 Hulstaert (MONGO) Tervuren

1960 Molin (BAMBARA, MALINKE) Issy
1961 Rodegem (RUNDI) Tervuren
1961 Ribas (KIMBUNDU) Luanda

1962 Mkandawire (TUMBUKA) Lusaka

Fairy-tales, Stories

1958 Herskovits (Dahomey) Evanston

1961 Tubiana (Zaghawa) Paris
1961 Walker + Idewu (Yoruba) New Brunswick
1961 Fuchs (Mimi) Stuttgart
1962 Ribas (KIMBUNDU) Luanda
1962 Ennis (Kimbundu) Boston
1962 Fuja (Yoruba) London
1962 Ogunbowale (YORUBA) London

1964 Postma (South Africa) Johannesburg

1964 Sidahome (Benin) London

1966 Johnston (Hausa) Oxford
1966 Mbiti (Kamba) Oxford
1967 Finnegan (Limba) Oxford

Songs, Epics, Poems

1958 Lasebikan (YORUBA) London
1958 Nyembezi (ZULU) Pietermaritzburg
1959 Gbadamosi + Beier (Yoruba) Ibadan

1961 Tescaroli (SUDAN) Bologna
1961 Gbadamosi (YORUBA) Ibadan

1963 Dampierre (NZAKARA) Paris
1964 Morris (HIMA) Oxford
1964 Ribas (KIMBUNDU) Luanda

1965 Schapera (TSWANA) Oxford
1965 Lacroix (ADAMAWA) Paris
1966 Sow (FULANI) Paris
1966 Babalola (YORUBA) Oxford

Chapter 4

AFRO-ARABIC LITERATURE

1. Hausa Literature

Hausa literature is comparatively well documented and analysed, so I shall merely quote from relevant works and add a few examples, which R. Prietze collected between 1904 and 1914.*

'The published poetic material in Hausa,' Greenberg writes, 'can be divided into two main categories. There is first the poetry of religious inspiration composed by the Mohammedan learned men, the *malams*. This poetry is circulated in written form and employs classical Arabic metres. It is usually sung without instrumental accompaniment. The other main type is that of the itinerant individual singer and drummer who sings in the interval between the dances. This poetry is unwritten; the subject matter is non-religious. Though the rhythm is quantitative, Arabic meters are not employed. As in classical Arabic poetry, each verse is divided into two hemistichs, but they are shorter than in Arabic poetry, averaging seven or eight syllables. Between these two types a middle position is occupied by the "singing master".'[1]

'The "singing master" gives himself the female title Zabia. He sometimes appears with solemn suite, partly musicians, notably the player of the *guremi* accompanying the song – a two-stringed zither with gourd sounding-board – and partly those who will help in collecting the gifts and who call out what these are, often with terrific exaggerations so as to extract a tip from the donor. The leader of a group of travelling scholars is also a *zābia*, surrounded by the choir of his companions, who sing an invocation of God after each of his verses – which does not stop him giving free vein to his student high spirits, for instance against the growling house-dog:

---

* The Hausa spelling of the texts collected by Prietze has been modernized by Professor Rössler of Marburg according to the rules of the Gaskiya Corporation, Zaria.

73

Mai gída yána múrnatá,
   karé na fúshi da ní;
mai ƙwaurí ya kwárkwaron mátsiyatá,
   mai bakí kamár kwarí.
Ban gá mutûm yána rówa bá,
   ba shi záya bá ka bá,
sái fa a gûn karé ɗán farká,
   karé ɗán harámíya.
Kó wace dábba ána cîn námanta,
   kái ba zâa cí ka bá.
Bâ ká da mágani sái háushi,
   faráutarka bâ mú cî.

'The master would welcome me in,
   But the miserable dog only growls.
His legs are so spindly thin,
   Like a quiver of arrows his jowls.
I've heard of the misers who won't spend a bean
   But never met anyone mangy and mean
Like this mastiff you meet at the door,
   Son of sin and the son of a whore.
You can eat almost all other animals' meat,
   But you, you damned dog, no one ever would eat.
Barking's the only real skill you can claim.
   You poisonous creature, we'd hate you as game.'

'Another "singing master" is the chief drummer of a ruling lord, whose deeds he must celebrate in song. But the main representative of poetry, its dreaded potentate, is the free minstrel who goes from place to place with his troupe and gives recitals. His reception by the public depends on how well he can handle the three types, *yabō* (praise song), *zambō* (lampoon) or *bēgē* (love song). The *yabō* is favourite because it brings in most money, and the singer will celebrate not only the ruler, the chancellor, the general, but also people whose social position is dubious, like a barber who knows how to tattoo girls attractively:

Yá máta tsúntsu carkí,
   yá máta alló, yá yi tambarí;
yá máta "bi tá da dubá",
   ín tá wúce, kówa yána dúbawá.[2]

'With Charki birds he has adorned her skin,
Patterned her arm and beautified her thigh.
"Just look at *her*" he might have branded in,
So folks all look at her when she goes by.'

The songs of the 'singing masters', as can be seen, belong to the general African *genre* of praise songs. Nor is the Islamic poetry in these songs all that pious. Here is an 'Admonition to invoke God's help in every undertaking':

Kóme záka yi, ɗán Adám,	Whatever you would do, O man,
ka ambací súnan rábbi.	Invoke the Lord's great name.
Idán ká kái ƙára ga rábbi,	If on the Lord you call for help,
aikin ba zâi ɓáci bá.	Your work will not go wrong.
Kó da sáta záka yí,	And if you would go forth to rob
kai ƙara gûn rábbaná.	Ask help from our good Lord!
Kó néman máta káke yi,	And if you would run after girls,
ka ambací súnan rábbi.[3]	Invoke the Lord's great name.

Now a lampoon, a humorous obituary to Gwaja, the over-officious henchman of the vizier Garko. The plant *dorawa* referred to in it is the poisonous *Parkia biglobosa*, the fruit of the tsada, the Nile acacia. Praise and mockery are mixed here, as in many African songs of this kind:

Námaɗótal sárkin ɗokí,	'Walkinfront, Lord Hurry's son,
zágín gabán zágí!	You before fore-runners run!
Námaɗótal Gwája,	Gwaja, Walkinfrontofall,
me záya fáɗi ka tsintá?	Do you pick up what will fall?
Mai abu na mútuwa	He who once the burials led,
Gwája, án bínne shi!	Gwaja now is buriéd.
Wasá dú án dáina –	Though his little games are done,
Gwája bai dáina bá.	Gwaja's poison lingers on.
Namaɗótal sannú da áiki,	Walkinfront, we see your plan,
Gwája ná sárkin Gárko!	Gwaja, Vizier Garko's man!
Doráwa kashé mai zarí,	Dorawa which swallows eater,
húntu kashé mai rigá!	Naked, of the armed a beater!
ƙyallí-ƙyallín tsáda,	Tsada's fruit that shines serene,
kyâun gáni daga báya!	Lovely from a distance seen!
Daníniya ná sárkin Gárko,	Garko's cruel snare and gin,
mai ɓádda wáwan baƙó!	Taking stupid strangers in!
Tínya mákanta idanú,	Cactus that infects the eyes,
wáwa ke sháfa ta!	Daubing it on them's unwise!

Tsarárriya mai rikíci,	Bean that never ripe will grow
wádda bá ta nuná!	Or bean shell to King Garko
Gayán-gayán ná sárkin Gárko	Just the sort that has you tricked,
wánda ba íya táro.[4]	Jumps about and can't be picked.'

Now a praise and love song to a girl without whose presence at the feast joy is missing:

Aiyaré ké gwidá ké ce,	'Hurrah for the maiden, you are she,
tá ɗan Alí mai wayó.	Sister of the son of Ali the clever!
Ní wasán da ke tsirára,	For the game one started naked,
ƙárya ba nâ yi mása wandó bá.	I would not pretend trousers were worn.
Domín abîn da bâ shi da róho,	What brings no good cheer in itself,
ní má ba zân mása róho bá.	I will not make cheerful either.
Bikí kadán bâ gwidá,	When the maiden is missing at a feast,
ní má ba zân íya múrna bá.[5]	I cannot make joy there either.'

Of the song below Prietze notes: 'In a burlesque duet a girl finds her lover "common"; he deduces that they fit together all the better for it.'

> *She*
> Tashí, tashí, ka bár míni gadóna,
> bakínka shína wárin tába!
> *He*
> Ní kuwá kadán bakína shína wárin tába,
> ke kuwá bakínki shína wárin gégo!
> 　　Matá karé
> 　　karé shíke áure,
> kurgúngumá kuwá sái buzúzu.[6]

> 'She
> Don't want you here in bed, so get up quick.
> Your vile smell of tobacco makes me sick.
> He:
> If my tobacco has so vile a smell,
> That's fine, because your breath is vile as well.
> Each dog must find
> His bitch as mate designed,
> Dung-beetle too only a moth can woo.'

Here is a rather horrifying 'lament of a slave-girl on the train through the desert':

> Alkáwari da báwan Túrawa
> bâ shi dáurewa.[7]
> Sún dauké ni, sún bá ga Túrawa,
> zásu kái ni Zaila.
> Wa ke kái ni kúkar Jangarai,
> in gáni alján.[7]

> 'Whites and slaves at peace can never
> Live together.
> They gave me to the Whites who maul me,
> To Zaila haul me.
> Who takes me now to Jangarai's breadtree
> The ghosts to see?'

Prietze comments: 'Jangarai is a town between Agades and Gameru, haunted by demons. You have to go through it in silence. Anyone who speaks disappears. Yet the slave-girl wishes to put herself under the protection of these ghosts; for in the Sudan there is a common idea that the black prisoners were dragged off to Zaila, there to be eaten by the Whites.'[8] Zaila is south of Djibouti, the port on the Gulf of Aden, from where the slaves were taken across to Arabia.

2. Swahili Poetry

Hausa and Swahili are influenced by Arabic in different ways. While Hausa *malams* often used the Arabic language to write down historic and religious texts, Swahili authors used only the Arabic script. There has thus been Swahili poetry written in Arabic letters for over three hundred years; the oldest Swahili manuscript so far discovered is *Utendi wa Tabuka*, a heroic poem written for the Sultan (Fumo) Laiti Nabhani, which bears the date 1728. Swahili poetry started by being mostly religious in content, but gradually became more secular. According to tradition it was Muyaka bin Haji from Mombasa (1776–1840) who brought 'poetry out of the mosque and into the market-place.'[1] Since the end of the nineteenth century Swahili has been written in the Roman alphabet.

Lyndon Harries has made an excellent study of *Swahili Poetry*. He says that although it 'derives from Arabic poetry, it cannot be considered an extension of Arabic poetry'; for it has 'an African background' and is 'an amalgam of two traditions.'[2] Since his book is easily accessible, I shall do no more than summarize his findings.

As in Arabic, there is a rhyme at the end of the verse, which is carried on for all verses till the end of the poem. Internal rhymes mark the end of each *kipande* (plural *vipande*), each part of a verse. Stylistically, the poems are classified according to the number of parts (*vipande*) to each verse (*baiti*). The metre is determined by the number of vocalized syllables (*mizani*) to a *kipande*: an eight-*mizani* verse, for instance, means a verse with eight vocalized syllables in each *kipande*.

Poems with four *vipande* to a verse are called *utendi*, and are used for epic, heroic, moralizing and didactic subjects, which are all connected with the glorification of Mohammed and Islam. Since the beginning of this century, however, *utendi* forms have been used for describing historical events–these form the largest part of Velten's collection (see p. 83)–and for the poetic treatment of oral traditions. The most popular form has eight *mizani* to a *kipande* (or sometimes seven). As an example, here is a humorous poem, the 'Song of the Stranger Come to Stay' (*Akala Shairi*):

Mgeni siku ya kwanza	'For the stranger his first day
mpele mchele na panza;	Rice and flying-fish provide,
mtilie kifuani,	Hug him, welcome him inside,
mkaribishe mgeni.	Stranger who has come to stay.
Mgeni siku ya pili	On the stranger's second day
mpe ziwa na samli;	Give him milk and butter too.
mahaba yakizidia,	Let love greatly grow in you,
mzidie mgeni.	For the stranger come to stay.
Mgeni siku ya tatu;	Stranger now on his third day,
jumbani hamuna kitu.	Three cups rice is all we've got
Mna zibaba zitatu,	Left for food. Cook, eat the lot
pika ule na mgeni.	With the stranger come to stay.
Mgeni siku ya ne	Stranger now on his fourth day,
mpe jembe akalime.	Send him off to help them hoe.
Akirudi muagane,	When he comes back bid him go
ende kwao mgeni.	Home, dear stranger come to stay.
Mgeni siku ya tano	Look at stranger his fifth day,
mwembamba kama sindano.	Thin as needle he has gone.
Hauishi musengenyano	Gossip now goes on and on
asengenyao mgeni.	'Bout the stranger come to stay.

Mgeni siku ya sita;	Stranger on the sixth long day,
mkila mkajificha;	When you eat he mustn't know,
mwingie vipembeni	In some hidden corner go,
afichwaye yeye mgeni.	Hide from stranger come to stay.
Mgeni siku ya sabaa	Stranger on the seventh day—
si mgeni a na baa.	Someone set the roof alight.
Hatta moto mapaani	Guilty man is known all right,
akatia yeye mgeni.	That's the monster come to stay.
Mgeni siku ya nane;	Tell the stranger his eighth day,
njo ndani tuonane.	Just come in a moment, then
Atapotokea nje,	Say when he goes out again,
tuagane mgeni.	Goodbye, stranger come to stay.
Mgeni siku ya kenda;	Tell the stranger his ninth day,
enenda mwana kwenenda!	Go in peace, my son, but go,
Usirudi nyuma,	Only don't come back, you know,
Usirudi mgeni.	Go, you stranger come to stay.
Mgeni siku ya kumi	Stranger now on his tenth day,
kwa mateke na magumi	Chuck him out with kick and clout!
Hapana afukuzwaye,	Chuck him, chuck him, chuck him out!
fukuzwaye, fukuzwaye yeye mgeni![3]	Out, you stranger come to stay!'

For love poems the form of the 'four-liner' started in the nineteenth century, each verse with eight *vipande*, a changing rhyme, and eight *mizani* to a *kipande*. This four-liner became more and more popular— for all subjects not inspired by Arab models. I give a modern example, a poem with two verses by Shaaban Robert, which, compared to the traditional form has two irregularities: the two verse endings do not rhyme with each other, but the first *vipande* of every line rhyme with each other, and so do the second *vipande*. It is called 'Quiver':

Ziaka tupu hutisha,	likiwa na mfuniko,
Adui atakupisha,	njiani kila wendako,
Bila ya kudhihirisha,	nia kwa tamko,
Stadi kubahatisha,	hatambui siri yako.
Ziaka bila mshale,	likifunikwa hutisha,
Hudhaniwa imo tele	mishale ya kufisha,
Ulimi vile vile,	siri yake hudumisha,
Usipomwaga nenole,	ovyo katika maisha.[4]

'When the lid on it is staying,   empty quiver quite impresses.
Enemy, his ambush laying,   feels the menace it addresses.
Left in doubt what game you're   at your plans he vainly guesses;
    playing,
And the quiver's not betraying   fearful secret it possesses.

When by lid it is protected,   empty quiver's still dismaying;
Arrowless, it's still suspected   full of arrows death-conveying.
Secret equally respected   by the tongue which "isn't
    saying" –
Till it blurts out, unreflected,   careless word to others straying.'

Shaaban Robert (1909–62) is outstanding among modern Swahili poets. Although his poetic inspiration is not particularly original, he expanded and modernized the vocabulary, and both in prose and verse created stylistic models adapted to modern times, which will be of importance for future Swahili poetry.

The most popular form of long verse, which was already common in earliest times, is the *gungu*-song with ten *mizani*, used both for dancing and for wedding songs, praise songs and serenades. Another type of wedding song, *mavugo*, has no rhyme, however, and no established metre measured in *mizani*. These songs come from folklore and are scarcely arabized.

The melodiousness and conciseness of the language, and also its facility for rhyming, have produced verses with all sorts of repetitions and permutations of words and *vipande*. It may look like mere jingle, a kind of poetic acrobatics, but in fact it enhances the rhythmic element and heightens the effect through repetition.

3. A Swahili Autobiography and Swahili Occasional Verse

'This is my story of what I know. But I have not finished yet. If it be God's will and I keep my health, I shall write a thousand times more next year. I shall describe everything from Zanzibar to Mrima, and give it to the very great sheik, my father, my teacher, my patron, my beloved Dr. Büttner. May God grant him health and His favour and all that is good, and grant it also to the Director . . . and to me likewise. And the Poor one of God the All-Highest, the servant of the Prophet Mohammed, Amur bin Nasur bin Amur Ilomeir, has written it in his own hand. And I have written it in Berlin, in return for presents. Completed on the 15th September 1892, in the year 1310 by Mohammedan reckoning, in Berlin.'[1]

So ends the 'autobiography' of Amur bin Nasur (1868–?) from Zanzibar, an expert on Swahili literature, who was brought to Berlin by Büttner as language teacher. He wrote his story in Swahili and in Arabic letters, and in it describes his birth, his youth, his journey to Europe and his experiences in Berlin. His style is the best traditional Swahili. His experiences are interesting because they show both how Europeans hoped to impress an African and also the things which fascinated him. Such an account supplies a background to the novels with a Paris or London setting written by modern African authors like Ousmane Socé (b. 1911), Bernard Dadié (b. 1916), Sembène Ousmane (b. 1923), Aké Loba (b. 1927), Ferdinand Oyono (b. 1929), Babatunde Horatio-Jones (b. 1930), etc. Here are a few extracts from Amur bin Nasur's book (taken from Büttner's rendering):

'First of all I Amur bin Nasur bin Amur Ilomeiri give an account of my journey to Berlin, to the Europe of the Germans. First I said to my mother when I was leaving Zanzibar: "Mother, if God grants me life, I am travelling to Europe." My mother said to me, "Why, what are you trying to find there, my son?" And I said to her, "I am going there to get known among the people and to seek my livelihood." Mother said to me, "All right then, my child, but don't forget us who are staying behind." And I said, "No, I will not, the All-Highest willing."

And I arose and said good-bye to my wife, Binti Rashid, and to my mother, but I did not say good-bye to the neighbours and the other people. And I boarded the ship by night. And those who brought me to the shore were my ayah [nurse] Siyenu and my brother Chalid bin Mohammed, and I slept till morning, and we sailed till the ninth hour when we reached Tanga, and there we stayed the night till day dawned. Then we sailed on till the sixth day when we saw Aden. At the time of the early prayer we sailed into Aden, and I went ashore there, and got into a carriage and rode into Aden. And so I had a look at the city of Aden and at the market of Aden, and in the harbour I saw Somalis who are customs guards there. And the city of Aden is like the city of Pangani, and there are big mountains there too. And now I saw the guns on the mountains, and below the mountains the people walked past them. Then on the seventh day we sailed on and after five days we reached the Suez Canal, and I went ashore into the town of Suez and saw the steam-trains and saw also horses and saw the palace of the Pasha, and I saw all that I saw. . . .'[2]

Amur bin Nassur travelled via Naples, Lisbon, Amsterdam, London and Hamburg to Berlin:

'And so I boarded the steam-train, the ship of dry land, and if a man walks from the harbour in Hamburg to Berlin, it will take him seven days, but by the land-ship he only takes five hours. So we left and travelled till we came to Berlin, and suddenly I was told, "Now we have arrived at Berlin", so I got out of the steam-train. Suddenly I saw Dr. Büttner, and he said to me, "Are you Amur bin Nasur?" And I said to him, "Yes, I am Amur bin Nasur." And the first thing he said to me then was, "So you have arrived safely?" And I said, "Yes." And he said to me, "The boat above and the waves below?" And I said, "Yes, praise be to God, the Lord of all worlds." And after that he said to me, "Well, now you have arrived in Berlin, so let's go home." And we arose and went to the house, and a meal was brought me, and I ate it and went to bed. And the next morning Dr. Büttner came and looked after me and asked how I was, and I told him, "I'm very well." . . .'[3]

Later on, during his stay:

'A pupil and friend of mine called Velten came and said to me "Please, Sheik Amur, can we go out together tomorrow?", and I said, "Oh yes." And we went out together and he instructed me in German customs.

And he said to me, "Have you seen horses dance to music? Have you seen horses which understand when you talk to them? Have you seen horses dance the polka?" And I said, "No, I haven't." And I thought, it isn't true, and I said, "You're only making fun of me." And he said, "No, I'm not, and if you don't believe me, you shall see it." I said to him, "When?" He said to me, "Tomorrow evening, God willing, you shall see it." And I slept till the morning, and we stayed till the evening. And he said to me, "Right, let's go and have a look at it tonight." And I arose and went, and saw people packed tightly together in a house, and this house was all of iron, and it is three times as big as the house of Shaksi [a rich man in Zanzibar], and we sat there. And suddenly horses came, ridden by women, and they danced, and then the women got off, and the horses were left and they danced. And as they were ordered by the women, they obeyed, and I was amazed. . . .'[4]

There were many things to amaze an African. 'Another day he said, "Today let's go to the theatre." And I went and saw people climb on to a wire and walk on it, and I was astonished, and then I

saw them making a city, and I saw houses and gardens, and
suddenly I saw nothing again. And then I saw sea and waves, and
people fishing, and others passing in boats, and mountain ranges.
And I thought, really it's the sea. And then I saw the sun going
down, and I was very frightened. And I thought it was all real, and
I asked my friend, "Are we here in Berlin or are we on the ship?"
And he said to me, "We are here in Berlin, but why do you ask me,
Amur?" And I said, "Oh, I was just asking." But in my heart I was
very frightened, but he knew nothing of that, and I was afraid.
And in the end we left, and I went home, and I thought about it
till the early morning. I couldn't go to sleep till morning. . . .'[5]

Amur also went to a panopticum, a zoo, a military parade, several
museums and several beer-houses. Bismarck presented him with a
flower. He expresses great astonishment and wonder at everything.
On the streets he writes:

'As for the tracks, they are five fathoms wide, and they are longer
than a man's eye can see. And the track where people walk is
separate, and the track where the carriages ride is also separate,
and every day these tracks look like a mirror, and there are people
here specially to sweep them, and every night they are swept, and
among these tracks or streets I have not seen one which is different, they were all just the same. And on the streets there are lamps,
and every lamp burns even better than the next, and these streets
are not made of small stones or big. They are first laid with pieces
and then with tar and then with paint, and when you look at them,
they are like silk, and I have never seen such streets as in Berlin . . .'[6]

Velten, the pupil and friend Amur refers to, later became a great
sponsor and patron of Swahili literature. In the introduction to his
book *Swahili Poetry* he wrote: 'I collected most of this collection of
Swahili poems in East Africa in the years 1893–96: others were sent
to me afterwards by their authors. All the poems were written down
in Arabic script. The whole collection of these Swahili poems is
mainly concerned with the wars in East Africa from the [German]
acquisition of the East African coast in 1888 till about 1900.'[7]

Velten gave the poets splendid gifts, and this is how the historical
chronicles, often very reliable, were put together, in the traditional
utendi metre of four *vipande* of seven or eight *mizani* (see p. 78). Of
a poem dealing with the 1894 rebellion of Hassan bin Omar in Kilwa,
Velten remarks: 'For an investigation at Kilwa into the history of
the war . . . I had taken along the poet as a literate Swahili, to help

me work through Hassan's extensive correspondence in Arabic. Consequently, being familiar with even the smallest details, the poet gives completely faithful accounts of all events.'[8]

As an example of this chronicle poetry, here are some verses from *Mkwawa's Death* by Mwenyi Shomari bin Mwenyi Kambi. Mkwawa was the sultan of the Wahehe, who after his defeat by the German colonial troops roamed the country as a fugitive, and finally, deserted by his last followers, committed suicide. (By 'the sea' the poet means German rule, and Vringa was Mkwawa's city.)

28 sikilizani habari
yake Mkwawa kabiri
alishikwa na ghururi
akicheza na bahari.

28 'Now hearken to the story
of Sultan Mkwawa the Great,
by pride he had been blinded,
and thought he could play
with the sea.

42 kachezea Jermani
dola ya Ulayani,
safu iliyo mbeleni
jamie dola nasari.

42 He dallied with the Germans
come here from distant
Europe,
a realm advanced in all things
above all Christian realms.

43 walimpiga mizinga
na bunduki za kuyunga,
saa moja hugonga
muji wameuhushuri.

43 They fired at him with
cannons
and with a mass of rifles,
Before an hour had passed
his city was destroyed.

44 akakimbia mjini,
akajificha mwituni,
akaisha maporini
siku nyingi dahari.

44 He fled from out the city,
to hide him in the wood,
from then on lived in
steppeland
for many endless days.

45 mara akakumbuka
miliki isha mtoka,
mpanda ngazi huchoka
akiwa mtu saghiri.

45 Suddenly he remembered
his realm now taken from
him,
weary of paths for climbing,
he found himself too small.

46 wakaua marijali
wakateka nyingi mali,
wala haina misali
idadi siikadiri.

46 The Germans killed so many
and took much booty off,
I cannot now report it,
measure how much they
took.

48 kakaa bwana umoja
   Mkwawa akimngoja
   muradi akizi haja
   Mkwawa kumdabiri

48 Only one man remained
   there
   to wait for Mkwawa,
   for this desire he cherished,
   to track Mkwawa down.

51 kaweka nyingi nabashi
   jamie katika inchi,
   Mkwawa kumnabishi
   kula panapo bandari.

51 Then he sent his spies out
   over all the country
   and in every place there
   to bring Mkwawa to light.

60 Mkwawa akibaini,
   watu wake wamehuni,
   wako kwa Jermani
   akili yake muduri.

60 And soon Mkwawa noticed
   his people had betrayed him.
   They sided with the
      Germans,
   it nearly drove him mad.

65 rohoni akijuta
   kufanyiza harbata,
   'wapi takwenda kifita,
   Muungu anisitiri?

65 In his heart he now
      regretted
   having begun the battle;
   "Where shall I hide now,
   that God can conceal me?"

68 ikamushika ziki,
   akaiona helaki,
   akitafuta riziki
   njaa ikamwaziri.

68 By poverty tormented,
   ruin before his eyes,
   for food he had to forage,
   by hunger driven on.

98 'nimechoka kukimbia,
   sina pa kujizuia,
   kula siku nauzia
   naona kunikesiri.

98 "I'm weary now of fleeing,
   I cannot hold out longer,
   The torments are increasing,
   My load's too heavy to bear.

100 shauri nnawambia,
    tajipiga bundukia,
    ni heri nikijifia,
    ukisha wangu umuri.'

100 So my resolve I make
      known,
    that I will shoot myself.
    It's better that I die now,
    so that all is over."

171 kad tamati shairi
    yake Mkwawa kebiri,
    alicheza na bahari
    kafa mauti fujara.

171 Now is the poem ended
    of Sultan Mkwawa the
      Great,
    he played with the sea
    and died a sinner's death.

172 nami nawapa hazari,	172 I give you all the warning:
msichezee bahari,	don't play with the sea.
mauti yako fujari	or your death will be a bad
hufa ukabusuri.[9]	one,
	you'll die a slow death.'

Although pro-colonial, this poem is not without dignity. Velten also included in his collection protest poems which reached him anonymously.[10] The praise songs in his honour[11] were well deserved.

REFERENCES AND BIBLIOGRAPHIES

1. Hausa Literature

[1] Greenberg, p. 125.
[2] Prietze 1931, pp. 88 f.
[3] Prietze, Haussa-Sänger, pp. 190 f.
[4] ibid., pp. 594 ff.
[5] ibid., pp. 566 f.
[6] Prietze 1931, p. 94.
[7] Prietze 1904, pp. 63 f.
[8] ibid., p. 63.

FUNKE, E.: Einige Tanz- und Liebeslieder der Haussa. In: Zeitschrift für Eingeborenensprachen, 11th year, Berlin 1920

GREENBERG, Joseph Harold: Hausa verse prosody. In: Journal of the American Oriental Society, vol. 69, New Haven, Conn. 1949

JOHNSTON, H. A. S.: A selection of Hausa stories, Oxford 1966

PRIETZE, Rudolf: Haussa-Sprichwörter und Haussa-Lieder. Kirchhain, N.-L. 1904

– Haussa-Sänger. 2 Teile in: Nachrichten von der K Gesellschaft der Wissenschaften zu Göttingen. Philolog.-histor. Klasse. 1916

– Lieder fahrender Haussaschüler. In: Mitteilungen des Seminars für orientalische Sprachen (MSOS), 19th year, part 3, Berlin 1916

– Gesungene Predigten eines fahrenden Haussalehrers. In: MSOS, 20th year, part 3, Berlin 1917

– Landwirtschaftliche Haussa-Lieder. In: Festschrift Eduard Hahn zum LX. Geburtstag. Stuttgart 1917

– Haussa-Preislieder auf Parias. In: MSOS, 21st year, part 3, Berlin 1918

– Lieder des Haussavolks. In: MSOS, 30th year, part 3, Berlin 1927

– Dichtung der Haussa. In: Africa, vol. IV, London 1931

RATTREY, Robert Sutherland: Hausa folklore, customs, proverbs, etc. Collected and transliterated with English translation and notes. 2 vols. Oxford 1913

ROBINSON, Charles H.: Specimens of Hausa literature. Cambridge 1896

SCHÖN, Jacob Friedrich: Magána Haussa. Native literature, or, Proverbs, tales, fables and historical fragments in the Haussa language. To which is added a translation into English. London 1885

2. Swahili Poetry

[1] Harries, p. 2.
[2] ibid., p. 3.
[3] Büttner 1892, pp. 141 ff.
[4] Robert 1947, p. 3.

BÜTTNER, Carl Gotthilf: Suaheli-Schriftstücke in arabischer Schrift-mit lateinischer Schrift umschrieben, übersetzt und erklärt. Stuttgart and Berlin 1892

–Anthologie aus der Suaheli-Litteratur (Gedichte und Geschichten der Suaheli). Part 3, Berlin 1894

DAMMANN, Ernst: Dichtungen in der Lamu-Mundart des Suaheli. Hamburg 1940

HARRIES, Lyndon: Swahili poetry. Oxford 1962

ROBERT, Shaaban: Maisha yangu. Edinburgh 1949 (Repr. 1962) (No. 739)

–Kusadikika nchi iliyo angani. London 1951 (No. 740)

–Adili na nduguze. London 1952 (No. 741)

–Marudi mema. London 1952 (No. 742)

–Pambo la lugha. Johannesburg 1947 (No. 743)

VELTEN, Carl: Prosa und Poesie der Suaheli. Berlin 1907

–Suaheli-Gedichte. In: Mitteilungen des Seminars für orientalische Sprachen, 21st year, part 3, Berlin 1918

WHITELEY, Wilfred Howell: The dialects and verse of Pemba. Kampala 1958

3. A Swahili Autobiography and Swahili Occasional Verse

[1] Büttner, part 2, p. 190.
[2] ibid., p. 167.
[3] ibid., pp. 169 f.

[4] ibid., pp. 171 f.
[5] ibid., pp. 172 f.
[6] ibid., pp. 179 f.
[7] Velten 1918, p. 1.
[8] ibid., p. 2.
[9] ibid., pp. 144, 146-9, 153, 161.
[10] e.g. Velten 1907, pp. 367–70.
[11] ibid., pp. 387–91.

BÜTTNER, Carl Gotthilf: Anthologie aus der Suaheli-Litteratur. Berlin 1894

HARRIES, Lyndon: Swahili prose texts. A selection from the material collected by Carl Velten from 1893 to 1896. Edited and translated by Lyndon Harries. London 1965

VELTEN, Carl: Reiseschildungen der Suaheli. Göttingen 1901

–Prosa und Poesie der Suaheli. Berlin 1907

–Suaheli-Gedichte. Berlin 1918, 171 S. (Off-print from: Mitteilungen des Seminars für orientalische Sprachen, 21st year, part 3)

Chapter 5

'APPRENTICE' AND 'PROTEST'
LITERATURE

1. Definitions

Anyone who writes begins as an apprentice. His school supplies him
with the tools: literacy and the models for him to follow. Many
writers remain imitators all their lives, while others sooner or later
achieve an individual style. Since the African civilizations had no
written alphabet of their own until they came into contact with Islamic
and Western civilization,* the African 'apprentice', learning to write,
is also an apprentice to foreign cultural influences. The term 'apprentice literature' may therefore serve as a convenient way to distinguish
literary works produced according to the instructors' pattern and the
standards of the script-bearing civilization. But of course the script
is not shed again afterwards, and the apprentice may even adopt the
foreign language as his own means of written expression. So where
does the individuality begin which will allow an author to stop being
an apprentice?

However convenient, the term 'apprentice literature' has its dangers.
There are many people in Europe who would like to dispose of all
modern African literature by giving it that name or at least putting it
in that category. For them only the oral tradition from Africa is
genuine, all 'letters' are derivative, a surrender to the spirit of Europe.
They forget, incidentally, that the European alphabets were not invented in Europe either.

So we must start with a clear definition of the term 'apprentice
literature': I shall use it to denote the literature which in its style
follows European models, and in its content adopts the ideology and
social forms of colonialism or approves them without argument or
reflection. Everything European is from the outset assumed to be
'superior', 'progressive' and better than the 'bad', 'bloodthirsty',
'savage', 'heathen', African traditions. The European commands and
instructs, the African obeys in action and conforms in thought.

* The syllabic scripts of the Vai, in Liberia, invented in 1834 by Duala Bukere,
and of the Bamoon in Cameroun, invented in 1903 by King Njoya, failed to
establish themselves as scripts for creative literature.

By content and attitude the Southern Bantu literature discussed in the next chapter could almost all be considered 'apprentice literature'. But it is not that in the narrower sense, because it is written in African languages and based stylistically on African oral traditions of story-telling. On the other hand, almost the whole of the early African 'protest literature' written in European languages is European in style and uses European arguments to oppose tutelage by Europeans; so I do not count this either as 'apprentice literature' in the narrower sense, but place it in the special category of 'protest literature'. Stylistically, apprentice and protest literature belong together, which is why I am dealing with them in one chapter. By content, however, 'apprentice literature', and all early literary works in African languages sponsored by European missionaries and officials (up to about 1950), belong together in one group, which might all go under the main heading of 'mission literature'.

No hard-and-fast line, of course, can be drawn dividing 'apprentice' and 'protest' literature. Between them there is a wide field of 'hedging' or 'neutral' works, For, to avoid having to approve their tutelage, many writers glorified the traditional life of the tribe and the tribal chiefs and heroes: this can be interpreted as a form of indirect protest. The novel *Mhudi*, for instance, by Solomon Tshekisho Plaatje (1877–1932), is a love story which has as its background the battles between Mzilikazi's Ndebele and the Barolong.

Another borderline case is the novel *The Story of an African Chief* or *Africa Answers Back* by Akiki Nyabongo (born about 1910) from Uganda. The Ganda prince Ati has a son Mujungu, to whom he gives the first name Stanley. He sends the boy to be educated by a missionary, but refuses to cut down his three hundred and seventy wives to one, the condition for having his son christened. At school Mujungu shows himself to be a proud character who without disrespect can neatly answer the missionary back.

He grows up and is designated as his father's successor. A smallpox epidemic occurs, on which he sends for European doctors by 'drum telegraph', uses his authority to get their vaccination programme carried out, but shows them that his African doctors have the better methods for healing fractures. He sends away all but one of the wives inherited from his father, but loses face by this and finds himself threatened by various difficulties, so he decides to carry out reforms less impetuously. The book is basically 'conformist', i.e. 'apprentice literature', but protests against the ways of the Europeans and the missions being brought in too fast.

In the volumes of the lyric poets 'conformist' and 'protest' poems are often to be found next to each other. Such is the case, for instance, with Dennis Chukude Osadebay (born 1911) from Nigeria, with a poem 'Young Africa's Thanks':

> Thank you,
> Sons and daughters of Britannia.
> You gave me hospitals,
> You gave me schools,
> Easy communications too,
> Your western civilization.[1]

and a poem 'Young Africa's Lament':

> I am half starved;
> I asked for bread they gave me stone.
> I am thirsty;
> I asked for water they gave me slush.
> They tell the horse to wait awhile
> Because green grasses would soon grow
> And dry Sahara would yield great streams.[2]

Such contrasts, however, show no inconsistency, but the real relation to colonialism, which gave with one hand and took away with the other, which brought technical progress but allowed the 'apprentices' neither their full development nor equality of rights. The Africans who accepted the innovations with enthusiasm were just the ones who would feel bitterest at this discrimination against themselves as individuals. So acceptance was constantly turning into resentment, the cry of protest is heard between the poems of conformity. Thus the poem by Jolobe, 'The Making of a Slave' (see below, pp. 110–12), stands out against the majority of his poems which are either conforming or non-committal; while there are 'protest' as well as 'apprentice' lyrics among Vilakazi's poems.

When written in European languages, both 'apprentice' and 'protest' literature follows European literary models. But many conformist, non-committal or 'mixed' works in African languages are also European in style and so count as 'apprentice' literature: for instance, Enoch S. Guma's novel *UNomalizo* (see p. 105) or the novel *Headman's Enterprise* by Samuel Yosia Ntara (born 1905) from Malawi, in which a hint of criticism can be read between the lines.[3] The biographies of African hero figures like Shaka, Moshesh, Cetewayo, etc., by Rolfes Reginald Raymond Dhlomo, and the plays about the same heroes and chiefs written in English by his brother Herbert, make a sort of protest by means of the issues which they avoid touching on.

The table on pp. 98–9 classifies some typical works by language, style and their attitude to colonialism. There are nine panels, from *A* to *I*, showing whether these works are conformist, non-committal, part conformist, part protest, or protest only; and whether their language and style are European, African or 'mixed', i.e. African language and European style. The other way round, European language and African style, only occurs with Peter Abrahams and takes us into the literature of most recent times. *A* comprises pure 'apprentice literature', but *B*, *D* and *E* also belong to this category. *C* contains the pure 'protest literature', but this might be said to include *B*, *F* and *I* as well. Almost all the Southern Bantu literature in Chapter 6 would go into the panels *D*, *E*, *G* and *H*. 'Mission literature' should take in panels *A*, *B*, *D*, *E*, *G* and *H*. The most recent Bantu literature, as prescribed by the South African government, which should rather be called *apartheid* literature, would go into Panel *D*, with a small part for *E*.

2. Apprentice Literature

The most typical work of 'apprentice literature' is the novel *Kavwanga* by G. Bolombo, written in French. All the Christians in it are good, noble, helpful and understanding. All the good 'heathens' are naïve, frightened, hungry for salvation. The few intelligent 'heathens' are sly, crafty, malicious, murderous and bloodthirsty. No 'apprentice' could ever have produced such a model of 'apprentice literature': it is by one of the 'tutors', a European missionary disguised under a pseudonym.

The plot is as follows. In the Congo village of Kitsako young Kavwanga grows up with his parents. The whole village is frightened of the white tax collector. Kavwanga's uncle Kasuya does not pay his tax although he has the money. He goes to prison and plans for revenge. The Father Superior of the Mission, full of deep Christian kindness, visits the village and leaves behind as teacher the catechist Sitéfani (Stephan), who draws the children to him. Kavwanga eagerly learns to read and write; he is fond of prayer and soon becomes Sitéfani's favourite.

But his uncle Kasuya has a hate against the whites and the people who submit to them. Kasuya belongs to a secret society, and has already drawn a brother of Kavwanga's into his net. On the basis of his false accusations Kavwanga's father is killed during the ordeal by oracle which a bribed 'fetish priest' administers. All this only confirms the young Kavwanga in his search for Christ. He attends the mission school, which is a day's journey away, and eventually enters a seminary. Zealous prayer also helps him to resist the temptations of the girls sent by his wicked uncle to seduce him. His mother's grief over her husband's death and her anxiety for her son bring her, too, into the bosom of the mission.

The 'Commander' is a good white, like the missionaries. Directly he comes to the village, he tells the assembled elders: 'In the first place, you elders, let us examine the question of roads. In this district there is not a single road for cars. To come here, I was obliged to use the *tipoya* [sedan chair]. Now, *I* have a car, the Territory has trucks; and I would like to use them on my next visit. That is why, if you agree, we shall immediately build a big road which will connect your village with the main route. At dawn tomorrow I will myself go with you and all the men, and we will look at the plans together. Starting the day after tomorrow you will get the ground cleared. I shall leave you one of my soldiers till you are completely finished. Do you see any difficulties?'

'None,' they reply without conviction, overcome by such a spirit of decision, but dismayed by the prospect of a laborious task.

'Let us go on to the next point, cleanliness. There isn't a single lavatory here. You use the bush. It is unclean. The soldier will show you the model of a simple clean lavatory. Each of the men will build one for his family. I insist on it. You understand?'

'Yes, Komanda.'[1]

Then the Commander prayed, and 'the boys couldn't believe their eyes. A White who prays! Like the Father, like Sitéfani. Oh yes, with his "Madamo" [lady] and his children, he is certainly a friend of the missionary, a good White, Anyhow, it was quite clear: everything he said, everything he meant to do, was for the natives' benefit. The Komanda loves the Blacks . . .'[2]

The boys represent the voice of the people; and there is this passage on the connection between work and Christianity:

'Christians must love work. Without it they become bad. Isn't that true?'

'It is true,' they cried.[3]

The sponsors of genuine 'apprentice literature' are always stressing its spontaneity. Thus Meinhof in 1911: 'Without any prompting from the missionaries Christian folksongs were produced, for instance in Togo, of which I would like to give some examples which I received from Professor Westermann in Berlin.'[4] Then follow songs and verses like these:

> Der Heiland ist nichts Totes,
> Christus der Lebensretter!
> Er hat den Tod besiegt, das Leben uns geschenkt!
> Wäre Christus nicht gekommen,
> Wo würden wir sein, im Himmel oder auf Erden?

> Dankt den Bremer Missionaren,
> Danket dem Herrn Jesu!
> Wären die Bremer Missionare nicht,
> Nie hätten wir das Heil erlangt,
> Nie, nie!
> Wäre der Herr Jesu nicht,
> So hätten wir kein Leben,
> Kein Leben, kein Leben.

> 'The Redeemer is not dead,
> Christ the saver of lives!
> He has conquered death, given us life.
> Had Christ not come,
> Where should we be, in Heaven or on earth?

> Thank the European missionaries,
> Thank the Lord Jesus!
> But for the Bremen missionaries
> We should never have gained Salvation,
> Never, never!
> But for the Lord Jesus,
> We should have had no life.
> No life, no life!'[5]

The reference to the missionaries does not contradict Meinhof's statement: it is probably the poem's only African element. For Africans are happy to write a praise song on strangers who are welcome, and this would apply to the missionaries. In the purely Christian song produced at many mission stations, enthusiasm, piety and Christian convictions were seldom allowed such free play. As a rule, in fact, the Europeans' influence served to flatten 'apprentice literature' rather than stimulating it. Spontaneous enthusiasm, which might otherwise have produced a number of independent creative works, was reduced to a 'seemly' European form.

Praise poems on people known to the occasional poets only by hearsay, like Queen Victoria, Kaiser Wilhelm, governors and colonial officials, or on objects like the Union Jack, the Tricolour or the new school-house–all these exist–were stimulated, if not actually ordered, by Europeans. As literary works they are without significance.

Much 'apprentice literature' in European languages is mediocre stuff. Where that is not the case, it comes from the few Africans who received a solid European education during the first quarter of this century. Three poets from Ghana should be mentioned here: Joseph Kwame Kyeretwie Boakye Danquah (1895–1965), Gladys Casely-Hayford (1904–50) and Raphael Ernest Grail Armattoe (1913–53); and an author from Dahomey, Paul Hazoumé (born 1890). Danquah also wrote in his mother-tongue, Twi, and was a distinguished scholar and politician.

The most important work from this group is Hazoumé's historical novel *Doguicimi*, which brings to life the old kingdom of Dahomey in the age of King Geso (1818–58). Hazoumé, of course, shows the African society of that period from the viewpoint of the Europeans, as a world hungering for Christian salvation and French freedom and humanity. But the action is closely integrated into a far-reaching description of the civilization and customs of the court of Dahomey, with its divine kingship and its precise ceremonial, the ritual sacrifices and the strictly organized 'regiments of women'. Thanks to Hazoumé's ethnological and historical studies–he is a correspondent in Cotonou for the Musée de l'Homme in Paris–each detail has an authentic ring, from the herald, who greets the sun in the morning, to the praise songs for the kings.

REFERENCES AND BIBLIOGRAPHIES

1. Definitions

[1] Osadebay, p. 14.
[2] ibid., p. 10.
[3] cf. Jahn, pp. 209 f.

DANQUAH, Joseph Boakye: Nyankonsem. London 1941 (No. 206)
DHLOMO, Herbert I. E.: The girl who killed to save. Lovedale 1935 (No. 859)

−Plays about Moshesh, Cetewayo, Dingane and others
DHLOMO, Rolfes Reginald Raymond: UDingane kaSenzangakhona. Pietermaritzburg 1936 (No. 862)
−UShaka. Pietermaritzburg 1937 (No. 863)
−UMpande kaSenzangakhona. Pietermaritzburg 1938 (No. 864)
−UCetshwayo, Pietermaritzburg 1952 (No. 866)
FIAWOO, F. Kwasi: Tɔkɔ atɔlia. In: Mitteilungen der Ausland-Hochschule an der Universität Berlin, 40th year, part 3, Berlin 1937.−In book form: London 1960 (No. 293)
GUMA, Enoch S.: U-Nomalizo okanye izinto zalomhlaba ngamagingiqiwu. Tsolo 1918 (No. 881)
(Nomalizo, or, 'The things of this life are sheer vanity'. London 1928; reprinted 1951. No. 882)
JAHN, Janheinz: Muntu. London/New York 1961
JOLOBE, James James Ranisi: UMyezo. Johannesburg 1936; reprinted in new orthography, 1965 (No. 902)
NYABONGO, Akiki K.: The story of an African chief. New York 1935. British edition, London 1935, has title: Africa answers back (No. 695)
OSADEBAY, Dennis Chukude: Africa sings. Ilfracombe, Devon 1952 (No. 500)
ƆSEW, Emmanuel J.: Nana Agyemaŋ hwehwɛ. Accra, London 1937; reprinted 1960 (No. 501)
PLAATJE, Solomon Tshekisho: Mhudi. Lovedale 1930 (No. 1106)
RIBAS, Oscar Bento: Flores e espinhos. Luanda 1948 (No. 1114)
VILAKAZI, Benedict Wallet: Inkondlo kaZulu. Johannesburg 1935; revised edition, 1965
−Amal'ezulu. Johannesburg 1945; reprinted in new orthography, 1962 (No. 1177)
−Zulu horizons. The Vilakazi poems rendered into English by D. McK. Malcolm and Florence Louie Friedman. Cape Town 1962 (No. 1180)

2. Apprentice Literature

[1] Bolombo, p. 62.
[2] ibid., p. 64.
[3] ibid., p. 85.
[4] Meinhof, p. 111.
[5] ibid.

ARMATTOE, Raphael Ernest Grail: Between the forest and the sea. Londonderry 1950 (No. 135)

BOLOMBO, G.: Kavwanga. Namur 1954 (No. 3548)

COUCHORO, Félix: Amour de féticheuse. Ouidah 1940 (No. 191)

DANQUAH, Joseph Boakye: The third woman. London 1943 (No. 207)

DHLOMO, Rolfes Reginald Raymond: An African tragedy. Lovedale 1928 (No. 861)

DIALLO, Bakary: Force-Bonté. Paris 1926 (No. 233)

EKOLO, Josef: Wie ein Schwarzer das Land der Weißen ansieht. Basel 1908 (No. 261)

HAZOUMÉ, Paul: Doguicimi. Paris 1938 (No. 306)

HERTLEIN, Siegfried: Christentum und Mission im Urteil der neo-afrikanischen Prosaliteratur. Münsterschwarzach 1962

KITSOKWE, Vetelo Ndunda: Erlebnisse eines Kambajungen. Leipzig 1906 (No. 671)

MARANGWANDA, John Weakley: Kumazivandadzoka. London 1959 (No. 961)

MEINHOF, Carl: Die Dichtung der Afrikaner. Berlin 1911

MISIPO, Dualla: Der Junge aus Duala. Frankfurt a.M., about 1930 (No. 389)

NTARA, Samuel Yosia: Headman's enterprise. London 1949 (No. 1083)

TABLE 3

'Apprentice' and 'Protest' Literature
Relationship to Colonialism

A [and B, D, E] : 'Apprentice literature'   C [and B, F, I] : 'Protest literature'   D, E, G, H : Southern Bantu literature Chap VI

A, B, D, E, G, H : 'Mission literature'   [D and E] : Apartheid literature'   ( ) : Unpublished works

Numbers after title refer to my Bibliography

Language, Style	Conformist	Hedging or half-and-half	Protesting
	A	B	C
EUROPEAN	Kitsokwe: Erlebnisse . . . 671	Plaatje: Mhudi 1106	Dhlomo, H. I. E.: Valley of a thousand hills 860
	Ekolo: Wie ein Schwarzer . . . 261	Dhlomo, H. I. E.: The girl who killed to save 859	Abrahams: The path of thunder 779
	Diallo: Force-Bonté 233	(Dhlomo, H. I. E.: Plays)	Abrahams: Tell freedom 809
	Dhlomo, R. R. R.: An African tragedy 861	Nyabongo: The story of an African chief 695	
	Misipo: Der Junge aus Duala 389	Ribas: Flores e espinhos 1114	
	Hazoumé: Doguicimi 306	Osadebay: Africa sings 500	
	Couchoro: Amour . . . 191		
	Danquah: The third woman 207		
	(Casely-Hayford: Poems)		
	Armattoe: Between the forest and the sea 135		
	Bolombo: Kavwanga 3548		

	D	E	F
AFRICAN LANGUAGE EUROPEAN STYLE	Ntara: Headman's enterprise 1083 Marangwanda: Kumazivandadzoka 961	Vilakazi: Inkondlo kaZulu 1174 Dhlomo, R. R. R.: UDingane 862 *Jolobe: UMyezo 902* Dhlomo, R. R. R.: UShaka 863 Fiawoo: Tɔkɔ atɔlia 293 Ɔsew: Nana Agyemaŋ hwehwɛ 501 Dhlomo, R. R. R.: UMpande 864 Danquah: Nyankonsɛm 206 *Vilakazi: Amal'ezulu 1177* Dhlomo, R. R. R.: UCetshwayo 866	(Waseluhlangeni)

	G	H	I
AFRICAN	(Amur: Khabari) (Mwenyi Shomari: Mkwawa) Mofolo: Chaka 994	Mqhayi: Ityala lama wele 1040 *Amu: 25 songs in the Twi language*	(Mqhayi: Praise Song on the Prince of Wales)

EUROPEAN LANGUAGE AFRICAN STYLE	Abrahams: Wild conquest 820	Abrahams: Mine Boy 772

Chapter 6

THE TRAGEDY OF SOUTHERN BANTU
LITERATURE

Neo-African literature in African languages begins in South Africa. After 1900 it made great strides, but these advances came to an abrupt end; and after brave but unsuccessful experiments in the 'thirties, it sank into insignificance. Since the end of the Second World War the only significant African literature from the south of the continent has been written in English by those who have left the country.

South Africa's three great Bantu languages, Sotho, Xhosa and Zulu, came to the fore one after the other, with an interval of about a decade between them; they produced talented authors and became literary languages. Each had a spiritual centre, a mission station and a publishing house. The mission was both help and hindrance: needing teachers and text-books, it educated, encouraged and supported the gifted; but they grew away from it and chafed at the pettiness of that simple pious world; or else, if they left pulpit and dais, they crumbled in a society which allowed them no right to development.

So their talents wasted away between hopes and despair, until the Nationalist Party came to power in 1948, forcing Southern Bantu authors into spiritual emigration; only authors who wrote English could risk physical escape to other countries. Finally in 1955 the law for Bantu education swept away the mission schools and with them the sparse remains of a semi-free literature. Anything allowed to appear since then scarcely deserves to be called literature: it is merely reading matter for beginners.

1. Sotho Literature

The first written document in the Southern Bantu languages was the translation of the Bible carried out by the missionaries. Collections of proverbs helped to preserve the vocabulary. In Sotho, where the development of a written literature began, the Bible was the only model that existed, for even Bunyan's *Pilgrim's Progress* had only

100

been translated into Xhosa (1867) and Zulu (1895). But nevertheless in 1906 the station of the Paris Evangelical Mission at Morija (Basutoland–now Lesotho) published a first novel by one of its former pupils, who was about thirty and worked as proof-reader in the mission printing press. His name was Thomas Mofolo (1875?–1948), and his book was called *Moeti oa Bochabela* (The Pilgrim to the East).

In content the book is pure mission stuff: Fekesi, its hero, is a young Mosotho who sees around him only 'black darkness', drunkenness, violence, vice, lies, robbery and disgrace. But in the belief that an almighty God must exist there, he wanders east across desert and fertile country to find God and the truth as he sees them in his dreams. On the sea coast he collapses, is found by three Europeans, on whose ship he is nursed back to health; they take him to Europe and bring him back on their next voyage. They give him happiness, understanding, Christianity, truth. 'He felt that most of the things they told him were the very things he was looking for. . . . . He asked and it was explained to him, and then he was taught to read and write. . . . He accepted all they told him, he believed them.'[1]

Mofolo too accepted all they told him, he believed them. He glorified Christianity in *Pilgrim to the East*, and condemned paganism in his next novel, *Chaka*, the first historical novel in modern African literature–and a masterpiece. But although in this book, which he probably wrote in 1908, he equated sorcery with death, the missionaries did not approve of it, and in fact it remained unpublished until 1925. Mofolo did penance, as it were, by writing another novel, *Pitseng*, a place-name meaning 'in the pot', which appeared in 1910: it shows a model Christian girl resisting all temptations and finally marrying an equally model Christian young man, to lead a model Christian life with him, which brings them both complete happiness.

The author had been disappointed, however, by the missionaries' narrow-mindedness; he withdrew from them and stopped writing. Instead he plunged into all sorts of business enterprises, bought himself a farm in East Griqualand, which was eventually taken away from him under the new race laws, and put everything he had left into a lawsuit to recover it. All this wore out his health, and in 1948 he died, an embittered old man.

The manager of the printing press and publishing house at Morija was Alfred Casalis; it was he and his colleague Edouard Jacottet who trained Mofolo and also encouraged him to write. Indeed, according to the Swiss Africanist, Peter Sulzer, these two alone stood up for him at the mission,[2] and after finally getting *Chaka* published Casalis resigned his position. It was afterwards translated into English, French, German and Italian, and has since become recognized as in the category of 'world literature'.*

The beginnings of Sotho literature between 1906 and 1912 were certainly impressive and raised high hopes: Sulzer calls it the 'Golden Age' of Bantu literature.[3] A whole team of authors was at work at Morija. Mofolo wrote his three novels; his friend Zakea D. Mangoaela (1883–1963), who also recorded the praise songs of the Sotho, took down stories; Mofolo's first teacher, Everitt Lechesa Segoete, wrote his novel, *Riches are Only Mist*–the story of a young Sotho who has a Road-to-Damascus experience; and E. Motsamai wrote his cannibal tales. These works are significant in uniting two opposites: their philosophy is wholly Christian, but their style is a continuation of African story-telling traditions. The Christian convictions were quite genuine, and the traditional style was not falsified by European literary models. Whether Ezekiel Mphahlele is right to see an influence of Shakespeare's *Richard III* in *Chaka*[4] can only be decided after an examination of the Sesuto original instead of Frederick Dutton's translation.

Mofolo and the others sincerely believed that Christianity was true and good, that it brought progress and could be combined with the beauty in their own tradition. The philosophy of that tradition, in which man and nature formed a unity, the awareness of a connection between all creatures and things in the world, did not contradict the Christian gospel of salvation and progress. Sulzer writes: '*Chaka* heard the voice of the grass; the wind which moves the rushes, the movement of the water from which the snake emerges, the mist which envelopes him who is "called"–all these are working for his call, they are an expression of something going on inside him. Similarly, the night sky beneath which Fekesi sets off for the East, the endless veldt he has to cross, the desert sand on which he nearly starves, are only

---

* It seems regrettable that such a work should not have been published for over fifteen years after it was written, and even then, it has been asserted, only in expurgated form with considerable cuts. The mission station no doubt owns the copyright, since Mofolo was an employee there when he wrote the book, but did this entitle them to leave it unpublished for so long? In any case, surely only an author has the right to make cuts in his work? Even if at this stage it is impossible to account for the puzzling circumstances, one may legitimately hope a completely unexpurgated edition of *Chaka* may now be produced. In making these remarks, I do not wish to detract from the achievements of the Morija Press: the whole of Sotho literature given in the list on pages 116–17 was published there, whereas only a few unimportant works came from other publishing houses, all after 1947.

the outer form of what is taking place in his soul. Inner and outer world come together in an inseparable unity.'[5]

In their general philosophy these works, in fact, were all of a piece.

2. Xhosa Literature

The second period is that of authors writing in Xhosa. Their spiritual centre was Lovedale, a Church of Scotland mission station. Even before this was established in 1824, Joseph Williams from the London Mission Society, who died in 1818, had been active as a missionary near there. He converted to Christianity Prince Ntsikana, who only survived him by a few months, and who composed hymns for the little community, although unable to read or write. One of them has come down to us, thanks to John Philip, who put it in writing and in 1828 published it in Xhosa and English. Here are two extracts, as translated exactly from Xhosa by Professor D. J. Darlow:

> Line 1 'He the Great God, high in Heaven . . .
> 2 Great "I am", of truth the Buckler,
> 3 Great "I am", of truth the Stronghold,
> 4 Great "I am", in whom truth shelters . . .
> 13 Then he cast his cloak about us,
> 14 Cloak of Him Whose hands are wounded,
> 15 Cloak of Him whose feet are bleeding,
> 16 See the blood that streameth for us . . .'[1]

In his original translation Philip grouped the parts together differently, changing round the lines and selecting the words in such a way that the 'praise song' with Christian content turned into something more like a conventional European hymn. Here is the corresponding passage:

> Line 5 'God is mighty in the Heavens,
> 11 For he alone is a sure defence.
> 12 He alone is a trusty shield,
> 13 He alone is our bush of refuge . . .
> 14 We supplicate to the Holy Lamb,
> 15 Whose blood for us was shed,
> 16 Whose feet for us were torn,
> 17 Whose hands for us were pierced.'[2]

The translation itself shows that the missionaries overlooked Ntsikana's artistic achievement and regarded his poetic style as an unsuccessful attempt to imitate European hymns. Consequently his work had no literary effect until almost a century later, when Lovedale at last became the centre of a creative Xhosa literature. This too begins with the search for God as its subject. The story of *U-Hambo luka Gqoboka* (A Journey Towards Conversion) (1909), by Henry M. Ndawo, shows a heathen finding Christianity after many battles with wild animals, elements and men. The first important author in Xhosa literature, however, is Samuel Edward Krune Mqhayi (1875–1945), whose novel *Ityala lama-wele* (the Lawsuit of the Twin Brothers) appeared in 1913 or 1914, though it had been written earlier.

'At this time,' Mqhayi writes in his autobiography, 'I published my book about the lawsuit of the twins. I had never thought much of it, and the manuscript had been lying about at home for a long time. So I was all the more surprised that it gained general approval among the Blacks and also among the Whites who knew Xhosa. It was introduced as a textbook in schools.'[3]

A contemporary of Mofolo's, Mqhayi also had Christian parents. He was teacher, secretary and co-editor of Xhosa journals. He wrote his stories and poems in the style of the oral tradition, often with much humour and always with dignity. He managed to preserve a considerable independence: when the mission world became too narrow for him, he withdrew to his small property in the country, where he helped and served his tribe's chiefs. This is what he says about it in his autobiography, showing a pleasant touch of irony:

'In 1922 I was invited to go to Lovedale as teacher and literary worker. With some hesitation I accepted the invitation, but realized that I was a bit out of place there. People did not agree with my views on the history of the Xhosa and on other matters. So I left, but luckily this caused no lasting misunderstanding between Lovedale and me; our relations are still friendly. This is largely due to Mr. Bennie,* whom I look up to as my elder brother and who knows how to point out my mistakes in a kindly way, when in my stubbornness and Xhosa pride I fall into the danger of acting against my own interests.

'Today I live in the small village of Ntabozuko, which belongs to the tribe of the Ndhlambe. I am in constant touch with the Chiefs and am often invited to attend public ceremonies and feasts. I take the chair at meetings of the Chiefs in Ciskei. I am the secretary of the Ndhlambe Chief. When the Prince of Wales and the Duke of Kent visited South Africa, I was asked to sing the praise songs on them.†

---

* General Inspector for Native Education.
† See below, pp. 279–80.

My little hill is on the main road between East London and King William's Town. The small town of Berlin is a mile and a half from my home.'[4] This is where Mqhayi died in 1945, revered by his tribe.

Apart from him there are John Knox Bokwe, Enoch S. Guma, Guybon B. Sinxo and James J. R. Jolobe, whose first books appeared between 1914 and 1924. Another who is in spirit one of the same school is Solomon Tshekisho Plaatje, a Tswana, the first South African author to write a novel in English. This was *Mhudi*, a heroic semi-historical idyll, written about 1918, which did not come out till 1930, when the padded 'Victorian' style was already decidely remote and antiquated.

A novel by Guma, which first appeared in Tsolo, is typical of the spirit of works by this school of writers. In *Nomalizo*, the eponymous heroine is beautiful, pious and chaste. Her schoolmate Mxabaniso, in whose parents' house the wicked heathens drink alcohol, lusts after her, becomes a teacher, gets a crony to abduct her, and tries to force her to marry him. But she is attached in a bond of quiet pious love to Rangela, her old school-friend and protector. Before she marries him, the wicked Mxabaniso plants stolen goods in the house of the bridegroom, who is arrested and sentenced to imprisonment for life. But the villain's accomplice is pricked by conscience, his confession brings the guilty man behind bars and the innocent to married bliss. 'Such is the story,' the novel concludes, 'of a girl who bore wonderful trials, yet never complained, because of the deep faith which she had, and because of putting her trust in God. Farewell, gentle reader.'[5]

The style is didactic and moralizing, with characters from stock, but quite effective in its simple narrative way. Nature has disappeared, the protagonists no longer live within a tribal framework in the open country; their realm of experience is the school, the settlement, the 'location'. It is nice, edifying, 'schoolboy' literature, which did not have to be silenced in 1924 when the Nationalist Boer Party under General Hertzog took over the government of South Africa for the first time. After all, these works had nothing more 'subversive' than morality to preach. Mqhayi published some verse for children and a biography, Sinxo a play for children and the 'Life' of a priest. Then there was a period of silence. After that Mqhayi and Jolobe were to write poetry again, but in the 'thirties the impetus came from another quarter.

3. Zulu Literature

It may not be mere coincidence that written literature in Zulu began in 1933, when the more liberal Smuts came back into the government. It began with a novel about Chaka, *Insila ka Shaka*, by John Langali-balele Dube, who before this had founded a school, written a treatise on education, and as early as 1904 started the Zulu weekly *Ilanga Lase-Natal* in Durban. The spiritual centres of this literature were the Catholic Trappist Mission in Mariannhill, the Zulu weekly, and the publishing house Shuter and Shooter in Pietermaritzburg. The most important authors in this group were Benedict Wallet Vilakazi (1906–47) and the brothers Dhlomo–Rolfes Reginald Raymond (19?–19?) and Herbert J. E. (1905–45) – who ran the weekly after Dube and wrote their work in both Zulu and English.

Vilakazi came from a Protestant family, was converted to Catholicism in the mission school at Mariannhill, and became a teacher. He continued his own education, and gained a matriculation certificate. After teaching at several schools, he became lecturer in Zulu at Witwatersrand University, Johannesburg, where he was awarded a doctorate. Cyril Lincoln Sibusiso Nyembezi, a don at Natal University, wrote of him in 1961: 'He was the first, and so far the only, African in South Africa to hold the degree of Doctor of Literature. Vilakazi's three novels are important because he made an attempt to write something which even grown-ups could enjoy. His first novel *Noma Nini* depicts the beginning of the period of transition for the Zulus with the arrival of the missionaries in Groutville; his second novel tells the story of the Mthethwa Chief Dingiswayo who was Chaka's guardian. The third novel *Nje Nempela* is based on the events of the Bambatha Rebellion of 1906.

'And yet among the Zulus Vilakazi is remembered more as a poet than as a prose-writer: he was mainly responsible for developing poetry whose form departed radically from the traditional *izibongo* (or praises). He experimented with European forms. He divided his poems into regular stanzas. He also experimented with rhyme.'[1]

His remarkable volume of poetry *Inkondlo ka Zulu* (Zulu Poems) appeared in 1935. Even before this the Sotho chief Bereng, in his praise songs to King Moshesh, had abandoned the strict form and introduced short lines and rhyme. English models had exercised a strong influence, so now the Africans were trying to reform their own poetry. Vilakazi had used all the European forms he knew and given theoretical reasons for his experiments. His essay on the development

of Zulu poetry is South Africa's only important work of literary
criticism. In it he examines first the rhythmic form of the traditional
Zulu praise songs, and finds that each verse has a caesura in the
middle, with two stresses before as well as after it; while the unstressed syllables are not counted, so that there can be up to four
unstressed syllables between the stresses. He gives reasons for cases of
deviation from this form.

There are no similar studies for the other Southern Bantu languages, so that it is hard to compare them. But I have the impression
that we find a quantitative metre in the traditional Sotho praise song:
each line as a rule has eleven vocalized syllables with regular and
often symmetrical sequences of sounds. Here are some lines from
Mangoela's collection of traditional praise songs:

> Otloanyana tsa chela mabaleng;
> Fate tsa foforeha makhapethla;
> Robele tsa phurusetsa matlung,
> Nonyana tse beelang lifateng![2]

> 'The grass fence was burnt to ashes,
> The trees lost their leaves,
> The sparrows left their nests,
> Those birds which built their tree-nests.'

With this *Lithoko* (praise song) I have marked the number of
syllables by dots: the vocalized 'ng' is a separate syllable, true diph-
thongs ('oa', 'ee') are one syllable. If it is not a *lithoko* but a poem or
a song (*thothokiso*), there may be only ten syllables in one line but
then twelve in the next. The two lines are now a unity, with the second
giving a comment or variation on a statement in the first. The 'action'
or 'message', therefore, is not continued. Here is an unpublished
modern example from Makitle Makitle:

> 10: O mosa o molemo satane,
> 12: Etsoe ke oa molimo hantle.
> 11: Oa mantlha oa mathomo morena.
> 10: O ne a botjoe ka joe le thata,
> 12: A khojoa ka morema-phofo oa tšepe.

> 'The devil is good and friendly,
> That's what he's son of God for.
> He is the first, the very first king.
> He was made from hard stone,
> He is created out of ore.'

Verses with different numbers of syllables are considered faulty or overloaded, and anyhow not beautiful.

Unfortunately Vilakazi did not examine the possibility of a quantitative metre in Zulu. Having nothing but English metre to draw on for comparison, he noticed only the number and order of the stressed syllables, although Miss Beuchat says: 'South-Eastern Bantu languages do not have stress.'[3] He did not consider other structures either, those obeying tonal laws, rhythmic sequences on a single beat, hendeca-syllables, etc.; although he mentioned that in Zulu the pitch affects meaning.

On the other hand, he examined the possibilities of rhyme with great thoroughness. According to Nyembezi, the difficulty of rhyming in Zulu is because each line ends with a vowel, whereas English also has closed final syllables; 'the English poet is, therefore, not hampered in the same way as is a Zulu poet'.[4] Vilakazi solves this problem like the Italian poets, to whom the same argument would apply, by using mainly feminine rhymes. But here there is the further difficulty that a number of consonants alter the value of the vowels.

'Zulu' cannot rhyme with 'mulu', he explains, because alveolar fricatives have no acoustic or phonetic relationship to bilabial nasals. 'The rhyme is beautiful to the eye, but it grates on the ear.'[5] So he examines which consonants may rhyme and which may not. In all this he starts with the assumption that the 'educated poets have to study the standards of Classical or European poetry which will help to rouse in them the finer and deeper feelings of every impact of the outer world upon their poetic souls.'[6] Although his study makes it plain how rhymes in Zulu cannot help having an artificial ring, he still wants them brought in.

'I do not believe in form; I rely more on the spirit of poetry. Form tends to reduce everything to mechanical standards and mathematical formulae. But we have to use some form to embody or clothe the beautiful spirit of our poetry. We have no definite form so far, and our starting point will be at the standards given us by the Western education we have imbibed at college. We are beginning the work which may be given perfect form in generations to come. I believe, therefore, it is absolutely necessary that, in composing some poems, we ought to rhyme and decorate our poetic images with definite stanza forms.'[7]

So college education had taught Vilakazi and his fellow authors that a poem is not a poem without rhyme and stanzas (verses). This was the standpoint of old-fashioned schoolmasters who failed to see the essence of lyric poetry and also the development of European poetry in the first decades of the twentieth century. Vilakazi wasted his talent in laborious experiments, though he was wise enough to recognize his mistake in the end. In his second and last volume of poetry, *Amal'ezulu* (1945), he had stopped using rhyme. His earlier conclusions, however, had the greatest influence on the other poets in Southern Bantu languages, almost all of whom tried thereafter to press their thoughts into the Procrustean Bed of textbook poetry from Europe's nineteenth century.

The best known of Vilakazi's experiments is his hymn to the Victoria Falls, in which he forced Zulu into blank verses and so into old-fashioned European grandiloquence:

> Gobhoza kuze kube nini manzi
> Agubha ngempophoma nokwesaba,
> Nobuhle. Yebo, ungaphazanyiswa
> Gobhoza nokujul' okungaziwa.
> UNkulunkul' ogcobe isimongo
> Sekhanda lakho ngomudwa wothingo
> Lwenkosikazi, nenkung' engapheli
> Egubuzele inzinyawo zakho.
> Ukuphe nezwi lokuqhaqhabuka,
> Namandl' okukhuluma naye yedwa,
> Laph' uthulis' imilomo yesintu
> Ngaphezu kwedwala lase Sibungu.[8]

(In J. Dexter Taylor's translation):

> 'Flow on, flow on forever, O ye waters,
> O wildly tossing cataract of terror
> And of beauty. Yea, brook no interruption.
> Flow on in depth unsounded and unmeasured.
> 'Tis God who hath with grace thy brow anointed,
> And crowned thy head with circlet of the rainbow,
> And with eternal mists thy feet enshrouded.
> He giveth thee the voice of mighty thunders,
> And audience gives in solitary grandeur,
> There where thou silenceth the mouths of mortals
> Upon the mighty cliffs of Isibungu.'[9]

It is only where the content fits the artificial form that we sometimes find a genuine poem like the one by the Xhosa James J. R. Jolobe, 'Ukwenziwa Komkhonzi'[10] (The Making of a Slave);

significantly, this is not contained in the English translation of his book of poetry *UMyezo* (1936) which appeared in 1946. In 1954, however, in my anthology *Schwarzer Orpheus* (Black Orpheus), I published a German translation of verses 1 to 3 and 9 to 12 based on the author's own English translation:[11]

Andisenaku6uza ndisithi kunjani na
Ukukhanywa yintambo yedyokhwe emqaleni
Ku6a ndizi6onele kwinka6i yomqokozo,
U6umfama 6amehlo busukile ndagqala
Ku6a ndiku6onile ukwenziwa komkhonzi
    Kwinkatyana yedyokhwe.

Ya6igudile intle, izalelw' inkululo
Ingaceli nto mntwini izingca ngo6unkomo.
Uthe umntu ma i6anjwe iqeqeʃwe ithambe,
Ezilungiselela ngokunga uya siza,
Ku6a ndiku6onile ukwenziwa komkhonzi
    Kwinkatyana yedyokhwe.

Inge ingamangala ikhusel' ilungelo,
Yangqingwa ya6iyelwa ngo6ulumko namava.
Amaqhinga ooyisa kufunw' iqo6ozeke.
Isizathu esihle singafihla u6u6i,
Ku6a ndiku6onile ukwenziwa komkhonzi
    Kwinkatyana yedyokhwe.

Ime buxe kuudinwa kungekho luvelwano,
Yasitʃho esikrakra isililo ibonga.
Kunyenyiswe kancinci uku6a iphefumle
Kwa6uya kwaqiniswa i6ulawa umoya
Ku6a ndiku6onile ukwenziwa komkhonzi
    Kwinkatyana yedyokhwe.

Ndiyi6one mva se yaqo6ozeka yathamba
Itsal' umbaxa-mbini wekhu6a etʃhoniswe
Waphelela ikhonza, ikhefuza igcuma.
Ukufa kukuqhutywa, impilo kuuzenzela
Ku6a ndiku6onile ukwenziwa komkhonzi
    Kwinkatyana yedyokhwe.

Ndiyi6one inyuka iminqantsa yomendo
Ithwele imithwalo enzima ixelenga,

Iludaka kuu6ila ingenisela omnye.
Incasa yomse6enzi yinxaxhe6a kuvuno
Ku6a ndiku6onile ukwenziwa komkhonzi
    Kwinkatyana yedyokhwe.

Ndiyi6on' ilambile ngaphantsi kwaloo m6uso
Iliso liinyembezi umxhel' ujacekile,
I6e ingasakwazi nokuchasa im6una.
Ithemba yimigudu ezond' inkululeko
Ku6a ndiku6onile ukwenziwa komkhonzi
    Kwinkatyana yedyokhwe.[12]

'Why need I to ask how it feels
To choke from yoke strap bound round the throat?
I've seen it myself in tender yoke ox.
Blindness has vanished and well have I pondered
For I beheld how a slave was made
    Of a young yoke ox.

Young, sleek it was, for liberty born,
Begging for nothing and proud of its being.
Men were determined to catch it and train it.
Advancing their aims, they pretended to help,
For I beheld how a slave was made
    Of a young yoke ox.

It tried to resist, defending its rights,
Surrounded it was, experienced they were.
Cunning prevailed, to break it they would.
Innocent reasons can hide an evil,
For I beheld how a slave was made
    Of a young yoke ox.

Wearied it stood still, no sympathy came.
Sad was its cry as it bellowed from pain.
They loosened a little so that it might breathe.
They tightened again its spirit to break,
For I beheld how a slave was made
    Of a young yoke ox.

I saw it years later softened and broken,
Pulling a plough, a two-furrow plough,
Sunk deep, shuffling, and groaning at work,
Death is being forced; life is voluntary effort,

For I beheld how a slave was made
    Of a young yoke ox.

I saw it ascend steep mountainous roads,
Loaded with burdens, earning a living,
Wet with much sweat enriching its lord.
The sweetness of labour is share in the harvest,
For I beheld how a slave was made
    Of a young yoke ox.

I saw it in want under this rule,
The eye with a tear, the spirit oppressed.
It no longer knew even how to resist.
Hope lies in efforts sweet freedom to gain,
For I beheld how a slave was made
    Of a young yoke ox.'

REFERENCES AND BIBLIOGRAPHIES

1. Sotho Literature

[1] Mofolo 1934, pp. 111 ff.
[2] Sulzer 1953, p. 252.
[3] Sulzer 1955, p. 90.
[4] Mphahlele, pp. 170 f.
[5] Sulzer 1955, p. 102.

MANGOAELA, Zakea D.: Lithoko tsa marena a Basotho. Morija, Basutoland 1921

MOFOLO, Thomas: Pitseng. Morija 1910 (No. 991)
–Moeti oa bochabela. Morija 1912 (No. 992)
    (The traveller of the East. London 1934 (No. 993))
–Chaka. Morija 1925 (Nos. 994–7)
    (Chaka, an historical romance. London 1931; a 'shortened and slightly simplified' edition was published under the title, Chaka the Zulu, London 1949; 8th impression, 1963 (No. 996))

MOTSAMAI, E.: Mehla ea malimo. Morija 1912 (No. 1019)

MPHAHLELE, Ezekiel: The African image. London 1962 (No. 1035)

SEGOETE, Everitt Lechesa: Monono ke moholi ke mouoane. Morija 1910 (No. 1123)

SULZER, Peter: Postface in: Mofolo, T.: Chaka der Zulu. Zürich 1953 (No. 995)
–Schwarze Intelligenz. Zürich/Freiburg i. Br. 1955

2. Xhosa Literature

[1] Shepherd 1945, p. 99.
[2] Shepherd 1955, p. 21.
[3] Westermann, p. 312.
[4] ibid., pp. 312–14.
[5] Guma 1928, p. 64.

BENNIE, William Govan: Imibengo. Lovedale: The Lovedale Press 1960. x, 276 pp. Nars+Es+Lyr–Anth (First published in 1935.) Cf. No. 756

BOKWE, John Knox: [Xhosa+engl.] U-Ntsikana. Ntsikana: the story of an African convert. 2nd ed. Lovedale: Lovedale Mission Press 1914. 67 pp. ill. (Biography)

GUMA, Enoch S.: U-Nomalizo okanye izinto zalomhlaba ngamagin-giqiwu. Tsolo, South Africa, 1918 (No. 881)
(Nomalizo, or, 'The things of this life are sheer vanity'. London 1928, also 1951 (No. 882))

JABAVU, Davidson Don Tengo: Bantu literature. Classification and reviews. Lovedale 1923

JOLOBE, James James Ranisi: UZagula. Intr.: J. K. Mather. Lovedale 1923 (No. 901); new ed. 1958. 86 pp.

KAKAZA, L.: UTandiwe wakwa Gcaleka [Xhosa: Tandiwe, a damsel of Gaikaland]. Cape Town: Methodist Book Room 1914. 70 pp. Ro

MAKALIMA, Gilbert B.: UNtsizi. Palmerton, E. Pondoland, 1924. 84 pp. Ro

MLOTYWA, Stephen: UNozipo. Lovedale: Lovedale Press 1923. 41 pp. Nar

MQHAYI, Samuel Edward Krune: Ityala lama-wele. Lovedale 1914 (No. 1040); abridged edition, Standard Xhosa spelling: Ityala lamawele. Lovedale: Lovedale Press 1961. vii, 105 pp., ill.
(The case of the twins. Transl. by Collingwood August. In: The New African, vol. 5, Nos. 1–3, London, January/April 1966)

–U-bomi bom-fundisi uJohn Knox Bokwe [Xhosa: Life of the Rev. John Knox Bokwe]. Lovedale: Lovedale Institution Press 1925. 92 pp. B

–Samuel Edward Kgune Mqhayi, ein südafrikanischer Dichter. (Autobiography.) In: Westermann, Diedrich: Afrikaner erzählen ihr Leben. Essen 1938

NDAWO, Henry Masila: Uhambo luka Gqoboka. Lovedale: Lovedale Institution Press 1909. 93 pp.

PLAATJE, Solomon Tshekisho: Mhudi. An epic of South African life a hundred years ago. Lovedale 1930 (No. 1106)

SHEPHERD, Robert Henry Wishart: Lovedale and literature for the Bantu. Lovedale 1945

– Bantu literature and life. Lovedale 1955

SINXO, Guybon B.: UNomsa. Lovedale 1922 (No. 1133)

WALAZA, Ngu I. I.: Inkwenkwe izala indoda [Xhosa: The son is the father of a man]. Johannesburg: Rosettenville 1929. Ro

WESTERMANN, Diedrich: Afrikaner erzählen ihr Leben. Essen 1938 (No. 57)

3. Zulu Literature

[1] Nyembezi, p. 7.
[2] Mangoaela, p. 177.
[3] Beuchat, p. 12.
[4] Nyembezi, p. 8.
[5] Vilakazi 1938, p. 128.
[6] ibid., p. 116.
[7] ibid., p. 129.
[8] Vilakazi 1957, p. 12
[9] Taylor, pp. 165 f.
[10] Jolobe 1961, pp. 66 f.
[11] Jahn 1954, pp. 36 f.; 1964, pp. 101 f.
[12] Jolobe 1951, pp. 66–7.

BERENG, David Cranmer Theko: Lithothokiso tsa Moshoeshoe le tse ding. Morija 1931 (No. 829)

BEUCHAT, P.-D.: Do the Bantu have a literature? Johannesburg 1963

DUBE, John Langibalele: U-Shembe [Zulu: Shembe]. Pietermaritzburg: Shuter and Shooter 1936. 117 pp. B

JABAVU, Davidson Don Tengo: The influence of English on Bantu literature. Lovedale 1943

JAHN, Janheinz: Schwarzer Orpheus. Munich 1954; new edition, enlarged, 1964 (Nos. 7+10)

JOLOBE, James James Ranisi: UMyezo. Johannesburg 1936, 1951; reprinted in new orthography, 1965 (No. 902)

KUNENE, Raymond: An analytical survey of Zulu poetry both traditional and modern. Unpublished thesis, University of Natal, Durban, no date.

MANGOAELA, Zakea D.: Lithoko tsa marena a Basotho. Morija 1921

MTIMKULU, Samuel M.: My life. Mariannhill: Mariannhill Mission Press 1930. 28 pp. A

NYEMBEZI, Cyril Lincoln Sibusiso: A review of Zulu literature. Pietermaritzburg 1961

SULZER, Peter: Schwarze Intelligenz. Zürich/Freiburg i. Br. 1955

TAYLOR, J. Dexter: Inkondlo kaZulu: an appreciation. In: Bantu Studies, vol. IX, No. 2, Johannesburg 1935 (With Taylor's translation of Vilakazi's poem 'Impophoma yeVictoria'.)

VILAKAZI, Benedict Wallet: Inkondlo kaZulu. Johannesburg 1935; rev. ed., reprinted in new orthography, 1965 (No. 1174)

–Noma nini. Mariannhill 1935 (No. 1175)

–The conception and development of poetry in Zulu. In: Bantu Studies, vol. XII, No. 2. Johannesburg 1938

–UDingiswayo kaJobe. London 1939 (No. 1176)

–Amal'ezulu. Johannesburg 1945 (No. 1177)

–Nje-nempela. Mariannhill 1955 (No. 1178)

–Zulu horizons: the Vilakazi poems rendered into English by D. McK. Malcolm and Florence Louie Friedman. Cape Town 1962 (No. 1180)

TABLE 4
Southern Bantu Literature

A : Autobiography
B : Biography
N : Novel
P : Poetry
Pl : Play
St : Story
Sts : Stories

*: work written though not published in year cited
(Brackets) : written in English

The numbers following the entries correspond to those in my *Bibliography of Neo-African Literature*

	SOTHO *Morija*	XHOSA *Lovedale* Place of publication (when not Lovedale)	ZULU *Mariannhill* Place of publication (when not Mariannhill)
		T: Tsolo J: Johannesburg C: Cape Town P: Palmerton, E. Pondoland	P: Pietermaritzburg J: Johannesburg D: Durban L: London
1906	Mofolo: *Moeti N 992		
1907			
1908	Mofolo: *Chaka N 994		
1909		Ndawo: UHambo N	
1910	Mofolo: Pitseng N 991 Segoete: Monono N 1123		
1911			
1912			
1913	Motsamai: Mehla Sts 1019		
1914	Mangoaela: Har'a libatana Sts 959	Mqhayi: Ityala N 1040 Kakaza: UTandiwe N C	
1915			
1916			
1917		(Plaatje: *Mhudi N 1106)	
1918		Guma: UNomalizo St Z 881	

1919			
1920			
1921			
1922		Sinxo: UNomsa N 1133	
1923		Jolobe: UZagula N 901	
		Mlotywa: UNozipo N	
1924		Makalima: UNtsizi N P	
1925		Sinxo: Imfene Pl 1134	
		Mqhayi: Bokwe B	
1926			
1927		Sinxo: Umfundisi N 1135	
1928	Sekese: Pitso 1126 Sts	(Dhlomo, R.R.R.: Tragedy N 861)	
	Maile: Ramasoabi Sts 948		
1929		Mqhayi: UDon Jadu B 1042	(Mtimkulu: My life A)
		Walaza: Inkwenkwe N J	
1930	Bereng: Lithothokiso P 829		
1931		Ndawo: UNolishwa N 1063	
1932			
1933			Dube: Insila N 871
1934			
1935		(Dhlomo, H.I.E.: Girl Pl 859)	Vilakazi: Noma nini N 1175
			Vilakazi: Inkondlo P J 1174
			Dhlomo, R.R.R.: UDingane B P 862
			Dube: UShembe B P
1936		Jolobe: UMyezo P J 902	Ndebele: UGubudele Pl J 1065
			Dhlomo: UShaka B P 863
1937		Ndawo: UNomathamsanqa St 1064	Dhlomo, R.R.R.: UMpande B P 864
			Vilakazi: UDingiswayo N L 1176
1938	Motsatse: Khopotso St 1020	Futshane: UJujuju St 877	
	Mofokeng: Sek'hona Pl 990	Mqhayi: UMqhayi A 1043	(Dhlomo, H.I.E.: Valley P D 860)
1939			
1940		Jordan: Ingqumbo N 909	
1941		Mqhayi: Inzuzo P J 1044	
1942			
1943			
1944			
1945	Mopeli-Paulus: Ho tsamaea P 1008		Vilakazi: Amal'ezulu P J 1177
	Matlosa: Molahlehi St 968		Dhlomo, R.R.R.: Indlela N P 865
1946	Ntsane: 'Musapelo P 1085	Swaartboi: UMandisa St 1158	
1947	Khaketla: Moshoeshoe Pl 918		
	Machobane: Mphatlalatsane St 942		
1948	Sentso: Matlakala P 1127		

PART THREE

The American Scene

Chapter 7

NINETEENTH-CENTURY
AFRO-AMERICAN LITERATURE

1. From Romanticism to Symbolism (Haiti and Brazil)

When an African is born in isolation into a different culture far from his home, he is likely to retain nothing of the culture of his forebears. But when many come in large groups to another continent, the traditional culture will survive. The slaves who were forcibly transplanted into the New World did not abandon their culture on board ship, but they might just as well have done so for all the impression that African culture made on the ruling classes of the New World. It therefore lived on unnoticed beneath the surface of official cultural life and, if noticed at all, was thought of as merely 'folklore'. It only managed to produce literary results towards the end of the nineteenth century in the days of 'naturalism', when Americans began to take a greater interest in the behaviour and speech of the 'lower classes'.

From the point of view of what was officially called 'literature', a writer with African origins was accepted only if he completely adopted the ruling, i.e. the European models of style. There was no other approach. None of the arbiters of literary taste doubted the universal validity of European norms. If you wrote at all, you had to adapt to these norms, anything else was wrong and got corrected. Africanisms were not recognized as such but regarded as mistakes and expunged. Marrant (see pp. 40–1), who doubtless spoke and wrote in a forceful Afro-American vernacular full of imagination and hyperbole, had to submit to drastic corrections like all other 'uneducated' persons. 'I have always preserved Mr. Marrant's ideas, tho' I could not his language',[1] writes 'Reverend Mr. Aldridge' in his introduction.

Probably, therefore, not much in the way of African style survived in nineteenth-century Afro-American literature. But until this has been thoroughly investigated, all writers of African origin remain 'under suspicion', as stated in Chapter 1, of perhaps belonging to neo-African literature. There are so many of them in the nineteenth century that I can here only refer briefly to the most important names.

The century started with Haiti's fight for freedom, which resulted in the first independent Afro-American state. But political liberty was not followed by cultural independence. Some grandiloquent patriotic liberation poems were written in the manner of the French Revolution, and a few pieces of verse for special occasions. The most original of these are by Juste Chanlatte, Conte de Rosiers, who produced them for use at the court of King Christophe. Césaire quotes them in his *La Tragédie du Roi Christophe*:

> Du guerrier généreux le trône est l'héritage,
> C'est le glorieux prix d'un cœur pur et loyal.
> Le sort toujours sourit aux talents, au courage;
> Qui sauve son pays, touche au manteau royal.[2]

'A noble warrior's heritage shall be the throne,
The glorious prize won by a heart that's pure and loyal.
To talent and to courage, see Fate's favour shown;
The man who saves his country gains the mantle royal.'

Chanlatte was the typical sycophant. As soon as the king was dead, his former flatterer joined the other side and called the king a tyrant, reacting in the way he himself described in two lines:

> De tout tyran, tel est l'infaillible destin,
> On l'encense vivant, et l'on rit à sa fin.[3]

'This is the certain fate of tyrants all:
Alive they're worshipped, jeered at when they fall.'

At this time such authors were adopting, somewhat belatedly, all the literary styles from France. Coriolan Ardouin (1812–35) poured out his anguish on the bosom of nature; Charles-Séguy Villevaleix (1835–1923) shed his tears by graves; Alibée Féry (1819–96) imitated the imitators of Greece and Rome; Pierre Faubert (1803–60) imitated Lamartine; Charles D. Williams (1849–95) took Victor Hugo as his model; Emeric Bergeaud (1818–58) wrote the first Haitian novel, *Stella*, published posthumously in 1859, an allegorical work in which Romulus represents the Blacks and Remus the Mulattos. Demesvar Delorme (1831–1901), inspired by Goethe's Werther and influenced also by Hugo and Dumas, portrayed the fateful love affairs of his two heroes, an Eastern prince and a certain Ulrich von Krussnacht. Louis Joseph Janvier (1855–1911) imitated Balzac. No works with Haitian themes were written till the second half of the century (see Chapter 8).

While in the United States a drop of African blood excluded a person from the enjoyment of civil rights, in Brazil to have an African grandmother was the stamp of a complete Brazilian. So almost all the great Brazilian writers of the century were half-castes; even so, most of them adhered to the European literary movements. If José de Natividade Saldanha (1795–1830) took political action against the slave trade, his verse shows no sign of this. Antônio Gonçalves Teixeira e Sousa (1812–81) wrote novels in which Afro-Brazilian folklore is described in a superficially picturesque manner, although in a poem on Brazil's independence he stresses the equality of Mulattos and Whites. The two heroes, the white Gonzaga and the mulatto Nunes, are attached to each other like Patroclus and Achilles. When Gonzaga is killed by a Portuguese, Nunes sacrifices his own life to avenge him.

Antônio Gonçalves Dias (1823–64), the world-famous romantic poet, was indeed the only specifically American poet recognized in Central Europe prior to 1900 (Longfellow, for instance, was regarded as an *English* poet). In one of Dias's early poems, 'A Escrava' (1846), he describes a slave-girl dreaming of the blazing sun and burning sand of the Congo, where her beloved waits for her by the moonlit stream under the banana tree–till the harsh voice of her master tears her from her day-dreaming. Here is the sentimental romanticizing of Africa which some critics have unjustifiably imputed to the poets of 'Negritude'.

Antônio Cândido Gonçalves Crespo (1830–82), who married a general's daughter in Portugal and there became an outstanding poet in the group of 'Parnassians', sometimes, but not very often, celebrated the beauty of a half-caste woman. Yet Bastide finds 'in the rhythm of his verse the sombre drum-beat which stems from the drops of his black blood.'[4]

Joaquim Maria Machado de Assis (1839–1908), founder of the Brazilian Academy of Literature, and for many years its President, is the most important representative of realism in Brazilian prose. He avoided slave subjects and drew characters, mainly from high society, with psychological acumen and deep irony. Admittedly he always portrayed Afro-American types in his novels with sympathy; but as he was only concerned with the perfection of his own art, he remained uncommitted in the struggle to free the slaves, which at that time was exciting the whole of Brazil.

Tobias Barreto de Menezes (1838–1908) was chiefly a philologist and philosopher, who devoted himself to the German language and German philosophy, especially that of Haeckel. He was the first to ask the sort of questions about his own identity which were later to play a big part in literature: 'Neither a pure Aryan nor a pure African nor a pure American–what am I then? An individual of a race or a sub-race, which is still evolving?'[5] It was a question which had a biological meaning for him but not a cultural one, since he (like all these writers) belonged intellectually to the middle-class society which was orientated completely towards Europe.

Only Luis Gonzaga Pinto da Gama (1830–82), who spent his youth as a slave, regarded this attitude as hypocritical, stressed the fact that he was African, became an ardent abolitionist, and wrote inflammatory satirical verse castigating the social snobbery of mulatto society with its European ways:

> Se os nobres desta terra empanturrados,
> Em Guiné têm parentes enterrados;
> E, cedendo à prosápia, ou duros vícios,
> Esquecem os negrinhos, seus patrícios;
> Se mulatos de côr esbranquiçada,
> Já se julgam de origem refinada;
> E curvos à mania que os domina,
> Desprezam a vovó que é preta-mina;
> Não te espantes, leitor, da novidade,
> Pois que tudo no Brasil é raridade![6]

> 'If all the upstart nobles in these regions,
> Whose ancestors to Guinea owed allegiance,
> From pride of birth or other vice besetting
> Their negro race are hastily forgetting;
> If each mulatto with his bleached complexion,
> To some compelling madness in subjection,
> Or in the hope of future status prizes,
> His black-as-pitch great-grandpapa despises:
> By novelties like these be not dismayed, sir,
> Such rarities–Brazil's new stock-in-trade, sir.'

Gama's satire is the reverse of romanticism. If he should dream of a white damsel with snowy neck and alabaster bosom, she will turn out to be a marble statue; whereas his real sweethearts are 'beautiful, the colour of night, embroidered with glittering stars.'[7]

Brazil's greatest poet, whom many consider among the finest poets anywhere, was also under the pressure of having to follow European literary models: this was João da Cruz e Sousa (1862–98), who was of pure African descent. A symbolist, he adopted a tragic symbolism of colour: white means the white man, the European, Christianity, virtue, but also sterility, the cold and death-bringing snow. Black is lust, fetishism, but also life, fertility, creative power and pain. So a phenomenon occurs, as Bastide writes, 'analagous to the Afro-Brazilian religious syncretism between Catholic saints and Yoruba *orishas*: the Christ of Cruz e Sousa turns into a carnal, lascivious Christ.'[8]

Although Cruz e Sousa saw African culture 'through European spectacles', he felt the presence of both cultures in himself. The tension between them gave his poetry power, beauty and a sombre brilliance. The time was not yet ripe for upsetting the scale of values inherent in his symbolism. As he could not resolve the tormenting conflict, he was drawn to the pessimism of Schopenhauer, who influenced the late romantics in Brazil as elsewhere. Cruz e Sousa then went a step further, to Baudelaire's Satanism. His poetry, therefore, has a 'nocturnal' side, in which blackness is beautiful. Bastide rightly calls him a forerunner of Negritude.

2. The Accounts of Escaped Slaves (United States)

In North America no writers of African descent came anywhere near the social status which the half-caste writers of Brazil could take for granted. Most of the North American writers were ex-slaves or direct descendants of slaves. The development of any sort of independent creative literature was out of the question. The writers subordinated themselves either to the abolitionists or to the 'Negro Churches'. For their fight against slavery the abolitionists welcomed first-hand narratives from those directly affected, while the 'Negro Churches' provided a certain degree of intellectual advancement for gifted Afro-Americans. Anyone who wrote from literary ambition tried to show that despite deficient education he could serve one of these two sponsoring movements as required.

We can divide the writers into two main groups. The first group had no literary ambitions. It consists of escaped slaves, preachers, sailors, teachers, soldiers, politicians etc., who were only 'occasional' writers. The other group contains 'professional' writers concerned with creative writing. I have subdivided the first group of writings into (a) autobiographies by escaped slaves, (b) works by preachers and pastors. The table on pages 140–1 shows the dates of publication; where several works have been written by the same writer, I have given the dates of his first and last publication. Furthermore, I have subdivided into major writers, whose names are shown in small capitals, important minor writers (names in italics) and other minor writers (names in roman). Afro-American literature in North America had been so well documented, especially in the thorough study of the subject by Vernon Loggins, that I can afford to be brief.*

The accounts by the escaped slaves served as political propaganda against slavery. They had an immense success, and were meant to have: the proceeds from these writings were an immediate source of help for the ex-slaves to set themselves up, and sometimes helped to free more of their fellow-sufferers. This also justified literary 'forgeries' (shown in brackets on the list): slave experiences which an abolitionist had recorded, arranged for maximum effect, and then published not as what he had been told but as autobiography by the slave concerned. In most cases there is no doubt of the authenticity of the story told; only the authorship is false.

Style too was subordinated to the political objective. No work reached the market 'uncensored'. The ex-slave was made to write in a way that served the cause. Anyone coming fresh from slavery had personal experiences with slave-masters and overseers, felt a hatred that was concrete but doubtless did not extend to abstract theory. Yet every kind of spontaneous excitement, outburst, oath, cry or invocation, which might have left its mark on the style and made the accounts into fascinating literary works of an Afro-American folk art, were suppressed by the editors. The political objective demanded that the institution of slavery should be castigated, but never the individual. The slave-owners' brutality, always described vividly and often with individuals named, was not to be represented as the result of fear, hatred, vindictiveness or psychological repressions, but as the effect of an inhuman system and of the demon alcohol.

Although it may be assumed that the slaves, especially the household slaves, knew the characters of their masters very well, descriptions of character are avoided in their accounts, for the slave should tell his story 'objectively', without anger or excitement. All Africanisms, all the special images and metaphors from the vernacular, were suppressed; for any excess of emotion, coarseness or thirst for vengeance was considered 'primitive' and could be used by opponents as counter-propaganda.

Even works in which a vivid Afro-American figure like Sojourner Truth (1792–1883) was represented in dialogue with comparative realism, were a 'find' for the defenders of slavery, showing the 'bar-

---

* In the bibliography for this chapter I have only listed works which I can quote as being thoroughly typical. For others see the table (pp. 140–41) and compare my Bibliography published by André Deutsch and Frederick Praeger.

barous heathenism' of the slaves. The touching though bloodless figures of Harriet Beecher Stowe's *Uncle Tom's Cabin*, with their nobility still unbroken in suffering, their Christian humility and piousness, their wise love of justice and their tender middle-class sensitivity, were therefore the models the escaped slaves had to personify in their accounts. Josiah Henson, who is supposed to have been the original Uncle Tom, spent all his life in the laborious but profitable role of resembling his literary embodiment. Frederick Douglass (1817-95), even when speaking before a big audience, had instructions to tell his story quite impassively. It was only when he was found to inspire his audience by getting carried away, that irony, sarcasm and passion were welcomed in his speeches–as enhancing their rhetorical power.

The ex-slaves' accounts were meant to show that the Afro-American slave not only had the same worth as the 'Euro-American' but that he was also the same sort of person as the average Euro-American middle-class citizen of that idealistic and romantic age. This, of course, he neither was nor could be. The only special qualities allowed were ingenuousness and naïveté–but no Africanisms, please, nothing 'barbaric' or 'primitive'! As a result, compared with later unexpurgated stories from ex-slaves, these eyewitness reports seem strangely colourless, uniform and flat, if one sets the hair-raising facts which produced them against the way they are presented.

Yet a brilliant author like Frederick Douglass succeeded in creating a literary work of enduring value, even though without anything Afro-American in style, a work which combined all the qualities required– objectivity, fairness and Christian values–with vividness, conviction and stylistic skill. The severe detachment of William Wells Brown, too, makes his life-story fascinating and thrilling to read even today. Three others who should be mentioned are Lewis Clarke, a striking exception–for he indulges in fierce abuse, especially against the women slave-owners; Henry Bibb, who speaks of 'superstition' among the slaves; and Samuel Ringgold Ward, who inserts personal anecdotes, some of them humorous.

Two slaves showed a talent for poetry. After the general emancipation Islay Walden travelled round peddling verses, asking for a piece of bread in return. He was awarded a scholarship to Howard University,* which completely spoiled his natural talent.

---

*Howard University was chartered in 1867 for the higher education of Negroes. General Oliver O. Howard, one-time head of the Bureau of Freedmen, was one of its founders and its President from 1869 to 1873.

Like him George Moses Horton (1779–about 1883) remained a slave until the general emancipation. For fifty cents a day he was hired out by his master as servant to the Principal of Chapel Hill University in North Carolina. He learnt to read and write, and then wrote love poems on commission for the students, in which he provided spiritual ardour as required. 'He was paid to compose verses by the young men of the University,' says Loggins, 'just as another slave in Chapel Hill at the time was paid to allow planks to be broken over his head!'[1] Horton hoped to buy his freedom through his private earnings, but did not succeed. His famous poem, 'On Liberty and Slavery' is to be found in many anthologies. His talent, which combines a subtle sense of rhythm with a flair for apt and often witty expression, is shown also in his 25-cent poems, like this one 'To Eliza':

> Eliza, tell thy lover why
> Or what induced thee to deceive me?
>   Fare thee well–away I fly–
> I shun the lass who thus will grieve me.
>
> Eliza, still thou art my song,
> Although by force I may forsake thee;
>   Fare thee well, for I was wrong
> To woo thee while another take thee.
>
> Eliza, pause and think awhile–
> Sweet lass! I shall forget thee never:
>   Fare thee well! Although I smile,
> I grieve to give thee up for ever.
>
> Eliza, I shall think of thee–
> My heart shall ever twine about thee;
>   Fare thee well–but think of me,
> Compelled to live and die without thee.
>
> Fare thee well!–and if for ever,
> Still for ever fare thee well![2]

3. The Writings of the Preachers

The founding of the African Methodist Episcopal Church in 1816 by Bishop Richard Allen, a former slave who had bought his freedom, began the development of the North American 'Negro Churches'. These soon developed into real 'churches of the people', and in them the African cultural heritage gradually asserted itself and found its specific Afro-American expression.[1] The Negro Church preachers soon developed a picturesque ecstatic style of preaching, with rhythmical emphasis and an evocative power which swept the congregations off their feet. Biblical and African elements were blended into 'Negro Sermons', and the stronger the African element, the deeper the effect. The art of the Negro sermon is an oral art; and when the preachers wrote down their sermons, they became self-conscious about them. You were no longer among your own people, you were writing for everyone. Because of this wider 'congregation' you had to appear respectable, in fact conventionally European. But sometimes African rhythms, stresses and images break through or shine out among the Biblical metaphors and figures. It would be a useful task to try to find all the Africanisms in the 'Negro Sermon' of that era.

The sermons of Haynes (1805) had nothing specifically Afro-American about them; indeed they were completely puritan in attitude. Absalom Jones went in for grandiloquent platitudes, Peter Williams used pathos; Cannon's sermons already showed hints of 'swinging rhythms'.[2] Alexander Crummell, on the other hand, who studied at Cambridge (England) and founded the American Negro Academy, composed his sermons in a well-bred conversational style. Theodore S. Wright wrote 'Prayer of a Colonizationist', satirizing with scathing irony the movement of those who wanted to resettle the Afro-Americans in Africa. The *Rise and Progress of the Kingdom of Light and Darkness* by Lorenzo Dow Blackson has for Loggins 'the originality and charm which distinguish the Negro folk song',[3] and he calls it the 'product of a pure African temperament'.[4]

The preachers' autobiographies, too, are freer in style, for they were not directly serving abolitionist propaganda.

Among the writings of the occasional authors the only ones of interest are those which were produced as a result of the 'resettlement' movement and which contained accounts of West Africa: the travel diaries of Daniel Coker, Paul Cuffe, Daniel H. Peterson and Martin Robinson Delany. They show the spirit in which these Afro-Americans thought of Africa. Peterson preached to his audience in New York: 'At the time when your ancestors were brought from Africa, the rights of man were but little understood; while Africa itself was a land of darkness, where the people made merchandize of each other, and entirely neglected the true worship of the Almighty God. The land from whence you came is still in darkness, and, in the fullness of time, we may be the instruments in the hand of the Lord for redeeming that very land from the darkness of ignorance and superstition, and planting the banner of the Cross in that wilderness of thorns from which our forefathers were taken.'[5]

4. Creative Literature in the U.S.A.

North America's creative Afro-American writers before the Civil War were particularly anxious to show achievements. They wanted to prove that they could compose poetry and write novels just as well as any white writer. This alone would compel respect from those who tried to bring them down to the level of animals. So they were not concerned to be original, for an originality alien to the taste of the full (and average) American citizen could again bring them the hated reputation of being 'backward' and 'primitive'. They did not follow particular literary movements like Brazil's writers: they did not have the education needed for this. They imitated whatever happened to be generally approved: Milton, Byron, Longfellow, Scott, Dickens, Poe, Spenser, Tennyson, Whittier, Thomas Hood, Thomas Hardy, Thomas Gray. Albery A. Whitman expressed his concern clearly: 'Someone of my race is sure to do everything that anyone else has ever done, and as none of my race have executed a poem in the "stately verse", I simply venture in.'[1] He produced in fact, two huge verse epics, which, though completely eclectic in form, were fluent and well constructed. The glory was in being the first to write epics.

William Wells Brown (1815–84) was the first United States Afro-American to write a play and a novel. The novel *Clotel, The President's Daughter*–in the second edition *Clotelle*–is in the vein of *Uncle Tom's Cabin*; it describes the changing fates of an almost white slave-girl and her noble black-skinned lover, of whom it is said: 'Dante did not more love his Beatrice, Swift his Stella, Waller his Saccharissa, Goldsmith his Jessamy bride, or Burns his Mary, than did Jerome his Clotelle.'[2] After heart-rending experiences Jerome and Clotelle escape from the terrors of slavery, he by flight to Canada, she as the wife of a French officer. A kindly providence brings them together again: Jerome, becoming prosperous in Canada, makes a journey to Europe and in the cemetery at Dunkirk meets Clotelle; she is there mourning her husband, who was killed in India years earlier. Their old love has never died, they marry and go for a honeymoon to Lake Geneva, where they hear a man in the next room bitterly reproaching himself. He is Clotelle's father, who sold her into slavery. So in the end all three are brought together in freedom, happiness and prosperity.

The play, *The Escape*, is much less stirring. The slave-girl Melinda loves the slave Glen, but her master lusts after her and entices her into a remote hut, where she rejects his advances with the splendid words: 'Sir, I am your slave; you can do as you please with the avails of my labour, but you shall never tempt me to swerve from the path of virtue.'[3]

Frances Ellen Watkins Harper (1825–1911) wrote poems, novels and stories full of heroism and emotion. They were very successful and her first two volumes of poetry apparently sold over 50,000 copies.

Frank J. Webb wrote one novel, *The Garies* (1857), which became well known. Loggins says 'While it lacks the verve and narrative force of Brown's *Clotel*, it is far more subjectively emotional.'[4] But I cannot agree with his judgement. The fate of two prosperous coloured families in Philadelphia is grippingly told; apart from a few *longueurs* and despite some sentimentality, the book has a powerful atmosphere. A jealous white relative plans a lynching party, hires a mob and stages a race riot. The realism of these scenes points ahead to Richard Wright. We have here no artificial melodrama but living people, whose motives are credible and whose actions and reactions are well dovetailed. Moreover, the scenes with the rascals and the confusions which lead to the inciter being himself beaten up as a 'nigger' show vigorous humour.

North America's only important Afro-American author in the nineteenth century is Paul Laurence Dunbar (1873–1906). With him, Afro-American folklore–despised and derided till then–becomes creative art for the first time: with him, in fact, a new age begins. I shall therefore be dealing with him and Charles W. Chesnutt in a later chapter (see pp. 149–51).

5. Two Poets from Cuba

The only slave who won his freedom through his poetry was a Cuban, Juan Francisco Manzano from Havana (1797–1854). At the age of eleven he was transferred from a gentle mistress to a sadistic one, who gagged him and tortured him brutally for the 'unnatural crime' of composing and reciting poetry; the tortures are immortalized in his autobiography. About 1822 he escaped, covered his tracks in Havana, and got married. Some men of position decided to obtain him his freedom after coming across his sonnet, 'My Thirty Years':

Mis treinta años

Cuando miro el espacio que he corrido
   desde la cuna hasta el presente día,
   tiemblo y saludo a la fortuna mía
mas de terror que de atencion movido.

Sorpréndeme la lucha que he podido
   sostener contra suerte tan impía,
   si tal llamarse puede la porfía
de mi infelice ser al mal nacido.

Treinta años ha que conocí la tierra;
   treinta años ha que en gemidor estado
      triste infortunio por doquier me asalta;

Mas nada es para mí la cruda guerra
   que en vano suspirar he soportado,
      si la comparo, ¡oh dios!, con lo que falta.[1]

'When on my time of living I reflect,
   Right from my cradle to the present date,
   Only with trembling can I greet my fate,
Governed much more by terror than respect.

I wonder at the light I still have got,
   Redeeming the dark suffering and shame
   Of this my life, if it deserves that name,
The long endurance of a hopeless lot.

For thirty years I've known this world of pain,
   For thirty years I've groaned beneath the war
   Of cruel oppression, lusting to pursue me.

But all the torment I've endured in vain
   Is nothing to what one day is in store,
   For her—oh, God!—who brought this torment to me.'

But Manzano did not get much joy out of his freedom. When he had already become famous as a poet through his publications, he was thrown into prison for 'conspiracy'; and after being discharged, wrote no more. His biographer Franco declares that in some works 'the black contribution to a new Cuban culture'[2] is shyly revealed in his exotic rhymes – but I doubt this. Once when a priest had tried to protect Manzano, his cruel mistress said in self-justification: 'You'll see, that fellow will be even worse than Rousseau and Voltaire.'[3] It was Manzano's fate to be overrated.

The famous national hero and romantic poet, Gabriel de la Concepción Valdés (1809–44), had an Afro-Cuban father; his mother was a Spanish dancer. Under a pseudonym of Plácido he wrote 'Arcadian', bucolic and patriotic lyrics, which contain hardly any African elements or even indications of his father's origins. Another Afro-Cuban poet of that period, Bartolemé José Crespo y Borbón, though contemporary with Manzano and Plácido, belongs stylistically to a later chapter (see p. 143).

6. Creole Poetry in Louisiana

In North America too there was a 'Brazil'. Louisiana, which had belonged to the United States since 1803, had a French-speaking and French-educated urban middle class in the Creoles, whose parentage was part French and part half-caste. An African grandmother in their family tree was considered a distinction rather than a disgrace. The poets from this class felt themselves to be American citizens with a French culture; the poet Armand Lanusse (1815–67), for instance, who was the head of an orphanage for coloured children, served loyally in the Civil War as a soldier in the Confederate Army.

But prejudice moved down from the North; and these authors, discriminated against as French, papists and 'niggers', escaped into their dream of French freedom and French elegance, in the beautiful echoes of French love poetry from the *ancien régime* to early Béranger. Yet the pressure and the repression increased. Michel Saint-Pierre (died 1866) had once been near to committing suicide. Camille Thierry (1814–75) and Victor Séjour (1817–74), both born in New Orleans, emigrated to France. Séjour's highly romantic plays were given a lavish production in Paris under Napoleon III, and his light comedies were great box-office successes. Joanni Questi (died 1869) remained in New Orleans as a journalist on the Creole paper, *La Tribune de la Nouvelle Orléans*, and compiled an *Almanach of Laughter*.

Most of these works, although colourful enough when written, have not stood the test of time. But every now and then there is a flash of something more, which is reminiscent of the Senegalese poet Birago Diop and his famous incantation: *Les Morts ne sont pas morts.*[1] For instance, in a poem by P. A. Desdunes, 'Les Vivants et les Morts', you suddenly come across these lines:

> Nous ne livrons pas aux sépultures
> Qu'un vêtement trop lourd pour nous;
> Nous n'avons de corps ni figures
> Et nous ne voulons rien de vous.
>
> Notre vie est indifférence.
> Invisibles sans nous cacher
> Nous passons dans votre silence
> Auprès de vous, sans vous toucher.[2]

'A garment heavy now for us to wear
  Is all we have abandoned to the grave.
We have no bodies and no faces there,
  From you there now is nothing that we crave.

Our life's indifference; and lost to view,
  Invisible, without the need to hide,
Amidst your silence we are passing through,
  Not touching you yet somewhere by your side.'

So even in this isolated area of Afro-American poetry, which is often neglected, we can sometimes hear the distant echo of Africa.

REFERENCES AND BIBLIOGRAPHIES

1. From Romanticism to Symbolism (Haiti and Brazil)

[1] Marrant, p. v.
[2] Césaire, p. 60.
[3] Vaval, p. 18.
[4] Bastide, p. 81.
[5] ibid., p. 47.
[6] ibid., p. 55.
[7] Sayers, p. 106.
[8] Bastide, p. 100.

ACKERMANN, Fritz: Die Versdichtung des Brasiliers Antonio Gonçalves Dias. Hamburg 1938
ALVES, Henrique Losinskas: Cruz e Souza – o Dante negro. São Paulo 1961

ARDOUIN, Coriolan: Poésies complètes. Port-au-Prince 1916 (No. 1252)

BANDEIRA, Manuel: Poesia e vida de Gonçalves Dias. São Paulo 1962

BARRETO DE MENEZES, Tobias: Obras completas. Rio de Janeiro 1926. 5 vols. (No. 2025)

BASTIDE, Roger: A poesia afro-brasileira. São Paulo 1943

BERGEAUD, Emeric: Stella. Paris 1859 (No. 1281)

CÉSAIRE, Aimé: La tragédie du roi Christophe. Paris 1963 (Nos. 1388-9)

CHANLATTE Juste, see ROSIERS

CRUZ E SOUSA, João da: Obra completa. Rio de Janeiro 1961 (No. 2055)

DELORME, Demesvar: Francesca. Paris 1873 (No. 1447)

–Le damné. Paris 1877 (No. 1448)

FAUBERT, Pierre: Ogé ou le préjugé de couleur. Paris 1856 (No. 1491)

FÉRY, Alibée: Essais littéraires. Port-au-Prince 1876. 4 vols. (No. 1492)

GAMA, Luiz Gonzaga Pinto da: Primeiras trovas burlescas. Rio de Janeiro 1861 (No. 2082)

–Trovas burlescas e escritos em prosa. Edited by Fernando Goés. São Paulo: Ediçoes Cultura 1944. 206 pp. (Últimas gerações, 4)

GONÇALVES CRESPO, Antônio Cândido: Miniaturas. Lisboa 187–? (No. 2084)

–Nocturnos. Lisboa 1882 (No. 2085)

GONÇALVES DIAS, Antônio: Primeiros cantos. Rio de Janeiro 1846 (No. 2086)

GOURAIGE, Ghislain: Histoire de la littérature haïtienne. Port-au-Prince 1961

JANVIER, Louis-Joseph: Une chercheuse. Paris 1888 (No. 1615)

MACHADO DE ASSIS, Joaquim Maria: Obra completa. Rio de Janeiro 1959. 3 vols. (No. 2127)

MARRANT, John: A narrative of the Lord's wonderful dealings with John Marrant . . . London 1785 (No. 2999)

NATIVIDADE SALDANHA, José da: Poemas offerecidos aos amantes do Brazil por seu autor Jozé da Natividade Saldanha, natural de Pernambuco, e estudante dos leis na Universidade de Coimbra . . . Coimbra: Imprensa da Universidade 1822. 136 p.

–Poesias . . . colleccionadas, annotadas e precedidas de um estudo histórico por Augusto Ferreira da Costa. Lisboa 1875. 319 pp.

–Poesias de Natividade Saldanha, precedidas por um estudo historico-biográfico por José Augusto Ferreira da Costa. Pernambuco: J. W. Medeiros 1875

POMPILUS, Pradel & FRÈRES DE L'INSTRUCTION CHRÉTIENNE: Manuel illustré d'histoire de la littérature haïtienne. Port-au-Prince 1961

ROSIERS, Comte de (Juste CHANLATTE): Recueil de chants et de couplets . . . Sans-Souci 181–? (No. 1891)

SAYERS, Raymond S.: The Negro in Brazilian literature. New York 1956

TEIXEIRA E SOUSA, Antonio Gonçalves: Cantos lyricos. Rio de Janeiro: Typographia imparcial de F. de Paula Brito 1841

–Filha do pescador. 1843

–A independencia do Brasil: poema epico em XII cantos. Rio de Janeiro: Typographia imparcial de Paula Brito 1847

–Maria ou A menina roubada. In: Marmota Fluminense, Nos. 295–315, 10th September–16th December 1852.

VAVAL, Duraciné: Histoire de la littérature haïtienne ou: 'L'âme noire'. Port-au-Prince 1933

VILLEVALEIX, Charles Séguy: Les primevères. Paris 1866 (No. 1989)

WILLIAMS, Charles-D.: Les voix du cœur . . . Paris 1886 (No. 2012)

2. The Accounts of Escaped Slaves (United States)

[1] Loggins, p. 108.
[2] Brown-Davis-Lee, p. 290.

BIBB, Henry: Narrative of the life and adventures . . . New York 1849 (No. 2300)

BOTKIN, Benjamin Albert: Lay my burden down . . . Chicago 1945 (No. 2165–6)

BROWN, Sterling Allen–DAVIS, Arthur Paul–LEE, Ulysses Grant: The Negro caravan. New York 1941 (No. 2171)

BROWN, William Wells: Narrative of the life . . . Boston 1847 (No. 2355)

–Three years in Europe . . . London 1852 (No. 2357)

CLARKE, Lewis Garrard: Narrative of the sufferings . . . Boston 1845 (No. 2407)

DOUGLASS, Frederick: Narrative of the life . . . Boston 1845 and Cambridge, Mass. 1960 (No. 2492)

–My bondage and my freedom. New York 1855 (Nos. 2494–5)

–Life and times . . . Hartford, Conn. 1881 (Nos. 2496–8)

HENSON, Josiah: The life of Josiah Henson . . . Boston 1849 (No. 2693)

–Father Henson's story of his own life. New York 1962 (No. 2699)

HORTON, George Moses: The poetical works . . . Hillsborough, N.C. 1845 (No. 2762)

LANE, Lunsford: The narrative of Lunsford Lane, formerly of Raleigh, N.C., embracing an account of his early life, the redemption by purchase of himself and family from slavery, and his banishment from the place of his birth for the crime of wearing a colored skin. Published by himself. Boston: The author 1842. iv, 54 pp. 4th ed. 1848

LOGGINS, Vernon: The Negro author: his development in America. New York 1931; reprint, Port Washington, N.Y. 1964

NICHOLS, Charles H.: Who read the slave narratives? In: Phylon, vol. XX, Atlanta, Ga. 1959, pp. 149–62

– Many thousand gone: the ex-slaves' account of their bondage and freedom. Leiden 1963

WALDEN, Islay: Walden's sacred poems. New Brunswick, N.J. 1877 (No. 3241)

3. The Writings of the Preachers

[1] cf. Jahn, pp. 217 ff.
[2] Loggins, p. 108.
[3] ibid., p. 309.
[4] ibid., p. 306.
[5] Peterson, pp. 49 f.

ALLEN, Richard: The life, experience and gospel labors . . . No place or date, subsequently New York 1960 (No. 2225)

BLACKSON, Lorenzo Dow: The rise and progress of the kingdoms of light & darkness . . . Philadelphia 1867 (No. 2303)

CANNON, Noah Calwell: The rock of wisdom . . . No place of publication given, 1833 (No. 2382)

COKER, Daniel: Journal . . . Baltimore 1820 (No. 2416)

CRUMMELL, Alexander: The greatness of Christ . . . New York 1882 (No. 2437)

CUFFE, Paul: A brief account . . . New York 1812 (No. 2443)

DELANY, Martin Robinson : Official report . . . New York 1861 (No. 2475)

HAYNES, Lemuel B.: Universal salvation . . . 6th ed. Boston 1807 (No. 2671)

JAHN, Janheinz: Muntu. London/New York 1961

JONES, Absalom: A thanksgiving sermon . . . Philadelphia 1808 (No. 2927)

LOGGINS, Vernon: The Negro author . . . New York, 1931; reprint
   Port Washington, N.Y. 1964
PETERSON, Daniel H.: The looking-glass . . . New York 1854 (No.
   3077)
WILLIAMS, Peter: An oration . . . New York 1808 (No. 3319)
−A discourse delivered . . . New York 1817 (No. 3320)
WRIGHT, Theodore S.: The colonization scheme . . . Newark, N.J.
   1840 (No. 2422)

4. Creative Literature in the U.S.A.

[1] Whitman 1885, p. 10.
[2] Brown 1955, p. 58.
[3] Loggins, p. 168.
[4] ibid., p. 249.

BROWN, William Wells: Clotel . . . London 1853. Revised and re-titled:
   Clotelle . . . Boston 1864 and Philadelphia 1955 (No. 2358)
−The escape . . . Boston 1859 (No. 2360)
DELANY, Martin Robinson : Blake, or, The huts of America. Serial
   story in: The Anglo-African, 1859–60
FARRISON, W. Edward: The origin of Brown's Clotel. In: Phylon,
   vol. XV, Atlanta, Ga. 1954, pp. 347–54
HARPER, Frances Ellen Watkins: see Nos. 2649–58
WEBB, Frank J.: The Garies and their friends. London 1857 (No.
   3287)
WHITMAN, Albery Allson: Not a man and yet a man. Springfield,
   Ohio 1877 (No. 3298)
−Twasinta's Seminoles . . . Rev. ed. St. Louis 1885 (No. 3300)

5. Two Poets from Cuba

[1] Franco, p. 92.
[2] ibid., p. 26.
[3] ibid., p. 25.

FRANCO, José L.: Juan Francisco Manzano, el poeta esclavo y su
   tiempo. In: Manzano, Autobiografía . . . 1937
MANZANO, Juan Francisco: Cantos a Lesbia . . . La Habana 1821
   (No. 1709)
−Flores pasageras. La Habana 1830 (No. 1710)
−Záfira. La Habana 1842 (No. 1712)

–Autobiografía, cartas y versos . . . La Habana 1937 (No. 1713)

–7 Poems in: Guirao, Ramón: Orbita de la poesía afro-cubana. La Habana 1938 (No. 1207)

PLÁCIDO (Gabriel de la Concepción Valdés): Poesías completas . . . Paris 1856 (No. 1850)

VITIER, Cintio: Lo cubano en la poesía. La Habana 1958

6. Creole Poetry in Louisiana

[1] Diop, p. 64; Reed/Wake, pp. 25–7.
[2] Coleman, p. 125.

COLEMAN, Edward Maceo: Creole voices . . . Washington 1945 (No. 2178)

DIOP, Birago: Leurres et lueurs. Paris 1960 (No. 237)

LANUSSE, Armand: Les cenelles. Nouvelle Orléans 1845 (No. 2198)

LAROQUE TINKER, Edward: Les écrits de langue française en Louisiane au XIXe siècle. Paris 1932

REED, John and WAKE, Clive (eds.): A book of African verse. London 1964 (No. 42)

SÉJOUR, Victor: Plays, produced in Paris: La chute de Séjan (1849), Richard III (1852), L'argent du diable (1854), Le fils de la nuit (1856), Les grandes vassaux (1859), Les mystères du temple (1862), Le fils de Charles-Quint (1864)

THIERRY, Camille: Les vagabondes . . . Paris 1874 (No. 3191)

TABLE 5

Works of U.S. Afro-Americans in the Nineteenth Century

A : Autobiography	Pl : Plays
B : Biography	Se : Sermons
N : Novel	Sp : Speeches
P : Poetry	St : Stories

Important authors in *italics*, interesting authors in SMALL CAPS (literary 'forgeries' in brackets)

Autobiographies of Escaped Slaves

William Grimes		1825
(Nat Turner)		1832
(Archie Moore)		1836
Moses Roper		1837
(James Williams)		1838
Lewis Clarke		1841
Lunsford Lane		1842
(Moses Grandy)		1844
FREDERICK DOUGLASS		1845
William Wells Brown		1847
(Julius Melbourn)		1847
(Zamba)		1847

Writings of Preachers and Clergy

Lemuel B. Haynes	Se	1805
Absalom Jones	Se	1808
Peter Williams	Sp	1808–1830
Richard Allen	A	c.1820
Noah C. Cannon	St	1833
(Jarena Lee)	A	1836
Robert B. Lewis	St	1836
Hosea Easton	Se	1837
Theodore S. Wright	St	1840
Jeremiah Asher	A	1850, 1862
Alex. Crummell	Se	1853, 1862
Dan. H. Peterson	A	1854

Creative Literature

John Boyd (Bahama)	P	1834
Ann Plato	P	1841
Daniel A. Payne	P	1850
William Wells Brown	N+Pl	1853–1858
James M. Whitfield	P	1853
Frances E. Harper	N+P+St	1854–1900
George B. Vashon	P	1854
Elymas P. Rogers	P	1855
Josephine Brown	B	1856
Frank J. Webb	N	1857
Martin R. Delany	N	1859
James M. Bell	P	1864–1870

William Douglass	Se	1854
Peter Randolph	A	1855, 1893
Israel Campbell	A	1861
L. D. Blackson		1867
John Jasper	Se	1882
Daniel A. Payne	A	1888
Charles B. Gordon	Se	1889
Singleton Jones	Se	1892

B. Clark	P	1867
A. A. Whitman	P	1873–1901
J. Willis Menard	P	1879
PAUL L. DUNBAR	P+St+N	1893–1914
Sanda	N	1894
Alice R. Dunbar		1895–1899
Mary W. Fordham	P	1897
C. W. Chesnutt	St+N	1899–1905
Pauline E. Hopkins	N	1900

Occasional Writings

James Forten (Letters)	1813
Prince Saunders	1816
Daniel Coker	1820
David Walker (Appeal)	1829
Paul Cuffe	1839
James McCune Smith	1841, 1854
Nancy Prince	1850
Daniel H. Peterson	1854
Martin Robinson Delany	1861
Henry Ossian Flipper	1878
John Mercer Langston	1894

Henry Watson	1848
Henry Bibb	1849
(Henry Box Brown)	1849
Josiah Henson	1849
J. W. C. Pennington	1849
(Sojourner Truth)	1850
Solomon Northup	1853
Samuel R. Ward	1855
(John Brown)	1855
Austin Steward	1857
(Mattie Griffiths)	1857
(Charles Ball)	1859
(Jermain W. Loguen)	1859
(Noah Davis)	1859?
(William Craft)	1860
(Linda Brent)	1861
(Aunt Sally)	1862
James Mars	1866
Elizabeth Keckley	1868
James Williams	1873
Jacob Stroyer	1879
Isaac Mason	1893

Poetry by Slaves

George Moses Horton	1829–1865
Islay Walden	1873, 1877

Chapter 8

'MINSTRELSY' AND VOODOO

1. The African Heritage in America

The African slaves shipped over to America, as already remarked, did not abandon their culture on board ship. Ramos gives a lively, if not very thorough survey of how they clung to their specific cultures in Brazil and the countries of the Caribbean. They adapted these cultures to the new conditions, stubbornly preserving everything they could. The rest they altered, improved and expanded, working influences in from Portugal, France, Britain and Holland. Religious syncretisms grew up like Candomblé in Brazil, Voodoo in Haiti, the Obeah cult in Jamaica, and many similar forms. Mixed languages were produced like Creole in Haiti, Papiamento in Curaçao and Surinaams in Guyana. New art-forms emerged and established themselves in music, dancing and 'folk literature'.

It would take many volumes to show Afro-American 'folk literature' with all its forms and expressions, its proverbs, tales, religious and secular songs, in so many different countries. Much has been collected and published, but there are only a few thorough studies which draw a comparison with African literature. One of these was made very recently by Verger, who listed many *oriki* (Yoruba praise songs) and other songs from Brazil and Cuba, and compared them with the corresponding ritual verses in Western Nigeria and Dahomey. Within the scope of this book I can only offer a brief select bibliography and treat in summary fashion the few forms which have become known throughout the world, the Negro Spiritual, the Blues and the Calypso (Chapters 9 and 10).

2. Extravaganzas and Slapstick Comedies (U.S.A. and Cuba)

During the nineteenth century Afro-American folklore had fully developed its special forms. But the Afro-American writers rejected this folklore and followed European schools and models. Struggling hard for recognition as citizens, they held everything African to be primitive, barbaric, backward and 'common'; especially as European and American travelling shows exploited such folklore, on their fleeting acquaintance with it, to obtain cheap comic effects.

At the beginning of the nineteenth century the 'Nigger Minstrels' were already starting up: itinerant white actors blacked their faces with burnt cork, put on gaudy clothes, played 'primitive' instruments, and imitated Afro-American songs and dances. They performed 'extravaganzas' in which two comic types were presented: the Negro dunderhead who misunderstands everything and does everything wrong; and the Negro dandy who would like to be a fine gentleman and exaggerates everything by his manner and dress. A silly way of talking, sprinkled with dialect words, and imitations of songs from the plantations or home-made compositions, extremely syncopated, were meant to suggest (or caricature) an Afro-American setting.

In 1848 four such performers formed a company, the 'novel, grotesque, original and unsurpassingly melodious Ethiopian Band, entitled the Virginia Minstrels'. In the Bowery Theatre, New York, they achieved the striking success so common when a social group in power has fun at the expense of a minority kept firmly in its place. So the Minstrel Show was born, America's first independent theatrical form. Soon there were minstrel troupes everywhere, with a regular programme in two parts: in the first part songs, jokes, ballads; in the second part variety numbers, sketches, burlesques. The show ended with a general song-and-dance number called the 'breakdown'.

After 1870 the Minstrel Shows turned into noisy mammoth entertainments with companies of up to a hundred performers. Their financial success also stimulated some real Afro-Americans to start their own minstrel groups.

Afro-American authors were understandably disgusted at their people being made laughing-stocks in this way. As has been said, this was one reason why they stubbornly adhered to European literary models. But from the perspective of today one can see that the Minstrel Show also had its positive side: for the first time white Americans were being influenced by Afro-American folklore, even though a travesty of it. Their ear was sharpened in advance for when they met the real thing.

In Afro-American written literature, too, folklore made its entrance through the backdoor of burlesque. In Cuba from 1838 on Bartolomé José Crespo y Borbón (1811–71), sometimes under the pseudonym of Creto Gangá, was writing carnival rhymes and farces including a piece called: 'A Slapstick Comedy, or the Marriage of

Pancha Jutía and Cañuto Raspadura' (1847). All the characters in it are Afro-American and it uses the local dialect. At the end of the play there is a wedding song:

Ya yo son libre	'Now I am free
Yo tá casá	I'll marry thee
mi su amo memo	My stupid master gave
me libertá.	Freedom to me.'
El Coro:	*Chorus:*
¡Guah! ¡Guah! ¡Guah!	'Guah! Guah! Guah!
¡Baila, carabela,	Dance and caravel,
maníalo la pata!	Shake him by the hand!
Cañuto son libre	Canuto is free
y casá cum Pancha.[1]	And marries Pancha.'

3. The Patriotic School (Haiti)

In Haiti the Emperor Soulouque's ignominious defeat in 1861 had one good result: it awakened the Haitians' sense of nationhood. Poems, novels and plays dealt with regional and national themes. Patriotic poets like Alcibiade Fleury Battier (1841–83) glorified the heroes of Haiti's fight for freedom:

Salut, ô Dessalines, ô Pétion, ô Guerrier!
Salut, brave Magny, modèle du guerrier!
Et toi, vaillant Lamarre, à la bravoure antique!
Et vous tous, fondateurs de cette République![1]

'Hail Dessalines, hail Pétion, hail Guerrier the fearless!
And hail to thee, brave Magny, a warrior so peerless!
And hail to thee, gallant Lamarre, in ancient valour grounded!
Hail all of you heroic souls who this Republic founded!'

Massillon Coicou (1867–1908) wrote *Poésies nationales* and historical plays like *Liberté, Les fils de Toussaint, L'Empereur Dessalines*; Vendenesse Ducasse (1872–1902) wrote a tragedy called *Toussaint au Fort-de-Joux*. And when these authors turned to their own history, they began to observe their own landscape as well, and eventually their own society and its problems. Oswald Durand (1840–1906) was the first poet in Haiti who tried, in Gouraige's words, 'to show the realities of Haiti in simple words and tender images.'[2]

'Until Durand,' Gouraige writes, 'it was the fashion to look at

nature in Haiti with the eyes of Lamartine and to recreate it in hackneyed literary phrases.'[3] Durand certainly captured Haiti's nature,
more especially its women, all the half-caste women, negresses, quad-
roons and octoroons, whose beauty, sensuality and charm he was
always celebrating–although these 'praise songs' have scarcely any
element of African style. In 1884 he created his famous ballad in
Creole to a *marabou* (half-caste) girl, 'Choucoune', thereby making
Creole a written literary language. Before this the only appearance of
written Creole was in the eighteenth century, when French colonial
settlers had sometimes collected the songs of their slaves. As song or
lyric 'Choucoune' is insignificant, a souvenir piece for tourists. Here
are the first two verses:

> Dèriè gnou gros touff' pingouin,
> L'aut'jou moin contré Choucoune;
> Li souri l'heur'li ouè moin.
> Moin dit 'Ciel! à la bell'moune.' (twice)
> Li dit: 'Ou trouvé ça, cher?'
> P'tits z'oézeaux ta pé couté nous lan l'air. (twice)
> Quand moin songé ça, moins gangnin la peine,
> Car dimpi jou-là, dé pieds moin lan chaîne! (twice)
>
> Choucoun', cé gnou marabout:
> Z'yeux li clairé com'chandelle.
> Li gangnin téte doubout . . .
> Ah! si Choucoun', té fidèle!–
> Nous rété causer longtemps,
> Jusqu'z'oézeaux lan bois té paraîtr' contents!
> Pitôt blié ça, cé trop grand la peine,
> Car dimpi jou-là, dé pieds moin lan chaîne![4] (twice)

> > 'Behine de big ole cactus tree
> >   I met Choucoune 'pon dat day.
> > She see me and she smile at me,
> >   "You lovely lady," I did say. (twice)
> > "You mean dis, sweetheart," she repeat.
> > De birdies roun' us smile so sweet. (twice)
> >
> > Oh jes' to think of it is pain,
> > Fo' sence dat day my legs in chain. (twice)
> > Her eyes so bright like candle shine,
> >   Choucoune, missie maraboo!
> > Her breasts dey standing out so fine,
> >   Choucoune, if you only true!

De two of us we talk so long,
All birds in wood show glad with song.
I best forget dat, too much pain,
Fo' sence dat day my legs in chain!' (twice)

At the end a white man comes with a little red beard, and Choucoune falls in love with him because he speaks French, and she gets a child by him—'her little belly's big an' roun' '. But the singer still loves her, although 'sence dat day my legs in chain!'

The plays and novels by these authors helped to get the vernacular accepted in written literature. Coicou wrote successful low comedies, especially the two plays *Féfé Candidat* and *Féfé Ministre* (1906), both inspired no doubt by Flaubert's *Le Candidat*. But Féfé is by no means consumed with ambition, he fights as hard as he can against becoming a candidate and a minister; the play is cruder, broader, more animated than its model. Ducasse too wrote some bawdy farces with verse dialogue which also uses the vernacular. 'In both him and Coicou,' Gouraige remarks, 'we find our customs depicted in their full vigour, combined with our Southern raillery.'[5]

The vernacular finally made its breakthrough in the novel. This obeyed the demands of naturalism, as formulated, for instance, by the novelist Frédéric Marcelin (1848–1917), who called for 'une littérature nationale' with 'la couleur locale'. An author should 'draw inspiration from our old customs, portray our mentality, present the exact photographic image of our passions, prejudices and virtues.'[6] Thus *La Vengeance de Mama* brought in for the first time an old man who brews African magic potions, with the aid of which the beautiful Zulma frees the country from the tyrant Télémaque. Justin Lhérisson also handled language naturalistically, and in *La famille des Pitite Caille* he returned to Coicou's theme of a candidate, this time an ambitious one but equally comic. The hero is given the advice in Creole: 'De fust condishuns fo' a peeple's cand'ate are bowin' an' shakin' hans. My fren', bow in front an' bow behine, bow to ev'ry women, to dirty negroes and clean negroes, to good women an' bad women . . .'[7]

Haiti's most important naturalistic novel is *Mimola*, the only work by Antoine Innocent (1874–1960). The plot is as follows. On her death-bed Aunt Rosalie, born in Africa, bids her daughter throw into the sea the casket she has had with her for a lifetime. The daughter, Madame Georges, carries out this wish, but is thereafter dogged by misfortune. Her husband dies and so do six of her seven children. She would do anything not to lose the last child, Mimola, as well. Doctors and Churches cannot help. In her convulsions Mimola keeps repeating the word 'Dan-Maoua', so Madame Georges seeks advice from an old friend of Aunt Rosalie's and receives the answer: 'Piti moé, gangnin mystè dans la vie que criol pas connin, tandé? Et bin, piti moé, Dan-Maoua cé nom nanchonm té gangnin là-bas, lan pays Whydah-Alladah-Dahomey.'[8] (My child, there are secrets in life which a Creole does not know, you understand? Well then, my child, the name Dan-Maoua was given to your mother over there in the country of Whydah-Alladah-Dahomey.)*

In simultaneous dreams Mimola and her mother learn that they will die unless they offer certain indispensable sacrifices to the ancestors. On the way they are joined by a widow and her son Léon, who have the same fears and are obeying the same visions. Léon, however, rejects the faith of his ancestors, but Mimola makes the three sacrifices required. She gets well and becomes a Voodoo priestess herself, while Léon the mocker goes mad.

The details of the various sacrifices and ceremonies are described by Innocent with almost photographic exactness. You get the impression, indeed, that the whole plot is only incidental to the scenes showing the cult. Innocent presents facts and reactions without any psychological or moral comments, except that he puts in evolutionist arguments here and there, trying to explain the country people's 'backward' behaviour. When the book first came out, it won few friends. Coicou and others thought Innocent should have 'indicated more clearly Mimola's hysterical temperament'.[9] Others considered the book too 'occult' and called for psychological, historical or 'scientific' explanations. This was really a period when people found it bad enough that the author should have adopted, as the ending shows, a pro-Voodoo attitude.

Yet Innocent had only done what the naturalistic school demanded: he observed everything photographically and wrote it down. But instead of an everyday setting, he chose the rites which were life and death to the rural population of his home country. He was the first writer to bring out the strong African element in Afro-American folklore. *Mimola* appeared in 1906. 'Twenty years later,' says Gouraige, 'several generations of writers agreed to give a verdict in Innocent's favour and to follow the path he traced. The Indigenists (see Chapter 12) may not always remember that they had a forerunner in Innocent, to whom they owed everything.'[10]

* Whydah and Alladah are towns in Dahomey.

4. 'Nigger Minstrels' in Literature

The military and economic defeat of the Southern States in the American Civil War effected only a temporary suppression of the Southern 'ideology'. Almost as soon as the storm was over, a wave of justification set in: white authors from the South idealized the 'good old days' of slavery, in which mild, kindly masters ruled over contented, loyal, grateful, cheerful and song-loving slaves. Freedom had turned the slaves into helpless, uprooted paupers who were incapable of acting on their own initiative while pining for the happy days of slavery.

This literature was a sort of literary Nigger Minstrel show: white writers made themselves spokesmen for the dark race. As the minstrels blacked their faces and popularized the crude comic types of the black buffoons and dandies, so these writers in their poems and stories showed ex-slaves longing for the old plantations and days of slavery. They created the touching but funny simpleton, whom the whole country was meant to see, and eventually did see, as the true representative of the Negro, an immature and childlike creature who neither desired nor deserved real emancipation.

Irwin Russell (1853-79) in his poems developed this ideology[1] and set its literary pattern. He made his ex-slaves speak in dialect to stress their 'primitiveness' and introduced the 'Negro sermon' into literature. Joel Chandler Harris (1848–1908) collected genuine folklore from the region of Atlanta in Georgia, 'Negro' songs and stories, which he arranged to suit the taste of the planter tradition. His 'Uncle Remus' stories had a terrific success. Thomas Nelson Page and Armistead C. Gordon, in the same tradition as Harris, laid it on with a trowel: the Negroes, as Wagner says, are 'above all an instrument of glorification for their masters.'[2] For example, an ex-slave on his death-bed tells his son to give all his savings, with which the son had hoped to buy his freedom, to the 'young master' impoverished by the Civil War, because the young master needed the money more:

> . . . say you kin work an' don't need none,
> An' he carn't, son.

> He ain' been use ter diggin'
> His livin' out de dirt;
> He carn't drink out a piggin,
> Like you. . . .[3]

The South's justification propaganda actually had the greatest success in the North about twenty years after the Civil War. 'That,' says Wagner, 'is the revenge of the plantation tradition for *Uncle Tom's Cabin*, and we find a former abolitionist of the stature of Thomas W. Higginson reading Thomas N. Page's *Marse Chan* and weeping hot tears over a slave-owner's death.'[4]

The most famous black author of the time, Paul Laurence Dunbar (1872–1906), owed his success with the white public chiefly to the fact that he adopted the planter ideology. He modelled himself on the verse of Russell, Harris and Riley, even of Page and Gordon. He was a *black* nigger minstrel, who also took part as an actor in various farces and was remarkable for his bawdiness. So he was a Negro who imitated the imitators of the Negroes.

Dunbar had only a cursory acquaintance with the South and with the days of slavery, which he had heard about, not experienced himself. So in his 'Corn Song'[5] there are the usual planter clichés: the 'Old Home', with Master sitting on the great white verandah, and hearing from afar the slaves' singing as they return from the maize fields with tired limbs but cheerful hearts. In the last verse the inevitable tears flow:[6]

> And a tear is in the eye
> Of the master sitting by,
> As he listens to the echoes low-replying
> To the music's fading calls . . .

Slavery appears purely idyllic. Even the worst punishment for a refractory slave, being 'sold down the river' into the deep South, is made light of in the poem 'Parted'.[7] On the other hand, the freed slaves are in despair when it comes to leaving their kind master, and at Christmas of all times:

Chrismus on the Plantation

It was Chrismus Eve, I mind hit fu' a mighty gloomy day—
Bofe de weathah an' de people–not a one of us was gay;
Cose you'll t'ink dat's mighty funny 'twell I try to mek hit cleah,
Fu a da'ky's allus happy when de holidays is neah.

But he wasn't, fu' dat mo'nin' Mastah'd tol' us we mus' go,
He'd been payin' us sence freedom, but he couldn't pay no mo'.
He wa'n't nevah used to plannin' fo' he got so po' an' ol',
So he gwine to give up tryin', an' de homestead mus' be sol'.

At this terrible news the women workers weep out loud, the men try to hide their tears. Then loyal old Ben comes up to Mastah (who is also crying), and addresses him as follows – note the disapproval for 'Mistah Lincum':

> Look hyeah, Mastah, I's been servin' yo' fu' lo! dese many yeahs
> An' now, sence we's got freedom an' you's kind o' po', hit 'pears
> Dat you want us all to leave you 'cause you don't t'ink you can
>   pay.
> Ef my membry hasn't fooled me, seem dat whut I hyead you say.

> Er in othar wo'ds, you wants us to fu'git dat you's been kin',
> An' ez soon ez you is he'pless, we's to leave you hyeah behin'.
> Well, ef dat's de way dis freedom ac's on people, white or black,
> You kin jes' tell Mistah Lincum fu' to tek his freedom back.

> We gwine wo'k dis ol' plantation fu' whatevah we kin git,
> Fu' I know hit did suppo't us, an' de place kin do it yit.[8]

Dunbar also wrote melancholy introspective poems, about feeling a sad clown or a bird in a cage, about his doubts and religious scepticism, the bitterness of life, an artist's despair that he cannot achieve the perfect love or the perfect song:

> To have come to sing the perfect song
> And only by a half-tone lost the key . . .[9]

He aspired to be another Shelley, and tried, in fact, to 'sing' like a European. Yet it was just the other half-tone in his songs that gave him his artistic individuality. In the musical quality of his poetry, not in its content, we recognize the African cultural heritage. He could no more deny this, try as he might, than he could deny his own mother. His poetry has an intonation of its own, which differs in a subtle way from our poetic conventions. The melody is shifted by the odd semi-tone, and the rhythm follows the beat rather than any strict metrical norm. Despite his conformist ideology, his poetry sounds truly Afro-American because of these qualities. His literary models only achieved a superficial resemblance, closer to parody than to the real thing.

In prose Dunbar was less happy. He wrote a book of short stories, *Folks from Dixie*, with dialogue which sometimes shows him on the track of the oral story-tellers both in spirit and in sound. But often he turned to themes he felt more worthy of his pen, and then proved no more than a moderate story-teller. Like Harris, Page and Chesnutt, he tried to draw inspiration from the oral Afro-American folklore, hoping to find thereby its original note and technique (in both senses of the word 'original'). What Harris and Page found was only something they took for naïveté.

Charles Waddell Chesnutt (1853–1932) worked out his 'Uncle Julius' very elaborately as a counterpart to Harris's 'Uncle Remus'. Chesnutt was a disciple of the naturalist school, and in *The Wife of His Youth*, for instance, placed the central figure of each story in an abnormal situation caused by racial prejudice. This method, of course, is far removed from oral story-telling, and it points forward to Richard Wright and the twentieth century.

At any rate Afro-American folklore made its breakthrough into literature, by whatever highways or byways; and it was this which allowed the African cultural heritage to remain alive and at work in North America right up to the present day.

REFERENCES AND BIBLIOGRAPHIES

1. The African Heritage in America

ADAMS, E. C. L.: Nigger to Nigger. New York 1928

BREWER, John Mason: Dog ghosts, and other Texas Negro folk tales. Austin, Tex. 1958

BROWN, Sterling Allen: Negro folk expression. I.: Folk tales and aphorisms. In: Phylon, vol. XI, Atlanta, Ga., 1950

BROWN, Sterling Allen–DAVIS, Arthur Paul–LEE, Ulysses Grant: The Negro caravan. New York 1941 (No. 2171)

BUTCHER, Margaret Just: The Negro in American culture. Based on materials left by Alain Locke. New York 1956

CABRERA, Lydia: Cuentos negros de Cuba. La Verónica 1940

–Porqué . . . Cuentos negros de Cuba. La Habana 1948

–El Monte, Igbo Finda, Ewe Orisha, Vititinfinda. Notas sobre las religiones, la magia, las supersticiones y el folklore de los negros criollos y del pueblo de Cuba. La Habana 1954

CARNEIRO, Edison: Antologia do negro brasileiro. Rio de Janeiro 1950

COURLANDER, Harold: The drum and the hoe. Life and lore of the Haitian people. Berkeley, Los Angeles 1960

HAURIGOT, Georges: Littérature orale de la Guyane française. Paris 1893

HERSKOVITS, Melville Jean–HERSKOVITS, Frances S.: Suriname folklore. New York 1936

HUGHES, Langston–BONTEMPS, Arna: The book of Negro folklore. New York 1958

HURSTON, Zora Neale: Mules and men. Philadelphia 1935 (No. 2869)

LANDECK, Beatrice: Echoes of Africa in folk songs of the Americas. New York 1961

MÉTRAUX, Alfred: Le vaudou haïtien. 5th edition. Paris 1958

MORE, Carlos: Le peuple noir a-t-il sa place dans la révolution cubaine? In: Présence Africaine, No. 52, Paris 1964

ORTIZ, Fernando: Los bailes y el teatro de los negros en el folklore de Cuba. Habana 1951

RAMOS, Arthur: As culturas negras no novo mundo. Rio de Janeiro 1937

(Die Negerkulturen in der Neuen Welt. Erlenbach-Zürich 1947)

SANTOS, Deoscóredes M. dos: Contos negros de Bahia. Rio de Janeiro 1961

SHERLOCK, Philip Manderson: Anansi the spider man. Jamaican folk tales. London 1959

SOUZA CARNEIRO, A. J. de: Os mitos africanos no Brasil: ciencia do folk-lore. São Paulo 1937

SYLVAIN-COMHAIRE, Suzanne: Contes du pays d'Haïti. Port-au-Prince 1938

TALLEY, Thomas Washington: Negro folk rhymes, wise and otherwise. New York 1922

VERGER, Pierre: Notes sur le culte des Orisa et Vodoun à Bahia, la Baie de tous les Saints et à l'ancienne Côte des esclaves en Afrique. Dakar 1957

2. Extravaganzas and Slapstick Comedies (U.S.A. and Cuba)

[1] Ballagas, p. 97.

BALLAGAS, Emilio: Mapa de la poesía negra americana. Buenos Aires 1946 (No. 1186)

BLESH, Rudi: Shining trumpets. New York 1946

CRESPO Y BORBÓN, Bartolomé José: El chasco ... Habana 1838 (No. 1423)

–Laborintos y trifucas de canavá. Habana 1846 (No. 1424)

–Un ajiaco, ó La boda de Pancha Jutía y Cañuto Raspadura. Habana 1847 (No. 1425)

–Debajo del tamarindo. Habana 1864 (No. 1426)

–Los pelones. Habana, no date (No. 1427)

DAUER, Alfons Michael: Minstrel(s). In: Longstreet and Dauer: Knaurs Jazz-Lexikon. München 1957

FRIEDENTHAL, Albert: Musik, Tanz und Dichtung bei den Kreolen Americas. Berlin 1913
WITTKE, Carl Frederick: Tambo and bones: a history of the American minstrel stage. Durham. N.C. 1930

3. The Patriotic School (Haiti)

[1] Gouraige, p. 46.
[2] ibid., p. 55.
[3] ibid., p. 56.
[4] Morpeau, pp. 23 f.
[5] Gouraige, p. 99.
[6] Marcelin 1903, p. 5.
[7] Lhérisson 1929, p. 51.
[8] Innocent, p. 17.
[9] Vaval, p. 166.
[10] Gouraige, p. 144.

COICOU, Massillon: Poésies nationales. Paris 1892 (No. 1411)
– Liberté, Play, produced 1894 in Haiti and 1904 in Paris
– Les fils de Toussaint, Play produced 1895 in Haiti
– Féfé Candidat, Comedy produced 1906 by Théâtre National, Port-au-Prince
– Féfé Ministre, Comedy produced 1906 by Théâtre National, Port-au-Prince
– L'empereur Dessalines, drame en deux actes, en vers. Port-au-Prince 1906? (No. 1415)
DUCASSE, Vendenesse: Toussaint au Fort-de-Joux. Play, produced 1896 in Haiti
DURAND, Oswald: Rires et pleurs. Corbeil 1896 (No. 1477)
GOURAIGE, Ghislain: Histoire de la littérature haïtienne. Port-au-Prince 1961
INNOCENT, Antoine: Mimola ou L'histoire d'une cassette. 2nd edition. Port-au-Prince 1935 (! 1937) (No. 1613)
LHÉRISSON, Justin: La famille des Pitite Caille. 2nd edition. Paris 1929 (No. 1667)
– La Dessalinienne. Port-au-Prince, no date (No. 1669)
MARCELIN, Frédéric: Thémistocle Epaminondas Labasterre. Paris 1901 (No. 1743)
– La vengeance de Mama. Paris 1902 (No. 1744)
– Autour de deux romans. Paris 1903 (No. 1745)
– Marilisse. Paris 1903 (No. 1746)

MORPEAU, Louis: Anthologie d'un siècle de poésie haïtienne, 1817–1925. Paris 1925 (No. 1217)

POMPILUS, Pradel & FRÈRES DE L'INSTRUCTION CHRÉTIENNE: Manuel illustré d'histoire de la littérature haïtienne. Port-au-Prince 1961

VAVAL, Duraciné: Histoire de la littérature haïtienne ou 'L'âme noire'. Port-au-Prince 1933

4. 'Nigger Minstrels' in Literature

[1] See Wagner, pp. 54–62.
[2] Wagner, p. 64.
[3] Gordon/Page, pp. 115 f.
[4] Wagner, p. 73.
[5] Dunbar 1960, p. 94.
[6] Wagner, p. 85.
[7] Dunbar 1960, pp. 234 f.
[8] ibid., pp. 219 f.
[9] ibid., p. 367.

CHESNUTT, Charles Waddell: Works: No. 2393–8
–The conjure woman. Boston 1899 (No. 2393)
–The wife of his youth. Boston 1899 (No. 2395)

CUNNINGHAM, Virginia: Paul Laurence Dunbar and his song. New York 1947

DUNBAR, Paul Laurence: Works: Nos. 2518–45
–The life and works. Naperville, Ill. and Memphis, Tenn. 1907 (No. 2518)
–The complete poems. New York 1913 and 1960 (No. 2519)
–Folks from Dixie. New York 1898 (No. 2523)

GLOSTER, Hugh Morris: Negro voices in American fiction. Chapel Hill, N.C. 1948

GORDON, Armistead C. and PAGE, Thomas Nelson: Befo' de war. Echoes in Negro dialect. New York 1891

HARRIS, Joel Chandler: Uncle Remus, his songs and sayings. New York 1880 and 1921
–The complete tales of Uncle Remus. Boston 1955

LOGGINS, Vernon: The Negro author. New York 1931; reprint, Port Washington, N.Y. 1964

PAGE, Thomas Nelson: In ole Virginia. New York 1887

RUSSELL, Irwin: Poems. New York 1888

WAGNER, Jean: Les poètes nègres des États-Unis. Paris 1963

Chapter 9

THE NEGRO SPIRITUAL

1. Content: Death and Rebirth

After being fêted in North America, the Fisk Jubilee Singers had a triumphal tour in 1873 through Europe's concert halls. The words and music in their entertainments were most unusual, although set in euphonious European harmonies and presented in the best *bel canto* manner. They were regarded as a magnificent novelty, as 'America's first home-grown contribution to music'. The programme notes, which tried to explain the phenomenon to audiences, were written in North America and entirely ignored the African cultural background.

Seward wrote of spirituals that they are 'never "composed" after the manner of ordinary music, but spring into life, ready made, from the white heat of religious fervour during some protracted meeting in church or camp. They come from no musical cultivation whatever, but are the simple ecstatic utterances of wholly untutored minds. From so unpromising a source we could reasonably expect only such a mass of crudities as would be unendurable to the cultivated ear. On the contrary, however, the cultivated listener must confess to a new charm, and to a power never before felt, at least of its kind. What can we infer from this but that the child-like, receptive minds of these unfortunates were wrought upon with a true inspiration, and that this gift was bestowed upon them by an ever-watchful Father, to quicken the pulses of life, and to keep them from the state of hopeless apathy into which they were in danger of falling?'[1]

Today we have a different view of the Spiritual and its origins. We may assume that it did not spring by divine providence into the brain of an untutored slave, but was the result of African and Western cultures meeting and mingling, in fact that it is neo-African 'folk literature'. Opinions differ only as to the proportionate parts played by the two cultures in the origins and meaning of the Spiritual.

The slaves shipped over to America had indeed lost their native languages in the United States. But they retained their philosophy of life, their religious practices, their form of poetry, song and dancing.

They absorbed their new environment within the framework of their own ideas and principles.

The White Americans completely overlooked this. Instead of a black beast of burden, without feelings anyone need bother about, the abolitionists saw the poor slave, a victimized helpless creature who suffered patiently and sang longingly of his lost freedom in plaintive numbers only designed to arouse pity. The slave-owners, on the other hand, and those who accepted the planter ideology propagated after the slaves were freed, saw the songs of the Afro-Americans as an equally naïve expression of childish, carefree happiness. For if people sang and danced, it meant they were cheerful and contented.

The debate between abolitionists and slave-owners, which lasted for decades, was thus carried on by both sides with arguments which rested on 'projections'. In the aristocratic planter society, you enjoyed yourself in song and dance; so when the Afro-Americans sang and danced, they too were enjoying themselves. The middle-class society of the abolitionists stood for the idea of freedom represented by the French Revolution; so the slaves were also yearning for such freedom and sang their songs of melancholy longing. No mention was made of the dancing. The latter-day puritans benevolently ignored it.

The Afro-Americans, however, knew little of song and dance as expressions of personal pleasure, and perhaps even less about individual freedom and the characteristic Western conception of 'human dignity'. What they did know from Africa were communities where people's rights and duties were defined and balanced by mutual dependence, within the framework of a religious system which penetrated every human activity, a system in which song and dance had important functions. They were also familiar with periods of trial and suffering, through the initiation rites and *rites de passage* practised by the African secret societies. In these the aspirant, whether young man or girl, must first 'die': he is torn from the community of his clan, put in 'ghosts' clothing, painted all over with 'ghostly' white, and has then to endure all manner of trials, ordeals and terrors, to pass tests of courage, often to learn a strange 'ghosts' language for his initiation period; so that he may at last be reborn with a new name, as a new person and a full member of the society.

Nothing shows so clearly as the words of the Spirituals that the Afro-Americans saw slavery as such an initiation stage. There are constant references to death as the precondition for rebirth in the true life. The Christian idea of death and resurrection, and the African idea of death and rebirth, are not all that far removed from each other. So the latter could be expressed through the former; and conversely, bits of Christian eschatology were absorbed into African religious concepts. The slaves joined the Protestant religious communities with a religious sense and forms of worship they would find akin to African religious forms. Such were the revivalist 'Camp Meetings' of the Methodists and Baptists, which aimed at personal conversion and rebirth, with the aid of chanted responses, psalms and anthems, all invoking God as in the Old Testament, and sermons full of rhythmical utterances.

The Christian vocabulary used can easily lead the Western observer astray as to the real meaning of the Spiritual. By Heaven he imagines the Christian Heaven, in which after death and resurrection man appears as a spirit. 'Heaven' in the Spirituals, however, signifies rather the place in this world where life is truly fulfilled. 'I got shoes . . . all God's chillun got shoes . . . when I get to Heaven, gonna put on those shoes . . .' After rebirth the new initiate is given clothes, shoes and a belt, and is allowed to sit down–'gonna sit all over God's Heaven'. In Africa these are all 'status symbols' for the adult and complete personality, status symbols given to the initiate by 'the Lord', i.e. the high priest or the ruler of that real community of living people which the initiate will enter after the ordeal of his 'death period', and which he invokes with passionate longing.

Death period, death, Hell and slavery are equated, and this period of suffering is contrasted with the time of responsible, fulfilled life in the social community, which is equated with Heaven, Zion, Jerusalem and Freedom. The Catholic idea of Purgatory is significantly absent in the Spiritual: the initiation rites serve as an education, not towards a remission of sins.

So the Afro-Americans went through the era of slavery not in apathetic despondency, nor in carefree cheerfulness, nor in sad longing for freedom. They had entered a rather protracted initiation process leading towards rebirth as a new personality; its unpleasantness, however, made rebirth certain. So they carried out the work demanded of them, while doing everything they could to shorten the initiation period, using the most effective means in their culture: they invoked the future in a magical way. The Spirituals were the songs of invocation which originated from this need and with this purpose.

2. Form: The Magic of the Word

In traditional African culture all life is based on religion. The universe consists of a structure of living forces which are hierarchically arranged. The 'thinking forces' are the most powerful forces by virtue of their control over the magic of the word, the *nommo*, and they are superior to all other forces, to the 'thing-forces', to the forces of time and space and of the 'how'. The thinking forces include living people, dead people, deified people, the ghosts and the gods. In the hierarchy of thinking forces, living people are on the lowest rung, yet the whole universe of forces depends on them. For it is only through them that all other thinking forces can go on affecting the world.

This limitation applies even to the gods. Their activity is either a past one which continues to work, or – with personified nature forces – a constant activity with a direction which never alters. Only through living people can gods produce changes. They are not transcendent, and their effectiveness is dependent on the living person. He invokes them by virtue of his *nommo*, his word magic, and indicates the activity proper to them. He brings the gods into his life, by realizing their latent capacities in himself. He does not accept their orders, but asks them to 'work'. In ecstasy, he takes them into himself, is ridden by them, personifies them, identifies himself with them. And through the 'sympathetic magic' of his *nommo*, his magic word, he invokes their activity, as handed down in myths, depicted in legends or demonstrated by historical actions, to bring the gods into his living presence, indicating to them the present concrete task. He nominates the gods as instruments of his will. His religious practice, therefore, is not contemplative as in Christianity, but evocative. In African religion, as in the religion of the Spiritual, faith is expressed through the invocation of God; in the Christian religion through the adoration of God.

The basic difference in religious attitude – which admittedly never stands out as something absolute and can only be interpreted in the light of the historical context – has led to different forms of expression. The Christian religion stresses God's omnipotence, and the believer adopts a passive attitude towards God. He must wait for God's grace, for God to call him. The direct experience of God, which comes only to those 'blessed with grace', is a mystical act of faith in a complete spiritual union with the divine. The highest linguistic expression of this mystical experience is silent utterance.

In African religion, on the other hand, which is man-centred, man has an active attitude towards the gods. Through the sympathetic magic of invocation he compels the divine power to unite with him in ecstasy. If the union does not take place, this is not the god's fault, but means the magic is too weak or inadequate. Magic is a technique.

The Christian believer makes himself God's tool, the African makes the appropriate god into man's tool.

Drums and other percussion instruments are indispensable for the practice of an African cult. In the Afro-American cults of Brazil and the Antilles, which have retained the religious function of the drums, particular gods (*loas, orishas*) are invoked by particular drum-beat formulas. These formulas are the *nommo* names with which the gods are invoked. In North America, however, the development of Afro-American religious ideas took a different course, because the Pro-testant–in fact often Puritan–slave-owners, unlike the Catholic slave-owners in Latin America, forbade the use of the drum. With this ban on drums the African gods lost their effectiveness. They could not be invoked, they were no longer accessible to the slaves' call, they were hurled into namelessness and non-existence.

Then the revivalist services of the Baptists and Methodists showed a way of filling the vacuum. The slaves found an opportunity to in-voke a god in the new language by calling the name without drums ('Lord, Lord!', 'Jesus, Jesus'). They got to know Bible stories, put images and figures from the stories into their own setting of religious expression, and 'africanized' the forms of worship in these services. In this meeting of Christianity and African religion, the Spirituals were born.

They grew out of a culture in which invocatory poetry is simply word magic: not the written word, but the word which is sung and danced. North America's slave-owners had banned dancing. The fore-runners of the Spirituals were the 'Ring-shouts' (round dances with song but without drums), and these were still completely African. Dancing was an essential element to bring the congregation into a state of ecstatic possession. 'As a rule the older Spirituals were danced,'[1] writes A. M. Dauer. But in time the dancing was suppressed. What remained was the clapping of hands and stamping of feet to show the basic rhythm, and an ecstatic movement of the body, an 'inner dance', a characteristic 'swinging' as a sign of ecstatic excitement. The frequent use of the word 'shout' is a memory of the Ring-shout.

Just as Biblical ideas entered the 'theology' of the Afro-Americans when they lost their African gods, so when they lost their drums and had to internalize the dance in North America, it led musically to the disappearance of African 'polymetry', where several different sorts of basic metre are heard simultaneously: e.g. one drum beats a four-four beat, another a three-four beat, a third a two-four beat. All that remained was 'polyrhythm', where the bars stand vertically under one another as in European music, but several rhythmic versions of the one metre are combined together, marked by different sets of instruments.

But although the slaves began to come to terms with European musical forms, they kept certain elements which were still distinctly African. Besides the statement-response scheme of a lyric's basic structure, there was the melodic technique which Dauer calls 'heterophony of variants', i.e. small tonal changes made by putting in related intervals and exchanges in the given tonal material. Other African elements retained were the off-beat technique, certain fixed cadences, changes of tone, intonation, pitch and timbre, 'dirty tone',* variations, paraphrases and slurring of the words, and many other devices which Dauer has expounded in detail to show the development of the typical Spiritual we know today.

The words of the Spiritual also remain African in style. Words and music are closely linked, which of course does not mean that the words are secondary. The sung magic of the word determines the Spiritual's content. The function of the words is to invoke the god, and this they do through 'statement' and 'response', whereby the god is summoned, as it were, to receive his mission in the human realm. Images are used which are introduced as symbols into the 'statement'. They recur as 'secondary themes' under the persistent *motif* of the 'response': the mood is heightened by repetition, not by dramatic tension. The images come in without any outside reference, since the symbol immediately reveals the sense. Because the Spirituals are an invocation, they have a very African 'imperative' quality. They do not describe a world as it is, but demand deliverance from affliction. Basically, therefore, they have a single but universal theme.

So the manifest suffering of the slaves, which literally 'cries to Heaven', is equated with the trials and torments of African *rites de passage* and initiation rites. Living forces of deliverance are invoked: forces which have brought about deliverance and 'salvation', and so should bring about the present deliverance and salvation–through a state of ecstasy. Noah saved his 'household' from the Flood, Moses led the Children of Israel out of Egyptian bondage, Joshua led them across the Jordan and into the Promised Land, David slew Goliath, God brought Daniel safe out of the lions' den, the Chariot of Fire took Elijah up to Heaven, Jesus rose from the grave, Gabriel's trumpets awakened the dead.

---

* 'Dirty' tone has a croaking and vibrant quality. The term applies to both vocal and instrumental music.

In each of these events the analogy is obvious : there is a progression from a testing period of affliction, Hell, slavery and distress, into life, complete humanity, blessedness, riches and abundance. According to African philosophy man has an inalienable claim to a complete and happy life (*magara*); sorrow and anxiety are diseases. A life without happiness is a death in life, worse than the real death–which in fact only leads to another existence in this world. The term *magara* signifies a life-force expressed in the living person by prosperity and happiness, which comes to that person through the influence of his dead ancestors. This influence can be diminished or increased, but he has a right to it vis-à-vis his environment.

Magara is different from the Western idea of human dignity, which has a moralistic connotation and which you either lack or fully possess through your relationship to society. But the extent of an individual's *magara*, although it too depends on the influence of others, does not depend on others' judgement.

Magara is also different from 'humanity', that sum of moral qualities and duties which arises from the fact that the other person in a situation is as much a human being as you are yourself. For *magara* is primarily a claim by the person, and only the person, on all his environment, including the gods. A duty arises from it, but this is secondary, based on recognizing that all forces are universally connected. This connection means that each person can only be happy when others are too, since otherwise the *magara* force is constantly flowing away from him and to the others. As a Yoruba proverb says, 'to eat together is not sweet when somebody has nothing to eat'. (The proverb goes on : 'when all have, it is sweet'.)

Finally, *magara* is different from the European idea of human rights, innate and unalterable, which the individual possesses on the basis of natural law. However man-centred, the African view of the world is not individualistic.

Magara can be so reduced that life is no longer life but a 'death'. If a person comes into this situation, a claim on the community arises, and the person uses juridical means to get his *magara*, his full life, restored. If this recourse fails, but only then, he uses magic. But if the community comes into this situation, a claim on the universe arises. To help itself, the community resorts to magic, mobilizes all spiritual forces, cites precedents, identifies with them, and exacts a full life for itself in communal ecstasy. Only the community can use these religious resources, whereas the Christian mystical experiences come only to individuals. To sing a Spiritual as solo would be absurd.

For the slaves, *magara* is greatly reduced. Their life is a 'death', but in ecstasy they are liberated into real life. They really *live* only in ecstasy, and then adjure the liberators with whom they identify. In the place of African god-forces Biblical figures have appeared who take over their functions. In the slaves' affliction these have one single function: liberation and salvation.

Noah, Moses, Joshua, Daniel, David, Jesus, Gabriel, God and the Chariot of Fire are only various image-forces for the same process. They function interchangeably and hold equal redemptive value. The degree to which their liberation is effective is determined not by the status of the figure in Christian theology but by the degree to which the ecstatically excited person is possessed. Jesus and the Chariot, God and the railway train, Noah and the wheel, are images of equal status.

3. Interpretation: Liberation or Salvation?

There are two common misinterpretations of the Spiritual, which have been well exposed by Schmidt-Joos: 'One school stresses the Christian character of these songs, which fits so neatly into the picture of the harmless Negro: he is not only happy, he is devout. In this view, the African, having no culture or tradition of his own, was eager to fill his spiritual vacuum with Christian concepts; he therefore took over hymns and chorales from the Whites, africanized them slightly, but in substance scarcely altered them. The other school finds a close relation between the words of the Spirituals and the social situation of the Negro slaves, and concludes that these songs were exclusively protest songs, in which every line had a metaphorical protest reference. For one school, in fact, the Spirituals contained merely hope for a better world beyond the grave, and so were very popular as a diversion from the brutalities of slave routine. For the other school, they speak indirectly yet distinctly of insurrection and rebellion.'[1]

But even if nowadays the two schools of thought can 'co-exist', on the understanding that Spirituals contained both rebellion *and* the hope of salvation, both ways of thinking still miss the point. For, on the one hand, we are dealing not with hope of salvation but with real salvation; and on the other, not with real rebellion but with magical liberation. Salvation and liberation form an inseparable unity, and come about not some time in the future or in the next world, but here and now through ecstasy, which snatches them from the future into the present, so that they liberate and save the individual for as long as the ecstasy lasts. In this ecstasy the individual recreates the pattern that will cast its magic spell to bring about his future complete liberation, after which he will not fall back again into affliction.

Christians see salvation as coming through the grace of God. Man can only hope for salvation, not demand it. Western revolutionary thinkers, on the other hand, see liberation as coming by the use of drastic methods like insurrection and rebellion. But in the Spirituals the ideas of liberation and salvation become united. They can be 'compelled' into existence through the power of ecstasy, which is sufficient in itself. It does not exclude, but also it does not necessitate, any tangible action or intervention. And of course there were slave risings whenever an opportunity occurred; for the world of the slaves was wider than the world of the Spirituals, i.e. it was not merely 'religious'.

The joyfulness of some of the Spirituals is not an expression of actual joy, but an instrument for conjuring up the joy of salvation. It transforms the future into the present and sets a magic pattern. Moreover, the 'ego' is not that of the singer. He does not express his personal experience but the collective experience of the community, the slaves, the oppressed, the singing 'congregation'. The individual here is not a single soul facing God; salvation is produced in and for the community.

After the Old Testament images Christian imagery gradually found its way into Afro-American 'theology'. But this is not uppermost in Spirituals like 'Oh meet me, Jesus, meet me in de middle o' de air', 'You may have all dis worl', give me Jesus', 'Come down, come down, my Lord, come down', etc. These are invocations of the same kind as 'Swing low, sweet chariot' or 'De gospel train's a comin' '. Christian influences are to be found in Spirituals like 'De harder yo' crosses, de brighter yo' crown,' 'Live a humble, humble, humble, Lord', etc. For the idea of a heavenly reward for earthly suffering is as un-African as the idea of Christian humility.

In the last example, by the way, it is not the Lord God who is called on to be humble. His name is being invoked to strengthen the slaves' testimony – very much an Africanism. Presumably it would be possible to establish an approximate chronology for the Spirituals by analysing the quantity and quality of the Christian elements they contain. The more Christian ideas in a Spiritual the later it was conceived. Moreover, there are a good many Spirituals where only the first verse is old and the other verses have been added later.

The full texts of many Spirituals are easily available, so I need not quote them here. The literature on the subject is quite extensive. On the other hand, there is so far no full analysis or study of the Spirituals in their relationship to Africa.

REFERENCES AND BIBLIOGRAPHIES

1. Content: Death and Rebirth

[1] Seward, pp. 121 f.

CURTIS-BURLIN, Natalie: Negro folk songs. New York 1918/1919
DAUER, Alfons Michael: Der Jazz: seine Ursprünge und seine Entwicklung. Kassel 1958; 2nd impression, 1962
DITON, Carl: Thirty-six South Carolina spirituals. New York 1928
JAHN, Janheinz: Negro Spirituals. Frankfurt a.M. 1962
JOHNSON, James Weldon: The book of American Negro spirituals. New York 1925
–The second book of Negro spirituals. New York 1926
KWALWASSER, Jacob: Two hundred songs. Atlanta, Ga. 1949
LOMAX, John Avery and LOMAX, Alan: American ballads and folk songs. New York 1934
–Our singing country. New York 1941
–Folksong, U.S.A. New York 1947
MARSH, J. B. T.: The story of the Jubilee Singers; with their songs. 7th ed. London 1877
SANDILANDS, Alexander: A hundred and twenty Negro spirituals. Morija, Basutoland 1951 and 1964
SCARBOROUGH, Dorothy: On the trail of Negro folk-songs. Cambridge, Mass. 1925
SEWARD, Theodore: 'Preface to the music' in Marsh: The story of the Jubilee singers . . . London 1877

2. Form: The Magic of the Word

[1] Dauer, p. 24.

DAUER, Alfons Michael: Jazz, die magische Musik. Ein Leitfaden. Bremen 1961
JAHN, Janheinz: Muntu. London/New York 1961
KAGAME, Alexis: La philosophie băntu-rwandaise de l'Être. Bruxelles 1956

TEMPELS, Placied: Bantoe-filosofie. Antwerpen 1946 (Bantu philosophy. Paris 1959)

ZENETTI, Lothar: Peitsche und Psalm. München 1963

3. Interpretation: Liberation or Salvation?

[1] Schmidt-Joos, p. 176.

FISHER, Miles Mark: Negro slave songs in the United States. Ithaca, N.Y. 1953

JACKSON, George Pullen: Spiritual folk-songs of early America. New York 1953

KREHBIEL, Henry Edward: Afro-American folksongs. New York 1919; reprinted 1962

LEHMANN, Theodor: Negro Spirituals. Geschichte und Theologie. Witten and Berlin 1965

SCHMIDT-JOOS, Siegfried: Gesang aus der Tiefe. In: Lilje, Hanns–Hansen, Kurt Heinrich–Schmidt-Joos, Siegfried: Das Buch der Spirituals und Gospel Songs. Hamburg 1961

WAGNER, Jean: Les poètes nègres des États-Unis. Paris 1963

Chapter 10

BLUES AND CALYPSO

1. Blues Form and Blues Logic

In contrast to the Spirituals, the Blues are secular songs. They are not sung in chorus but by an individual singer. The Blues-singer describes first-person experiences, but only such as are typical of the community and such as each individual in the community might have. The singer never sets himself against the community or raises himself above it. He differs from a 'magician' poet in that he does not instruct the community, nor is he its spokesman to the outside world. Even a Blues like 'Poor Man's Blues' should be considered as a monologue sung before like-minded people. The Blues-singer differs from a European poet, and also from the anonymous author of folk-songs, in that he describes typical experiences in the first person. Descriptive songs in the third person are not Blues but work-songs (like 'John Henry') or ballads. Even a 'Trench Blues' is to be understood as a first-person experience which is typical of the group. In theme, therefore, the Blues is strictly defined.

It is also strictly defined in form. The Blues-singer composes words and music within strict rules, which are fixed by the Blues melody scheme.[1] Both words and music are improvised, but improvisation is never just making up at random, as is often believed. It succeeds only within the framework of strict rules, which offers the improviser a 'sure-fire' success. For as soon as he has started, and created the first line, his train of thought follows the rules, and idea after idea falls into the given form.

Like the Spiritual, the Blues consists of statement and response. It has six-line verses (much the commonest form) when the 'statement' is repeated, or four when it is not. The six lines, however, are sometimes written as three, the four as two. The 'statement' is not repeated when the 'response' is made into a chorus, which is then sung after a number of different 'statements'. In 'talking Blues', instead of 'statements' a story is told without being sung.

A Blues verse, then, is based on the African scheme of statement

166

and response, not the European scheme of two or four lines, although it looks as if you would only have to repeat the first half of such a verse in European poetry to make a Blues purely in form. There has been a good deal of confusion about this, particularly since Leonard Bernstein apparently thinks he has shown how to create a 'Macbeth Blues' from two of the lines in the play by simply repeating the first line:

> I will not be afraid of death and bane,
> I will not be afraid of death and bane,
> Till Birnam Forest come to Dunsinane.[2]

But before going into the internal structure of the Blues verse, let me deal briefly with its external form. Jean Wagner writes: 'Each verse contains four accents, but the unaccentuated syllables are some-times counted according to a metric scheme more complex than the classical one, which knows only binary and tertiary rhythms: here is the specifically Negro or African rhythmic element. It follows that a more or less indefinite number of unaccentuated syllables can be put between the stresses, which may make a Blues verse quite lengthy, so that it has to be presented typographically in two lines of equal or unequal length.'[3] The statement part and the response part have mas-culine endings and rhyme with each other.

In form and content the response part must provide a genuine 'answer' to the statement: I call this Blues logic. It is achieved in two ways: either the response part expands, illuminates, justifies, explains or gives grounds for the statement; or it offers an antithesis to them, so that statement and response form a confrontation. 'Justifying' and 'confronting' Blues logic are not mutually exclusive, there are even Blues with response parts which are both justification and confronta-tion. The response in such cases presents the essence of the statements, of the whole Blues indeed, like this verse from 'Outskirts of Town':

> Statement: I see you wigglin' and gigglin', baby,
>   Makes me mad as I can be.
>   I see you wigglin' and gigglin', baby,
>   Makes me mad as I can be.
> Response: We got eight children, baby,
>   Don't even one of them look like me.[4]

The response, indicating that none of the children is the singer's own, certainly gives grounds for his being angry with his woman! But in all the verses of this Blues the man's relations to his unfaithful woman are also put as antithesis to her relations with other men and the consequences arising therefrom (confrontation). The two lines of the statement, moreover, are contrasted in this verse, but in other verses one line justifies the other. By justification *and* confrontation the point of the song is enhanced.

Blues logic gives the verses a particular thought structure. If applied to the artificial Blues verses constructed out of European poetry or songs, it would give them a different sense. For instance, there is a poem by Eichendorff, which has been adapted as an English song by F. W. Farrar, 'The Broken Ring'. This could be put into apparently correct Blues form by repeating the first two lines, as in verse 2:

> She gave a true-love token,
> She breathed a plighted vow;
> She gave a true-love token,
> She breathed a plighted vow;
> That ring she gave is broken,
> That troth is slighted now.

But lines 5 and 6 do not really provide a 'response'; they continue the story, with the ring breaking. For 'Blues logic' this should be in the 'statement', to be justified, explained, etc., by 'that troth is slighted now'—which would of course spoil the Blues verse-form:

> She gave a true-love token,
> That ring she gave is broken.
> She gave a true-love token,
> That ring she gave is broken.
> That troth is slighted now,
> (That's why the ring is broken).

Pedantically speaking, too, it is the ring that suffers from the woman's infidelity, not, as Blues logic demands, the first person singular, the singer!

The last verse in the English adaptation would come nearer a real Blues, with response amplifying statement, except that again there is no first-person experience but in this case a generalization:

> Death, of the friends I number,
> The kindliest and the best,
> Death, of the friends I number,
> The kindliest and the best,
> In thee the wronged ones slumber,
> In thee the weary rest.

There is a well-known English drinking song with a first verse which repeats the 'statement' and gives a 'response' extending it:

> Come, landlord, fill the flowing bowl,
>> Until it doth run over,
> Come, landlord, fill the flowing bowl,
>> Until it doth run over,
> For tonight we'll merry, merry be,
>> Tomorrow we'll be sober.

Except for the feminine ending of the rhyming lines and the fact that line 5 is repeated three times in the tune, this comes near the Blues form. In a real Blues, however, the response does not take the form of a request or demand, nor is this example quite Blues logic, for 'tomorrow' opens a new statement; and of course the song is for chorus, not an individual singer.

Perhaps we could do something with Herrick's famous poem:

> There is a lady sweet and kind,
>> Was never face so pleased my mind.
> There is a lady sweet and kind,
>> Was never face so pleased my mind.
> I did but see her passing by,
>> And yet I love her till I die.

But no, this won't work at all. For one thing, the second lines of 'statement' and 'response' do not rhyme with each other. In any case there is no real response; for line 5 brings a new statement, while line 6 (taken as response) is against Blues logic; *and yet* means confrontation, but 'loving till I die' can only be *because* of the lady being sweet and kind. 'And yet' refers to the second 'statement' 'I did but see her passing by'. In 'Blues logic', a 'response' to different 'statements' must be justification, confrontation or both at the same time; but never justification towards 'statement' A and confrontation towards 'statement' B.

In fact there are very few verses in European poetry which are or could be completely like Blues verses in their basic structure, quite apart from the details of content. Nor have I even found any European folk-songs (which might be thought more likely to provide an example) with any great similarity of form.* This only underlines the

---

* Translator's note: The author has analysed the verses of a German folk-song he found which comes nearest to a Blues in form and content, in order to show the

strict rules of Blues form which, as has been said, are the key to the Blues-singer's success. The strict rules are not something which fetters him, but part of the equipment which gives him security in improvisation–for of course he cannot make cuts or corrections afterwards!

2. Blues and Folk-song

Improvisation and strictness of rules distinguish the Blues from the folk-song, which is not improvised but has just 'grown': the pattern is usually supplied by a particular tune, words being added afterwards. The priority of the tune is clear from the fact that the stresses in sense and for singing can be very different: e.g.

'Come, landlord, fill the *flow*ing bowl' (singing stress) instead of
'Come, landlord, fill the flowing *bowl*' (sense stress) or
'Good king Wences*las* looked out' (singing stress).

There are doubtless many other examples; whereas, in a Blues, sense stress and singing stress always fall in the same place. This is why the melody is not stiff. It is flexible within the Blues structure, the scaffolding of rules, and can, indeed must, fit the sense stresses of the word. There are thus variations of tune from verse to verse. In folk-song the tune has priority, in Blues the words.

But there is another essential difference. The folk-song is unsophisticated, while the Blues might be called self-conscious folk poetry. Its charm is made by irony, often at the singer's own expense, with double meanings and ironical points scored. The folk-song takes itself seriously, the Blues makes fun of and satirizes itself through understatements and exaggerations. The Blues continues the techniques of African praise- and mocking-songs; and these distinguish it from the *chanson*–for in the Blues the wit is always put in as a means only, never as an end in itself taking precedence over the sense. The Blues always has its reference to the social background.

The nearest thing to the Blues in European lyric-writing would probably be some poems by Heine which are like folk-songs but are selfconscious and sometimes ironical. The comparison leads to further points about the Blues. Here are two verses, one from the 'Blue Ghost Blues', and verse 4 from the eleventh poem in Heine's cycle 'Katharina':

differences which still remain and thereby show what a real Blues is like. This poem would be almost impossible to render adequately in English; hence I have omitted it and, with his approval, referred to the two English lyrics above.

Blues	*Heine*
I feel cold arms around me,	'I feel so sad and lonely,
Ice lips upon my cheek.	Like weeping out my heart.
I feel cold arms around me,	I feel so sad and lonely,
Ice lips upon my cheek.	Like weeping out my heart.
My love is dead,	This picture so reminds me,
How plainly I can hear her	Of when we had to part.'
speak.[5]	

Both verses are near to folk-song. Blues structure and 'Blues logic' are preserved. But Heine's response has a reference beyond the verse – 'this picture' points to other verses in the poem, which contain descriptions of nature; whereas the Blues verse is self-contained. Its response part is never allowed to refer to another verse, though it may refer to the whole theme of that Blues, and in fact is considered particularly happy when it does so (as we shall see later). Descriptions of nature, however, cannot occur in a Blues, for they are not a primary first-person experience.

The first two verses of Heine's 'Lotusblume' (Lotus-flower) look almost like real Blues verses, but demonstrate a further difference:

'The two of us must really	She is an ailing kitten,
Make quite a curious pair.	He's like a dog in pain.
The two of us must really	She is an ailing kitten,
Make quite a curious pair.	He's like a dog in pain.
Weak in the legs the loved one,	I think they both have something,
And lame the lover there.	The matter with their brain.'

Here is first-person experience, statement-response scheme, Blues form, Blues logic, self-contained verses, pointed wit and irony. Only the experience is not typical, it is individual.*

Being lame cannot be the subject of a real Blues, *becoming* lame at

---

* There is a so-called Blues which includes a statement about being lame, but although in content something like the Heine verses above, it is not even a first-person song, has no justification or confrontation and shows other divergencies from Blues form and logic. It is in fact a ballad:

> Old man Ben, he's so bent 'n' lame;
> Old man Ben, he's so bent 'n' lame,
> He loves his baby 'n' he ain't got a job to his name.
>
> She's got a head like a monkey, feet like a bear,
> Mouth full of tobacco, squirting it everywhere,
> But she's his baby, he loves her just the same;
> She's his Garbo 'n' he's her big he-man.[6]

most–through typical circumstances. Man's fundamental normality,
his original perfection in body and mind, is the basis not only of all
Blues but of all African and Afro-American poetry.

3. The Right to Live and 'Magara'

An individual's right to life and to an intact 'perfect' life, which is
defined by the term *magara* (see above, Chapter 9), is the central
theme of the Blues as well. In 'Silicosis Blues' this inalienable right is
stressed at once, in the first verse:

> Now, silicosis,
>> You made a mighty bad wreck of me.
> I said, silicosis,
>> You made a mighty bad wreck of me.
> Robbed me of my right to live,
>> And I am as worried as I can be.[7]

In contrast to the life-force which is exercised (*nommo*), there is
magara, the life-force which one possesses, which one wants to in-
crease, and which can be diminished by the influence of others. Anyone whose *magara* is diminished tries to reinforce it, to restore his full
life-force. For this purpose he uses communal ecstasy with others in
religious practice, through common invocation with magical song;
and in North America the result is the Negro Spiritual. He also uses
non-ecstatic invocation as an individual in secular practice, through
songs of mockery and accusation; the result in North America is the
Blues.

For the individual Afro-American there are two possibilities in
respect of his *magara*, the life-force which belongs to him: either he
has 'the full life', or he hasn't and tries to get it. If he is in adverse
circumstances–which would be normal for an Afro-American in
North America–he can either state his lack of *magara* and express
the fact that he hasn't got it, wants to have it, and knows how to get
it, thereby providing himself with *magara* through invocation; or he
can state that despite the adverse circumstances he has kept his full
life-force and express how he uses it against his adverse environment.
He can even boast of his *magara*, to draw more of it to himself evoca-
tively. The Blues expresses nothing else but these attitudes. It does
not express a sad or a happy mood, but demonstrates the attitude
caused by the loss of life-force or leading to the gaining of life-force.
The use of Blues as a synonym for 'melancholy', which goes back to

a misunderstanding of the musical mood of the Blues, especially the 'blue notes', has led to much confusion.

Blues logic also has the *magara* reference. The statements often deal with the general situation, the circumstances, the other person, the 'object'. The response then turns to the subject, the first person, the subjective testimony, the self in its *magara* relationship:

Rosetta's Blues

> The sun goes down,
>> The stars begin to shine.
> The sun goes down,
>> The stars begin to shine.
> Before the ev'nin's gone,
>> Your man will be mine.[8]

This verse confronts a normal phenomenon of the external world with something remarkable, the abundance of the singer's *magara*, which is what she is here demonstrating: 'I am so strong that all men succumb to me.' The singer demonstrates the abundance of her *magara*.

In the 'Hand-Reader Blues' the singer says that he has not got *magara*, doesn't even long for it any more, because he thinks it hopeless:

> Bad luck is in my family,
>> And there ain't nobody home but me.
> Bad luck is in my family,
>> And there ain't nobody home but me.
> I was a fool for thinkin'
>> That my happy days would ever be.[9]

The *magara* relationship is expressly presented at the crucial place in the structure, often in the response part of each verse, and always in the response part of the last verse. It thus holds together the separate verses and makes a Blues out of the sequence of verses. The response part, therefore, can without breaking the rule answer the statement indirectly as well, as here in the 'Poker Woman Blues':

> I gambled away my money,
>> I gambled away my shack.
> I gambled away my money,
>> I gambled away my shack.
> Same way I lost it,
>> Same way I'll get it back.[10]

The response part does not justify the loss; it confronts the bad luck in gambling, a temporary circumstance, with the inevitable luck of a person who has the 'full life' in all abundance and flaunts it. The response thereby points beyond the verse: not into another verse, however, but to the whole theme of the Blues, the *magara* reference. In the same way many African praise songs (see pp. 62 et seq.) are held together by a *magara* reference.

All that has been said applies equally to the Blues with a simple or an extended chorus. The chorus is only an expanded response part, which gives the same answer every time to the statements of the different verses. Since all responses point anyhow towards the *magara* reference, which can never alter in one and the same Blues, the forming of the chorus is a consistent development; indeed it makes improvising easier. The Blues without a chorus, however, is able to make more points.

The work-song also follows the statement-response scheme, and also expresses the *magara* reference. But it differs from a Blues in being unselfconscious, without irony or double meanings. A work-song is straightforward. If it describes a third-person instead of a first-person experience, it comes near to being a ballad.

Strictness of form, Blues dialectic and the relation of every verse to the *magara* reference at the time, give the Blues so firm a structure that the improvising singer seldom fails in his verses. In the 'Hitch-hiking Woman Blues' the response part of the second verse has obviously gone wrong:

> Yes, you's a hitch-hikin' woman,
>> You can dummy-ride with me.
> Yes, you's a hitch-hikin' woman,
>> You can dummy-ride with me.
> I jes' had my crank-case cleaned, mama,
>> My motor won' give out on me.
>
> The wind is blowin'
>> Right through my windshield,
> The wind is blowin'
>> Right through my windshield,
> When I go to drivin' slow and easy, mama,
>> Tell me jes' how you do feel.

The singer found no proper response, and one can hear on a record the dismay in his voice at the unsuccessful emergency solution. So he correctly put as a statement in the next verse what was against Blues logic as a response:

> I'm drivin' slow and easy, mama,
> > Don't you feel all right?
> I'm drivin' slow and easy, mama,
> > Don't you feel all right?
> The way I'm riding you now, baby,
> > Some day'll make you fuss and fight.[11]

But, as I have said, failed verses are very rare. The famous 'St. Louis Blues', however, is altogether irregular. It is not, in fact, a genuine improvised Blues but has been put together by William Christopher Handy from Blues parts which in themselves are regular. Here we can recognize the transition to the commercial Blues 'hit'.

4. The Calypso

Like the Negro Spiritual and the Blues, the Calypso has recently become generally known in its commercialized form, especially through the success of Harry Belafonte. The Calypso comes from Trinidad, afterwards growing popular in Jamaica as well, and is based on the rhythm of the *paseo*, a moderately quick rumba. Originally it was an extempore part-song according to the Afro-American statement-response scheme, arising out of duelling games and dances, in which commissioned 'choir-leaders' or 'chantwells' (from the French 'chanterelles') improvised mocking songs about the opponents in a baton contest (*Batonyé*). The original Calypsos, as Borneman[1] emphasizes, still had exclusively Creole-French words, with a structure from which the present curious rhyme-scheme has arisen, a scheme not to be found elsewhere in English verse. The 'chantwell's' statement is followed by the choir's 'response', which in the course of time turns into a refrain. On the music of the Calypso, Dauer writes: 'The genuine Calypso is distinguished by its polymetric basis, its strong off-beat phrasing, its simple sequence of dominant chords, and the use of archaic or artificially formed words with many syllables conglomerated in a very small space of text.'[2]

In the Calypso, public events are celebrated, things which concern everybody. If the Calypso singer sings from his own experience something valid for all, demonstrating a general need, he approaches the style of the Blues singer. Mainly, however, he fulfils the function of a newspaper, singing news and comment, and is also the gossip columnist and political conscience. His song has the completely African function of the praise song or more often the mocking and satirical song. It voices public opinion, with the audience confirming in the chorus what the singer has expressed, as in the first verse of a Calypso on the Trade Unions:

> Dalley says in our Trade Unions
> There are too many dissensions,
> No wonder the movement can't take a grip,
> Too many people want leadership.
> And while they're quarrelling bitterly
> It's the poor workingman pays the penalty.[3]

Or again, here is the last verse of a Calypso on the Montego Bay Conference, where the question of a Federation of the West Indies was discussed:

> Federation without self-government
> Is nothing but a left-handed compliment.
> We'll find ourselves reverting eventually
> To nothing but a glorified Crown Colony.
> We must stabilize these West Indies with a parliament,
> Make them a Commonwealth for our betterment,
> For without the fullest representation
> Then, I ask you–What's the use of Federation?[4]

1948 was a year of food shortage in the West Indies, and in a Calypso from that year, 'Small Island Pride', the singer tells how he sent his girl into town, but she didn't return because a Chinese merchant gave her a pound of rice. The chorus goes:

> All they talk is rice the biggest sweet man in Town
> Ah fuss ah frighten to send me girl in Town.
> Rice is the biggest sweet man in Town
> Ah fuss ah fraid of these Chiney men in the Town.
> Rice is the biggest sweet man in the Town
> Ah fuss ah fraid ah lost me girl for ah pound.[5]

When a famous person dies, the Calypso turns into a praise song. Here is the last verse of a mourning Calypso sung after the death of Gandhi:

> In the death of the Mahatma
> The world has lost a great spiritual leader,
> A real true saint, good upright and
> A beautiful soul and a noble man.

> Millions are weeping in sympathy
> Over this terrible tragedy.
> So let us join with them and sing, R.I.P.,
> May he rest in peace in eternity.[6]

The African custom of improvising a praise song directly after a well-known person dies has survived in Africa even in places where a European *lingua franca* is used. In a bar in Lagos the Ibo band of 'The Three Night Wizards' improvised a praise song in English on the death of a Nigerian politician, Dr. Manuwa Manfo Henshaw, in a plane crash. The band played a Highlife dance rhythm, and the singer started by calling out Henshaw's names, then gave the news and linked together in a loose form his memories of the deceased:

> Doctor Manuwa Manfo Henshaw,
> Oh Doctor Manfo Henshaw!
> Nigeria mourn for Henshaw,
> Doctor Henshaw!
> Henshaw went to Zaria for a certain conf'rence.
> Return back to Lagos
> He visited Mr. Elua.
> Going back to Calabar
> He got an unlucky plane
> That was going to Tiko
> Per Enugu and Calabar.
> Henshaw down! He come down!
> He was among the persons
> That died in the plane-crash.
> I could remember him in Owerri,
> Henshaw was there as a doctor,
> A nice man, a better man,
> A peaceful man, a sorrowful man.
> Oh, Henshaw a sportsman
> All over Nigeria,
> Mister Manfo Henshaw
> Everywhere in Nigeria.
> I do remember in nineteen forty-four
> He enlisted me in the army.
> Oh, Henshaw, Doctor Henshaw,
> May you rest in peace!
> Henshaw! His wife and some children
> In Calabar,

> Long life in his mambo
> Wherever they go in their life.
> Whenever a man is dead, he's gone for ever,
> Whenever a man is dead, he's gone for ever.
> Doctor Henshaw, a nice man,
> He's dead!
> A news and a story and a hist'ry
> All over in Nigeria.
> Whenever a man is dead, he's gone for ever,
> Whenever a man is dead, he's gone for ever.[7]

But let us return to Trinidad, where carnival time is Calypso time, and many a poor wretch may win a prize for the Calypso he has made up. The jury is the whole audience, whose applause is the deciding factor. The best Calypsos appear in the Hit Parade. The singers tend to give themselves poetic names, under which they become famous: the Calypsos on the Trade Unions, Gandhi and the Montego Bay Conference were by Atilla the Hun; the name has been Caribbean-ized by changing the two t's for two l's.

Here are two verses from 'The Too Foot Santipead', which are by 'Young Growler':

> Ah mamer something is biting me
> In the middle of the night shouted Dorathy
> Oh what ah mistery
> Its ah Too Foot Santipead
> (She said) Look it day look it day look it day
> Hold it in your hand and dont let it get away.

> Yes siree I lying in my bed
> Oh what a scandal in my head
> In the darkness I heard ah Fumbling
> This time Dorathy was grumbling
> Mar it is stinging me
> So bring the Light and Let me see
> (She said) Look it day look it day look it day
> Hold it in your hand and don't let it get away.[8]

The famous Calypsos of the Carnival, of course, are mainly humorous gossip-column stuff full of innuendo, sometimes also a weapon; to be the subject of a Calypso is sometimes 'no joke'. Some of the most successful Calypsos are based on a concrete event, but have a chorus where the audience can join in the singing and dancing, taking the dance movements from the Calypso's words. Here, for instance, are the first three verses and the last verse of 'The Story of Lion's Lost Watch':

> Tick Tick Tick Everybody looking
> Tick Tick Tick See them how they searching
> Tick Tick Tick That's all they hearing
> But they couldn't find out where the watch was hiding.

> What a confusion
> When a fellow lost his watch on a Railway Station
> A saga girl name Emelda
> Was suspected to be the burgular
> She had no purse, no pockets in her clothes
> So where she had the watch hidden goodness knows.

> Tick Tick Tick etc.

> So on suspicion
> They took her to the nearest Police Station
> Then called a Matron
> To examine every piece of clothes she had on
> Well every piece was examined with care
> They even made Melda comb out her hair
> They searched till they couldn't search no more
> And the watch ticking harder now than before.

> Tick Tick Tick etc.

> The Matron then got an idea
> That she can find the watch around somewhere
> She said she had an incentive
> And will find the watch if given prerogative
> To diverse Melda entirely
> And search her as if she crazy
> Well to that the Inspector did decide
> So the Matron turned Melda's inside outside.

> Tick Tick Tick Everybody looking
> Tick Tick Tick See how they searching
> Tick Tick Tick That's all they hearing
> But they couldn't find out where the watch was hiding. . . .

Excitement now in the station
Matron searching by inspiration
Watch ticking louder and louder
And the Matron moving up closer
Then convinced that there's no doubt
Pushed her hand up inside Melda's mouth
And you know de idea did come true
For when they found the watch it was ten to two.

Tick Tick Tick Everybody looking
Tick Tick Tick See how they searching
Tick Tick Tick That's all they hearing
And at last they found out where the watch was hiding.[9]

REFERENCES AND BIBLIOGRAPHIES

1. Blues Form and Blues Logic
2. Blues and Folk-song
3. The Right to Live and 'Magara'

[1] cf. Dauer 1964, p. 23.
[2] Shakespeare, Macbeth, Act 5, Scene 3.
[3] Wagner, p. 33.
[4] cf. Breman, p. 123.
[5] Lennie Johnson on Brunswick 87504 LPBM.
[6] Background of the Blues, Iain Laing. (Workers' Music Assoc. Ltd. 1944–out of print).
[7] cf. Berendt, p. 25.
[8] Silverman, pp. 273 f.
[9] William Jazz Gillum on RCA Victor 202964.
[10] Blind Blake on Paramount 12810.
[11] Black Ace on Arhoolie FS 101.

ALLEN, William Francis–WARE, Charles Pickard–GARRISON, Lucy McKim: Slave songs of the United States. New York 1867. New editions, 1929 and 1951

BERENDT, Joachim Ernst: Schwarzer Gesang II: Blues, englisch-deutsch, München 1962

BREMAN, Paul: Blues. En andere werdllijke volks-muziek van de noord-amerikaanse neger. The Hague 1961

CHARTERS, Samuel B.: The country blues. New York 1959

DAUER, Alfons Michael: Der Jazz. Seine Ursprünge und seine Entwicklung. Kassel 1958; reprinted 1962

−Jazz, die magische Musik. Bremen 1961

−Wie der Blues gesungen wird. In: Jahn, Janheinz: Blues und Work Songs. Frankfurt a.M. 1964

DOWNES, Olin und SIEGEMEISTER, Elie: A treasury of American song. New York 1940

GREENWAY, John: American folksongs of protest. Philadelphia 1953

HANDY, William Christopher: A treasury of the blues. New York 1949

JAHN, Janheinz: Blues und Work Songs. Frankfurt a.M. 1964

JONES, LeRoi: Blues people. New York 1963 and London 1965

KREHBIEL, Henry Edward: Afro-American folksongs. New York 1914. New edn. 1962

LOMAX, John Avery and LOMAX, Alan: American ballads and folk songs. New York 1934

−Negro folk songs as sung by Leadbelly. New York 1936

−Our singing country. New York 1941

ODUM, Howard Washington and JOHNSON, Guy B.: Negro workaday songs. Chapel Hill, N.C. 1926

OLIVER, Paul: Blues fell this morning: the meaning of the blues. London 1960

SHIRLEY, Kay: The book of the blues. New York 1963

SILVERMAN, Jerry: One hundred and ten American folk blues. New York 1958

WAGNER, Jean: Les poètes nègres des États-Unis. Paris 1963

4. The Calypso

ATILLA THE HUN (Pseudonym): Calypso on review. Souvenir collection, 1948. Port-of-Spain, Trinidad, 1948

BORNEMAN, Ernest: Der Mond über Trinidad. Eine Einführung in die Volksmusik der Insel. Radio script, Radio Bremen

CONNOR, Edric: Songs from Trinidad. London 1958

DAUER, Alfons Michael: Calypso. In: Longstreet und Dauer: Knaurs Jazz-Lexikon. München 1957

Chapter 11

THE 'NEGRO RENAISSANCE'

1. 'Race-consciousness' and 'Class-consciousness'

Much has been written about the phenomenon which Alain Locke (1886–1954) christened the 'Negro Renaissance'. Before I discuss opinions, here is a brief resumé of the facts.

In the pleasure-bent era after the First World War 'Negro music' created a furore; Cake-walk and Charleston conquered the dance-floor; Negro actors and 'a Negro setting' were introduced to the stage by Eugene O'Neill (1888–1953) with *Emperor Jones* (1920) and *All God's Chillun Got Wings* (1923); and New York's high society flocked of an evening to the bars and cabarets of Harlem. It was the era when 'black came into fashion'.

Along with the Afro-American bands, singers, dancers and actors, a great many writers were in the limelight. Their 'propaganda chief' was Carl Van Vechten (1880–1964), star critic and successful author, who 'discovered' Harlem's folklore. In his luxury apartment on Central Park he brought together the stars of Harlem and the cream of society – suddenly quite free from colour prejudice; and his best-seller *Nigger Heaven* (1926) made Harlem a viable literary and social environment. He had the purest of intentions. If, he thought, there was communication between the élite of white society and the élite of coloured intellectuals (which white society had hitherto ignored), and if in addition Harlem became popular with the middle classes, some prejudices were bound to die. His success proved him right: since then to admit to race prejudice in public has been considered uncouth and ill-bred in New York society.

White society, and with it the American public, was surprised at the number of talented people among their coloured fellow-citizens and at their imaginative powers; perhaps even more surprised to realize that 'Negroes' could produce literary works at all.

The 'ballyhoo' brought all Negro writers to the fore, good ones as well as mediocre, so long as they followed the fashionable trend; and this meant that some talented writers found support and encouragement, while others no doubt had their talents aroused by it. But such talents did not appear 'out of the blue', any more than the Spirituals had done. In 1912 the first collections of poetry by Claude McKay (1889–1948) had appeared (though in London, not America). In the same year the important novel, *Autobiography of an Ex-Colored Man*, by James Weldon Johnson (1871–1938), was printed, though at the author's expense. In 1927 the book came out in a new edition, as a great discovery, with a foreword by Van Vechten.

Three collections of poetry by Fenton Johnson (1888–1958) were published between 1913 and 1916, also at the author's expense. The early poetry of William Edward Burghardt DuBois (1868–1963) did not appear till later, scattered through various magazines. It included 'A Litany at Atlanta', written in 1906, which became a literary model for several writers. A small publishing house in Boston, the Cornhill Company, had printed a few bolder works, including *The Band of Gideon* by Joseph Seamon Cotter Jr. (1895–1919); but the bigger publishers, if they published 'Negro' works at all, took those in the spirit of Dunbar and his successors.

The argument between DuBois and Booker Taliaferro Washington (1858?–1915) paved the way intellectually for the Negro Renaissance. In 1895 Booker Washington declared that 'the agitation of questions of social equality is the extremest folly',[1] and found a shrewd compromise formula: 'In all things that are purely social we can be as separate as the fingers, yet one as the hand in all things essential to mutual progress'.[2] This was agreeable to the Whites of the Industrial North and those of the agricultural South, so he gained the support of both for his Tuskegee Training Institute, which trained coloured people for crafts, trade and industry.

Washington had renounced political struggle, higher education and the civil rights guaranteed by the constitution, which meant that he acknowledged the inferiority of all Afro-Americans. DuBois, on the other hand, stood for political equality,[3] i.e. the franchise, and above all for education up to the highest level for the 'talented tenth'. In 1910 he founded the N.A.A.C.P. (National Association for the Advancement of Colored People), which defended the rights of Afro-Americans mainly by legal action, and also the magazine *Crisis*, which defended them by propagandist means.

Higher education, of course, was only for the coloured middle class, which had completely taken over the values and prejudices of American middle-class society, and did not wish to be reminded of its past, of Africa, or the days of slavery. In their eyes, the peasants of the South, who had created and maintained a hybrid culture from African and European elements, were primitive and backward and did not merit equal rights; Booker T. Washington's obsequious tactics would still do all right as far as these poor wretches and their economic progress were concerned.

We find, for instance, in Otis M. Shackelford's novel *Lillian Simmons* (1915): 'She could understand why Jim Crow cars and all other forms of segregation in the South were necessary, but she could not feel that it was fair to treat all colored people alike, for after all they were not all alike.'[4] And as late as 1928 we find in Nella Larsen's novel *Quicksand*: 'Why, she wondered in furious protest, should she be tied up with this despised black race?' The inequality was stressed, thereby demonstrating the 'high level' of the deserving. It was beneath the dignity of the coloured middle class, it was just not done, to play Blues or Boogie-Woogie at home. The important thing was to show you belonged to the culture of the West. The writer, above all, had to be 'cultured', in the narrow bourgeois sense which degrades the writer to the status of a 'culture symbol', an admirer of 'higher values', a model of conventionality and respectability.

While still quite young, DuBois flirted with socialist ideas, but even so he always remained the spokesman of this ambitious middle class. He despised the Harlem 'craze', and when under its impetus the 'folk' elements emerged – Blues and Spirituals, memories of slavery, longing for Africa – he fought the trend fiercely, an arch-priest of respectability. As LeRoi Jones writes in an excellent modern study, 'the adjustment necessary for the black man to enter completely into a "white" American society was a complete disavowal that he or his part of the culture has ever been anything else but American.'[5]

Ignoring history and repudiating an Afro-American subculture was the basis for a bond between the middle class and socialist intellectuals. The former saw Afro-Americans oppressed as a race, the latter saw them oppressed as a class. But both believed they had first to educate the victim of oppression before they could liberate him. The middle class declared him a potential bourgeois citizen, which the tilling and cotton-picking land-worker neither was nor, with his separate culture, wanted to become. The socialist intellectual declared him the chosen spokesman for all the world's oppressed, which he also neither was nor could be, since his special history and typical everyday experience were different from those of all other oppressed people.

If their theories were to work, both schools of thought had first to persuade the Afro-American that he must reject his history and his culture, and that, by thus discarding his only real possession, he would eventually win some worthy prize. The middle class promised him 'full equality with the Whites', the socialists that he would no longer be a Negro. If you look closely at these promises, both are essentially the same: colourless in every sense, degrading–and utopian. For in any case they didn't work out. However 'educated' the black man might be, he remained a 'nigger' for the middle-class citizen. And however class-conscious as a proletarian the black man felt, it was the white worker in the North who refused to have him in the trade union, and the white proletariat in the South, not the white capitalist, who lynched him.

Many writers were led astray by the utopian slogans of emancipation. In 1958, two years before his death, Richard Wright could still maintain: 'If they [the Negro writers] became immersed in the main current of American life, it could result in the disappearance of a Negro literature as such. A similar result would mean that the conditions of life which in the past defined the Negro's nature have ceased to exist, and therefore that Negroes are Negroes only because they are treated as Negroes.'[6] The same sort of half-truth might have been written by DuBois. Both defined the Blues as pure dirges, both saw only the social aspect of Afro-American folk literature, both thought of the Afro-American as someone without a separate culture of his own. Jones remarks: 'There is still, for all the "race pride" and "race consciousness" that these spokesmen for the Negro Renaissance claimed, the smell of the dry rot of the middle-class Negro mind: the idea that, somehow, Negroes must *deserve* equality.'[7]

In the last resort neither race-consciousness nor class-consciousness could help the Afro-American; doors were opened to him only by his 'culture-consciousness'. When he played his banjo well enough, when he sang his religious songs and composed verse in his special way, he found an audience and readers, and was asked out to dinner–first of all by aristocrats like Carl Van Vechten. That was the reality. For it was only among the aristocrats that he did not have to pass a test in respectability and was not catechized on his creed. Culture and talent were the tickets of admittance there, though naturally, with the inevitable snobbery, some people got in on forged tickets. The average middle-class citizen and the average working-man found it much harder to eliminate their conventional prejudices.

Defenders of the race and defenders of the class paid homage, like complacent provincials, to 'white culture': anything that was not quite 'white' they called folk culture, were ashamed of it and offered it as a sacrifice. There was no 'leader of the masses', who would have spoken up for the rights of an Afro-American sub-culture; so there was no 'Negritude'. The vacant place was taken by an usurper: in 1916 Marcus Garvey landed in Harlem.

He came, he saw, he conquered. He was a man of the masses, and they had somehow realized that none of the old attitudes would do. Garvey saw what was needed and drew his conclusions. He did not write any great poetry, he lived it. The people demanded History, his answer was the slogan of Mother Africa. The people demanded unity and greatness, his appeal to them was 'Africans, unite!', and he appointed himself provisional President of a free Africa. The people demanded dignity, he appointed black dukes and duchesses, 'knight commanders of the Distinguished Order of Ethiopia, and knight commanders of the Sublime Order of the Nile'.[8] He drove through Harlem in regal pageantry, awarded orders and distinctions, appointed nursing sisters of the 'Black Cross', created an African Legion, an 'Orthodox African Church', and a shipping company, the 'Black Star Line'.

But Garvey knew neither Africa nor the Afro-American sub-culture in the United States. Instead of reviving the prestige of the despised reality and restoring to the oppressed a pride in their cultural achievements, he pursued a dream. His idea of Africa came out of the textbooks or the stupid stereotypes which Vachel Lindsay in 1914 had used for his blood-and-thunder vapourings:

... THEN I SAW THE CONGO, CREEPING THROUGH THE
   BLACK,
CUTTING THROUGH THE JUNGLE WITH A GOLDEN TRACK.
Then along that river bank
A thousand miles
Tattooed cannibals danced in files;
Then I heard the boom of the blood-lust song
And a thigh-bone beating on a tin-pan gong.
And 'BLOOD!' screamed the whistles and the fifes of the
   warriors,
'BLOOD!' screamed the skull-faced, lean witch-doctors;
'Whirl ye the deadly voo-doo rattle,
Harry the uplands,
Steal all the cattle,
Rattle-rattle, rattle-rattle,

Bing!
Boomlay, boomlay, boomlay, BOOM!'. . .
BOOM, steal the pygmies,
BOOM, kill the Arabs,
BOOM, kill the white men,
HOO, HOO, HOO.[9]

Instead of African reality Garvey showed his supporters the White man's stereotype of Africa. Instead of rehabilitating their syncretist religion, he propagated the pseudo-religion of his racial myth. Instead of defending their right to be themselves in America, he abandoned their claims, believing in his blindness that the Black man in America had 'no place, no right, no chance, no future'.[10]

His home-to-Africa movement did not lure anyone over the ocean, so his bubble burst. Without any grasp of political realities, he made himself into a Ruritanian monarch. Nevertheless, without his bold visions, his ideas like 'Africa for the Africans', 'African personality', and DuBois's pan-African ideals, would not have achieved the strength which, in conjunction with the political circumstances of the time, made them such a dynamic force after the Second World War.

The Afro-American poets, dramatists and novelists stood at the cross-roads of all these different trends; erratically and irresolutely, they supported now one trend, now another. The era of the 'Negro Renaissance' gave an impulse to many movements, but was not a unity and so created no literary style of its own.

2. How Important is the African Heritage?

All the critical works on the period have had an assimilationist bias, and have scarcely made any attempt to differentiate between styles. There are surveys by Sterling A. Brown (born 1910), J. Saunders Redding, Benjamin G. Brawley, Frederick W. Bond and Earl E. Thorpe. The prose has been investigated by Hugh M. Gloster and Robert A. Bone, the drama by Loften Mitchell and the poetry by Jean Wagner.

In Gloster's study, 'the themes, attitudes and background of the works under examination . . . rather than literary craftmanship, are of major importance'.[11] He sees the works of the Afro-Americans as merely a separate form of North American literature which has been produced by discrimination against the coloured people; with their social emancipation that form is destined to disappear.

Bone at least recognizes a cultural aspect, but draws the same conclusions. He writes that the Afro-American novel is 'at once alike and different from the novels of white Americans . . . While it follows, usually after a short lag, the main historical development of the American novel', it has 'in addition a life of its own, which springs from the soil of a distinctive minority culture. . . . It is no accident that approximately 85 per cent of the novels written by American Negroes deal principally or exclusively with Negro characters in a Negro setting. This racial emphasis is simply a literary echo of cultural reality. Whether this reality is desirable or not is another matter. When and if the minority becomes fully integrated into American life, tendencies towards cultural autonomy will presumably disappear.'[12]

So Bone too considers the separate culture as simply the result of racial discrimination, not as part of the African heritage. To his mind the Afro-American novel is torn between two diverging trends, assimilationism and black nationalism. He regards the struggle for assimilation, which would mean giving up the cultural heritage, as the progressive element, while nationalism is at once the conservative and the revolutionary-cum-separatist element. He quotes Brown's statement that 'the integration of the Negro artist means his acceptance as an individual to be judged on his own merits, with no favour granted and no fault found because of race.'[13]

This is true enough, but applies only to the individual and completely excludes the cultural aspect, which in the present context is crucial. For American society must accept the Afro-American cultural heritage, just as it has done with the European-American one, before it can completely integrate the Afro-American. He will then cease to be a cultural 'beggar', and will become the creator of something of special quality in America's culture. 'The liberation of the Afro-American,' writes the Nigerian essayist E. U. Essien-Udom, 'lies in an understanding, appreciation and assertion of his Afro-American and African cultural heritage.'[14] Through this approach, part of what Bone calls 'nationalism' gains a positive value; for the vague term includes two quite different phenomena. One is the race-consciousness disastrously emphasized on both sides of the 'Colour Line', the other is the culture-consciousness which has been largely ignored or else given a wrong, because 'racist', slant.

Jean Wagner, focusing on the poetry of the Negro Renaissance, sees the cultural aspect more clearly than Bone, but is the most thorough assimilationist of them all. In the 637 pages of his book,

Les poétes nègres des États-Unis, seven writers are dealt with in detail and a dozen more cursorily. His method is biographical and psychological: he examines the poets' character and attitudes in the light of their poems, on the grounds that 'in the eyes of many, writings are only worth as much as their writers' personalities'.[15]

So the book begins with a quasi-moral judgement of highly doubtful validity, which leads on logically to questions about writers' religious attitudes. Wagner writes: 'We have linked the study of racial feeling with a study of religious feeling; this is because we acquired the conviction very early in our researches that a sort of symbiosis must exist between the two.'[16]

Although I have very little idea what is meant by 'racial feeling' (*sentiment racial*), I consider it just as legitimate to enquire about the psychological reaction to prejudice as about a writer's attitude to God; only, all this has nothing to do with the history of literature. Wagner himself admits: 'This work, then, is not strictly a study of literary history.'[17] For the literary historian an author's life and his moral and religious attitudes are only important in so far as they contribute to an understanding of his work. But a moral judgement on the author must never influence the aesthetic judgement on his work.

Wagner's study proceeds in the opposite direction, with morality and religious attitude leading to aesthetic judgements, and producing conclusions which in essence had been already fixed from the outset. He writes: 'Is it not striking that James Weldon Johnson, Langston Hughes and Sterling Brown, who were the main artisans of the revival of the popular Negro forms, were at the same time the main critics of the Christian faith and ended in various degrees of disbelief; whereas Claude McKay, Jean Toomer and Countee Cullen, whose poetry developed entirely outside any "folk" influence on form and language, were also the great Christian poets of the Negro Renaissance?'[18]

So far this is an objective observation, which contrasts the styles and religious attitudes of the 'folklorists' and the 'spiritualists'; but now comes the judgement: 'With the folklorists, it is the collective which produces the poetic function; it is that which gives the poet his language, the framework for traditional forms for his poetic inspiration, the themes for his poetry derived from daily life, and finally his feelings.'[19]

In other words, the 'folklorist poet' is not really a poet at all, but only an instrument: language, form, content, feelings, belong not to him but to the group, the collective. On the other hand, there is a viewpoint also legitimately held by modern literary historians, that it is individualist expression in poetry which is of secondary importance; that the palm must be given to the poet who can make himself the spokesman for his time and the interpreter of his group. For my own comments on the African poet's relation to his group, I would refer the reader to my book *Muntu*.[20]

Wagner continues: '. . . the individual does not live an autonomous life; he is completely taken over by the group and only exists through it; his inner life atrophies and disappears. The spiritualists are revealed by comparison as the champions of individualism, . . . they reject the dialect and poetic forms which folk poetry could offer them, as if afraid that with the form a particular way of thinking might be imperceptibly imposed on them. They have no sympathy, either, with that light-hearted histrionic art which folk poetry usually goes in for, and their concerns are too serious to fit the half-humorous expression customary with folk poetry. Their own poetry is an eminently individual art, a secret dialogue of the human being with himself—or with God, which is the same thing—in the course of which a personality patiently analyses itself, explores its own frontiers and defines the links with the outer world which it has freely chosen. Without forgetting their own race, however, these poets penetrate deeply enough into the black soul to discover there the fundamental aspirations common to men of all races. As already indicated by their poetic form, they are searching beyond racial contingencies for universal values.'[21]

In other words, anyone who renounces the forms of Afro-American folklore and writes a typically Western individualist poetry, finds God in his heart and 'rises', as Wagner says elsewhere, 'to the level where a *rapprochement* between the races becomes possible.'[22] God and the Western world are practically identical for Wagner, and the Devil is black. So in 1963 the middle class and the socialists, who wanted the Afro-Americans to give up their separate culture as a condition for being emancipated, found a new ally in a fanatical Christian. His verdict is a foregone conclusion: the evil in Afro-American poetry is represented by the influences from folklore, the Blues, the preacher style, the Spiritual, in short, all Africanisms—which he tracks down with the zeal of a police inspector. His book, indeed, is as exciting in its way as a police file, in which every poem becomes incriminating evidence; and we can be grateful for his detective work in tracking down Africanisms. This alone makes the book valuable for us.

LeRoi Jones declared that owing to 'the attempts by the black middle class to whiten the culture of this country . . . only in music has there been any significant contribution to a formal American culture . . . the only vector out of American culture impossible to eradicate. It signified the existence of an Afro-American, and the existence of an Afro-American culture.'[23] But Wagner's investigation is so thorough that he proves the existence of that culture in poetry as well as music.

Moreover, he is conscientious enough to expose various sins, i.e. Africanisms, among the 'spiritualists' as well. But Jean Toomer (born 1894) soon abandoned the literary life to join a religious community; Countee Cullen (1903–46) wrestled with God conscientiously all his life; and Claude McKay (1889–1948) broke with communism in 1937, to be baptized as a Catholic in 1944. So Wagner feels able to grant absolution to all these.

References and Bibliographies at end of Chapter 13.

Chapter 12

THE 'GOLDEN YEARS'

As has been said, the Negro Renaissance literature is not a unity. I shall mention here only the typical works of its various trends; these trends are illustrated through the chronological table on pages 210–13. But even this table is by no means complete; and the bibliography to this and the next chapter refers, apart from other secondary literature, only to those works which are not in the table or in my *Bibliography of Neo-African Literature*. (See page 284.)

Between 1900 and 1920 the great mass of Afro-Americans lived on the land and did not concern themselves with literary activity. Only writers from the thin middle-class stratum, the 'talented tenth', mostly light-skinned half-castes, praised the achievements of the 'race', especially of the intellectual élite. The mere production of any literary work was considered evidence of intellectual abilities.

One group demanded privileges for 'the educated' in protest novels, or demonstrated how 'white' they really were physically and psychologically. Some did this by writing best-seller novels in which one of the main subjects was 'passing', 'declaring yourself white'. A few, like William Stanley Braithwaite (born 1878), even abandoned the conflict theme completely and wrote 'white' literature. The most important works of the whole group are James Weldon Johnson's novel *The Autobiography of an Ex-Colored Man* (cf. p. 183) and DuBois's novel *The Quest of the Silver Fleece*. The latter is overloaded with ideological and didactic matter, but in an idealistic way anticipates the equivalence of race and class.

Another group, led by Sutton E. Griggs (1872–1930) with his novel *Imperium in Imperio* (1899), took 'protest' to the opposite extreme of nationalist separatism, demanding that the Afro-Americans should have their own black state within the state. This was an idea revived in the 'thirties by the Communist Party. In the drama, 'protest' includes historical plays, which glorified the freedom fighters and leaders of slave risings.

A third group, represented above all by Oscar Micheaux (born 1884), propagated Booker T. Washington's theories; shrewd Negroes renounced equality, devoted their talents to economic progress and achieved wealth. Their critical works censured laziness, negligence and immorality in their own group. The writers named so far have scarcely any relation to folk literature; and it would doubtless be futile to look for any Africanisms in their work.

Poetry was still written in the wake of Dunbar and, if it used dialect at all, used his artificial sort which reflected the 'Negro' stereotype of 'Minstrelsy'. Only Claude McKay, while still in Jamaica, of course, used his rural native dialect realistically, describing the hill farmers' troubles in *Songs of Jamaica* and castigating Kingston city life in *Constab Ballads*. Fenton Johnson (1888–1958) was alone in sometimes adopting stylistic forms from Afro-American folk culture, if without much skill.

The trends began to change in 1920. A new group caught up with the descendants of the privileged class of Freed Negroes (those who had been free before the Civil War). A mass of former land-workers had 'invaded' the towns of the North during the war, and a Bohemian, urban, intellectual élite broke away from them: this was the élite of the Negro Renaissance. Their spiritual centre was Harlem, the New York 'ghetto' into which over 300,000 coloured people had poured. This militant protest was led by Claude McKay, whose most famous poem, with its *leitmotif* of 'fighting back', is the sonnet 'If we must die':

> If we must die, let it not be like hogs
> Hunted and penned in an inglorious spot,
> While round us bark the mad and hungry dogs,
> Making their mock at our accursed lot.
>
> If we must die, O let us nobly die,
> So that our precious blood may not be shed
> In vain; then even the monsters we defy
> Shall be constrained to honour us though dead!
>
> O kinsmen! we must meet the common foe!
> Though far outnumbered let us show us brave,
> And for their thousand blows deal one deathblow!
> What though before us lies the open grave?
> Like men we'll face the murderous, cowardly pack,
> Pressed to the wall, dying, but fighting back![24]

McKay, however, was not 'nationalistic' in Bone's sense, he only intensified DuBois's claims, aiming like DuBois at complete integration.

This comes out in his style too: he had given up dialect and used the sonnet, the strictest of typically European verse-forms. In another sonnet, 'America', he writes:

> Although she feeds me bread of bitterness,
>   And sinks into my throat her tiger's tooth,
> Stealing my breath of life, I will confess
>   I love this cultured hell that tests my youth.[25]

The 'cultured hell' was the city life of the 'twenties, and it had the same characteristics all over the world. It was hectic, and it was also anti-bourgeois, revolutionary, romantic. But there was something special about it in Harlem. A talented younger generation had grown up here, who regarded jazz, the era's distinctive music, as their own creation, and could identify themselves with the various intellectual movements of the period.

Thus, in Europe, it was the fashion to be proletarian; in Harlem they felt they had always been that. In Europe the modern-minded expressed their contempt for the traditional values of bourgeois civilization; in America the bourgeois world order had obstructed the progress of dark-skinned people, declaring them incapable of civilization. In Europe it was fashionable to revel in the exotic, in sensuality, strength and 'primitive art'. In Harlem they embodied these qualities; they *felt* exotic, sensual, primitive, radiating strength. In Harlem, in fact, they could claim to be all the things people in Europe admired and longed to be. But whereas the new movements made people in Europe adopt a 'sick' bitterness, nihilistic disgust with the world, and a general feeling of extreme decadence, in Harlem the same movements made them cheerful, out to enjoy life, and more self-confident than they had ever been before. 'Renaissance Harlem,' Bone writes, 'is a place of love and laughter, not of struggle and oppression.'[26]

The exotic as well as the proletarian and anti-bourgeois identification can be seen even in the first poems of Langston Hughes (1902–1967). 'The Negro Speaks of Rivers', which appeared in June 1921 in DuBois's magazine *Crisis*, reflects the spiritual bond between all black people (in the vein of Garvey):

> I've known rivers:
> I've known rivers ancient as the world and older than the flow
>   of human blood in human veins.
> My soul has grown deep like the rivers.

I bathed in the Euphrates when dawns were young.
I built my hut near the Congo and it lulled me to sleep.
I looked upon the Nile and raised the pyramids above it.
I heard the singing of the Mississippi when Abe Lincoln went
   down to New Orleans, and I've seen its muddy bosom turn
   all golden in the sunset.

I've known rivers:
Ancient dusky rivers.

My soul has grown deep like the rivers.[27]

In his poem, 'The Negro', which appeared in *Crisis* in January
1922,[28] Hughes puts together various identifications: the mythical
one with Africa,

> I am a Negro:
>   Black as the night is black,
>   Black like the depths of my Africa;

the social identification, which was to come into the foreground in
the Depression years,

> I've been a slave:
>   Caesar told me to keep his door-steps clean.
>   I brushed the boots of Washington.

> I've been a worker:
>   Under my hand the pyramids arose.
>   I made mortar for the Woolworth Building;

consciousness of the poetic tradition,

> I've been a singer:
>   All the way from Africa to Georgia I carried my sorrow
>   songs.
>   I made ragtime;

and the race protest,

> I've been a victim:
>   The Belgians cut off my hands in the Congo.
>   They lynch me now in Texas. . . .[29]

Negro history, which the middle-class assimilationists hoped to
ignore, was cultivated again, mainly thanks to the Association for
the Study of Negro Life and History, founded by Carter G. Woodson
in 1915. Jean Toomer travelled to Georgia, to identify himself with

the people, the land and the consequences of slavery. His book *Caine*, 'a potpourri of stories, sketches, poetry and drama',[30] with rural background was highly praised by the critics, though it sold very badly. As literature it is certainly more cogent than many equally expressionist works in Europe at that time; but the public was right to find a deficiency in Toomer. He was a 'spiritualist' (in Wagner's sense), and did not strike a distinctive Afro-American note.

Countee Cullen wrote poetry full of self-probing and introspection, and used classical European verse-forms. He too asked himself the question, 'What is Africa to me?'[31] But the answers his introspection brought up were only the usual clichés about the African personality, together with a hackneyed exoticism. He felt he was ill-starred in three ways, being illegitimate, with homosexual inclinations and a black skin. He reproached God for his own existence, and finally identified himself with the 'Black Christ',—in the poem of the same title—whose ethic is 'white',[32] as Wagner shows (i.e. the conventional ethic, with all its prejudices, of the American middle class). Besides producing some unforgettable poetry, Cullen wrote a novel, *One Way to Heaven* (1932), which gives a realistic picture of Harlem's religious life and a satirical portrait of its upper class. In this he belatedly joined the Harlem-style writers, just because he found Van Vechten's view too superficial. But he never tried to discover the African cultural inheritance, though he sometimes came near to it unwittingly.

It was not till 1926 that laughter at last broke through: Van Vechten's *Nigger Heaven* and Langston Hughes's *The Weary Blues* appeared in the same year. The former started the Harlem craze, the latter brought the Blues into written poetry, making Hughes a bard of his people. It is true that he too sometimes looked for the African heritage in the stereotypes offered by Lindsay. When he did, he became sentimental and flat. But in between the romantic and exotic extravagances inspired by Garvey, he always returned to the true rhythmical basis, which he experienced as jazz, as ragtime, swing, Blues, boogie-woogie and be-bop—and turned into poetry. Even here there is some incidental ranting:

> All the tom-toms of the jungle beat in my blood
> And all the wild hot moons of the jungle shine in my soul[33]

—together with a melodramatic anti-civilization note which is extremely European in origin:

> I am afraid of this civilization,
> So hard, so strong, so cold . . .[34]

But Hughes afterwards left this vein to Fenton Johnson, who managed to extract from it some shattering nihilist poetry.

Wagner holds it against Hughes that his Blues are not authentic, but mere night-club entertainments and opiates, 'laughing to keep from crying'. But the Blues, like the men who wrote them, were indeed brought to town by the people from the country. Nor had Blues been dirges in the country; in fact they became more dirge-like in town (Chapter 10). And if countless Blues were produced in an urban environment, it shows the power, adaptability and continuing liveliness of this Afro-American medium.

Where Hughes adopted the Blues form, his verse has proper Blues logic and *magara* reference; and it sings and swings to its Blues or Jazz rhythm:

> Cabaret, cabaret!
>> That's where ma man an' me go.
> Cabaret, cabaret!
>> That's where we go,
> Leaves de snow outside
>> an' our troubles at de door.[35]

And here is 'confrontation' logic in a verse like:

> When I was home de
>> Sunshine seemed like gold.
> When I was home de
>> Sunshine seemed like gold.
> Since I come up North de
>> Whole damn world's turned cold.[36]

But Hughes varies too: there are poems with him which have no Blues form and yet have Blues logic: others which move in the rhythms of different jazz forms. The Afro-American rhythms in his poetry would be worth a thorough study.

In 1927 James Weldon Johnson also discovered the 'folklorist' line. With 'God's Trombones' he introduced the preacher style into written poetry, without daring, however, to use dialect, which had been in disrepute since Dunbar and 'Minstrelsy'. Yet his images are so directly placed and his rhythms so typical that the Afro-American folk style of the sermon keeps its stirring power. Here is an extract from the poem, 'Listen, Lord':

> Lord, have mercy on proud and drying sinners—
> Sinners hanging over the mouth of hell,
> Who seem to love their distance well.

> Lord–ride by this morning–
> Mount your milk-white horse,
> And ride-a this morning–
> And in your ride, ride by old hell,
> Ride by the dingy gates of hell,
> And stop poor sinners in their headlong plunge.
>
> And now, O Lord, this man of God,
> Who breaks the bread of life this morning–
> Shadow him in the hollow of Thy hand,
> And keep him out of the gunshot of the devil.
> Take him, Lord–this morning–
> Wash him up and drain him dry of sin.
> Pin his ear to the wisdom-post,
>
> And make his words sledge-hammers of truth–
> Beating on the iron heart of sin.
> Lord God, this morning–
> Put his eye to the telescope of eternity,
> And let him look upon the paper walls of time.
> Lord, turpentine his imagination,
> Put perpetual motion in his arms,
> Fill him full of the dynamite of thy power,
> Anoint him all over with the oil of thy salvation,
> And set his tongue on fire.[37]

Claude McKay had meanwhile swung over to the Van Vechten line of the Harlem style with his anti-civilization novels *Home to Harlem* and *Banjo*, which became best-sellers, and his volume of stories *Gingertown*. Only Hughes looked for a line of his own in prose; he set his first novel, *Not Without Laughter*, in a small mid-West town.

In 1928 Rudolph Fisher had already struck a satirical note, thereby heralding the end of the era. At the end of the 'Golden Twenties' Marc Connelly's religious play in dialect, *The Green Pastures*, came to Broadway; and with it the preacher style, even if watered down by considerable 'Ministrel' clichés. Then followed the great Wall Street crash.

References and Bibliographies at end of Chapter 13.

Chapter 13

THE DEPRESSION

1. 'Depression' Writers

For a year after the shock, practically nothing appeared from Afro-American writers. A few works came out in 1931, including the great satire by George Schuyler (born 1895), *Black No More*, which reduced 'ad absurdum' the whole race question. The dark-skinned Dr. Crookman succeeds in turning Blacks into Whites within three days by electric gland-control; hair and features are also transformed.

' "But is the transformation transferred to the offspring?" persisted the Negro newspaperman.

' "As yet," replied Crookman, "I have discovered no way to accomplish anything so revolutionary, but I am able to transform a black infant to a white one in twenty-four hours."

' "Have you tried it on any Negroes yet?" queried a sceptical white journalist.

' "Why, of course I have," said the doctor, slightly nettled. "I would not have made my announcement if I had not done so. Come here, Sandol," he called, turning to a pale white youth standing on the outskirts of the crowd, who was the most Nordic-looking person in the room. "This man is a Senegalese, a former aviator in the French army. He is living proof that what I claim is true."

'Dr. Crookman then displayed a photograph of a very black man, somewhat resembling Sandol but with bushy Negro hair, flat nose and full lips. "This," he announced proudly, "is Sandol as he looked before taking my treatment." '[38]

Bone summarizes the rest of the action as follows: 'As more and more Negroes vanish into the white population, panic seizes the nation. Race leaders tremble, for their profitable business and uplift organizations are faced with ruin. In the South the social structure completely disintegrates. Jim Crow facilities lie in idleness; ostensibly white couples have coloured babies; the Knights of Nordica (Ku Klux Klan) is taken over by former Negroes; and the party of white supremacy loses its *raison-d'être*. The national balance of power is upset, and Black-No-More becomes the chief issue of a presidential compaign. In the end, life returns to "normal" when someone discovers that the ersatz Caucasians are a shade lighter than the garden variety. Segregation is promptly restored, based this time on the desideratum of a dark skin!'[39]

Although Schuyler's satire sets out to hold up colour prejudice to ridicule, he was not an author who believed in an Afro-American sub-culture. Following in his wake, Wallace Thurman (1902–34) wrote a satirical novel *Infants of the Spring* (1932), in which he tried to sum up the Negro Renaissance: 'Individuality is what we should strive for. Let each seek his own salvation. To me, a wholesale flight back to Africa or a wholesale allegiance to Communism or a wholesale adherence to an antiquated and for the most part ridiculous propagandistic program are all equally futile and unintelligent.'[40]

The Harlem style, which of course was not what it pretended to be, was bound to end in satire. For these intellectuals in Harlem were no more primitive, exotic or 'aboriginal' than intellectuals in the European capitals. Langston Hughes, who under the impetus of the Harlem style had felt 'all the tom-toms of the jungle beat in his blood', wrote more soberly in 1931, though without rejecting the African heritage–which he now recognized in its true perspective:

> So long,
> So far away
> Is Africa.
> Not even memories alive
> . . . Save those that songs
> Beat back into the blood.[41]

After the excitement and the ballyhoo were over, some authors rediscovered their individuality, while others looked for new ties. But all of them, consciously or unconsciously, still faced the problem of whether to accept or reject their African heritage.

So satires finished off the Harlem style. But now the days of laughter were gone, and Afro-American writers were very badly hit by the Depression, suffering as much as Negro workers from the effects of the motto 'last hired first fired'. The 'Federal Writers' Project', however, a social assistance enterprise established by the Roosevelt government, kept unemployed writers going by using their talents on work of public interest.

'The chief project of the Agency,' Bone writes, 'was the compilation of an "American guide"–a handbook of the forty-eight states which might serve as a kind of American *Baedeker*. According to Sterling

Brown, who was the FWP's Editor of Negro Affairs, the project turned up a vast store of information about the American culture which might well have formed the basis for a new regional art. The significance of the FWP for the Negro novelist, however, lay not so much in the realm of source material as in the extracurricular activities which surrounded the project. . . .

'The Federal Writers' Project was more than a job; it was a milieu. Most of the writers joined the government workers' union, an affiliation which brought them into direct organizational ties with the American labour movement . . .

'The roster of Negro writers connected with the FWP reads like a *Who's Who* of contemporary Negro literature. Richard Wright, Claude McKay, Arna Bontemps, Roi Ottley, Willard Attaway, Margaret Walker, Ralph Ellison, Frank Yerby and William Motley participated at one time or another.'[42] (So did Fenton Johnson and Sterling Brown.) 'Working in the same office on the same job with whites, these colored writers had an unprecedented opportunity to break out of their closed world. The white world which they entered, to be sure, was not "typically American", nor could they have entered if it were. It was in large measure a Stalinized world, but at least it was prepared to accept Negroes on a basis of social equality.'[43]

As 'job' and 'milieu', the Project gave rise to different literary movements. One used the local folklorist and historical material collected in research and turned it into literature. Sterling Brown studied the dialect of the rural South, and allowed the tone of the folk ballads and the country Blues to bear fruit in his poetry. Not that he merely took over the pure form; sometimes he welded together divergent popular models, making them into new and harmonious unities. The title poem of his collection *Southern Road* has Blues verses but no Blues logic: as in a Work-song the 'action' is continued in the response part, and the statements are regularly interrupted by exclamations like 'hunh!' and 'bebby!' The combination of Blues and Work-song is deliberate. One can see this from the way the poem 'Swing Dat Hammer' begins like a work-song. Later it goes:

> Gal's on Fifth Street–hunh–
>   Son done gone;
> Gal's on Fifth Street–hunh–
>   Son done gone;
> Wife's in de ward, bebby,
>   Babe's not bo'n.

My ole man died–hunh–
　　Cussin' me;
My ole man died–hunh–
　　Cussin' me;
Ole lady rocks, bebby,
　　Huh misery.[44]

In the poem, 'Market Street Woman' Brown combines Blues verse
and Blues logic with the ballad form (i.e. using the 'third person'
instead of the Blues 'first person'):

Market Street woman
　　Is known fuh to have dark days,
Market street woman,
　　Noted fuh to have dark days,
Life do her dirty
　　In a hundred ornery ways.

. . . Put paint on her lips,
　　Purple powder on her choklit face;
Paint on her lips,
　　Purple powder on her choklit face;
Take mo' dan paint
　　To change de luck of dis dam place.[45]

Prose also benefited from the folklorist and historical studies. Zora
Neale Hurston (1903–60), George Wylie Henderson (born 1904)
and George W. Lee (born 1894) portrayed the rural South with folklorist realism. Arna Bontemps (born 1902) wrote two realistic historical novels: *Black Thunder*, on the slave rising of Gabriel Prosser
in Virginia in 1800; and *Drums at Dusk*, on the rebellion of Toussaint
Louverture which in 1804 led to Haiti's independence. In the Depression even Claude McKay tried to find a bridge to the folklore of his
native region. His novel *Banana Bottom* shows a Jamaica woman
brought up by missionaries who reverts to the Afro-American Obeah
culture.

The movement stemming from the Project milieu struck a bitter
note of class struggle. It used crude realism to describe typical experiences of oppression suffered by coloured workers in industry and
on the land, and made these symbolic of treacherous capitalist exploitation. Race and class were equated. Almost all Afro-American
writers joined this movement. Its most militant representative was
Richard Wright: in the four short novels in the collection *Uncle Tom's*

Children he gives an unvarnished and unforgettable account of the brutality shown by the Whites to their coloured fellow-citizens, from the lynching of adolescents to the sexual exploitation of defenceless coloured women. In the fourth novel he draws the ideological consequences: a Black Christian preacher comes round to leading a protest march, in alliance with White workers, against the ruling exploiter class.

In his novel *Native Son* Wright successfully produced a universal symbol of the wretch oppressed and hemmed in by his environment, made aggressive by despair: Bigger Thomas is driven to murder by abysmal fear. 'Estranged from the religion and folk culture of his race',[46] the scared coloured adolescent was meant to symbolize not only American conditions but to serve as a universal example of society's responsibility for crime.

The identification of race and class led logically to works in which the protagonists of the novels are not 'Negroes' but rootless or proletarian Whites. Examples of this are *Let me Breathe Thunder* by William Attaway (born 1912), books by Frank Yerby (born 1916), and *Knock on Any Door* (1947) by Willard Motley (born 1912). The hero of this last book, the Italo-American Nick Romano, is so like Bigger Thomas that Bone goes so far as to say it borders on plagiarism.[47] Wright's skill and impact had produced a school which was to make its mark in the 'forties.

During the Depression almost all Afro-American writers, whether novelists or poets, joined in this race-class equation. Sterling Brown, Langston Hughes, Randolph Edmonds (born 1900), William Attaway in *Blood on the Forge*, and others, combined it with the folklorist movement. Almost all of them, however, abandoned it later, mostly (like Wright) in the Second World War. Their reasons for the change of mind were various. Claude McKay, who was like a barometer, always registering an imminent change in the weather, left the Communist Party as early as 1937. Afterwards, on finding his way to the Catholic Church, he wrote Christian poems with content illustrated by the following extract:

> Around me roar and crash the pagan isms
>   To which most of my life was consecrate,
> Betrayed by evil men and torn by schisms,
>   For they were built on nothing more than hate:
> I cannot live my life without the faith . . .
>   And so to God I go to make my peace.[48]

Langston Hughes had always rated the Afro-American cultural heritage higher than any ideology. In his autobiography *I wonder as I wander*, in connection with his stay in the Soviet Union, he talks of why he never joined the Communist Party: 'Once I gave as my reason for not joining the Party the fact that jazz was officially taboo in Russia, being played only in the *declassé* Metropol Hotel, and very badly there. "But jazz is decadent bourgeois music," I was told, for that's what the Soviet press had hammered into Russian heads. "It's my music," I said, "and I wouldn't give up jazz for a world revolution." '[49]

2. Development of Style

At the beginning of the twentieth century Afro-American folk culture and the written literature of the middle-class writers of African descent were almost unrelated to each other. The only works of folk culture accepted into official literature were non-committal 'notes' like Chesnutt's *Conjure Woman* and a distorted pseudo-realistic dialect, half comic and half bombastic.

In the 'twenties folk literature penetrated into the towns, creating separate urban forms such as the city Blues and the Gospel Song. The sentimental demand of the period for anything exotic or primitive, and the folklorist studies, were influences which helped to get the forms and rhythms of Afro-American folk poetry introduced into Western writing: Blues, preacher style, ballad and work-song. This had been started from sheer exuberance in Harlem, but later spread to Chicago and Washington as well.

With the onset of the Depression the extravagant incidentals of exoticism were shown up and 'debunked' in satires. Several authors withdrew into the individualism recommended to them; but this gave the individual neither seclusion nor freedom and led back into the integration problems of the nineteenth century. Even when he completely renounced his cultural separateness, American society did not offer him social integration.

In the Depression Afro-American writers were concerned with the sufferings of real people, and this promoted a deeper knowledge of their social problems as well as their folk culture. The literary consequences were two schools of writing connected by theme but disparate in style. One school rejected the African heritage so as to be universally representative, but only succeeded in this aim where it stated the problem in a local and particular context. The other school stressed the folklorist element, and as a result, like Afro-American music, gained universal status and influence.

Only the most important writer of each school remained creative after the Second World War: the two extremes, Richard Wright and Langston Hughes. Neither wrote his maturest works until much later, about 1960.

REFERENCES AND BIBLIOGRAPHIES

Chapters 11–13

The Negro Renaissance – The 'Golden Years' – The Depression

Titles appearing in the chronological table pp. 210–13 are not given in the bibliographies except where necessary for the inclusion of further details.

[1] Washington, p. 223.
[2] ibid., pp. 221 f.
[3] DuBois, p. 58.
[4] Shackelford, p. 142.
[5] Jones, p. 127.
[6] Wright 1961, p. 69.
[7] Jones, p. 134.
[8] Johnson 1930, p. 254.
[9] Hughes/Bontemps 1949, pp. 250 ff.
[10] Johnson 1930, p. 258.
[11] Gloster, pp. viii f.
[12] Bone, p. 2.
[13] ibid., p. 8.
[14] Clarke, p. 89.
[15] Wagner, p. ix.
[16] ibid., p. x.
[17] ibid., p. xi.
[18] ibid., p. 575.
[19] ibid.
[20] Jahn, pp. 148 f.
[21] Wagner, pp. 575 f.
[22] ibid., p. 577.
[23] Jones, pp. 130 f.
[24] McKay 1922, p. 53; Hughes/Bontemps 1949, p. 333; Bontemps 1963, p. 31.

[25] McKay 1922, p. 6; Hughes/Bontemps 1949, pp. 331 f.
[26] Bone, p. 66.
[27] Hughes 1959, p. 4.
[28] vol. 23, No. 3 (whole No. 135), New York, January 1922, p. 113.
[29] Hughes 1959, p. 8.
[30] Gloster, p. 128.
[31] Cullen 1925, pp. 36 ff.; Hughes/Bontemps 1949, pp. 121–5; Bontemps 1963, pp. 83–6.
[32] cf. Wagner, pp. 362–82.
[33] Hughes 1926, p. 102.
[34] ibid.
[35] Hughes 1927, p. 64.
[36] ibid., p. 23.
[37] Johnson 1927, pp. 13 f.
[38] Schuyler 1931, p. 14.
[39] Bone, p. 90.
[40] Thurman 1932, p. 240.
[41] Hughes 1931, no pagination; Hughes 1959, p. 3.
[42] Bone, p. 113.
[43] ibid., pp. 113 f.
[44] Brown 1932, p. 46.
[45] ibid., p. 70.
[46] Wright, p. 10.
[47] Bone, p. 179.
[48] McKay 1953, p. 49.
[49] Hughes 1956, p. 122.

A. Literary Works and Anthologies

BONTEMPS, Arna: American Negro poetry. New York 1963 (No. 2164)

BROWN, Sterling Allen–DAVIS, Arthur Paul–LEE, Ulysses Grant: The Negro caravan. New York 1941 (No. 2171)

BUTCHER, James W.: The seer. In: Brown–Davis–Lee: The Negro caravan. New York 1941

CALVERTON, Victor Francis: Anthology of American Negro literature. New York 1929 (No. 2176)

CLARKE, John Henrik: Harlem, U.S.A. The story of a city within a city, told by James Baldwin, Sterling A. Brown, Elizabeth Catlett, Alice Childress, John Henrik Clarke, Countee Cullen, Ossie Davis, Lorraine Hansberry, Ollie Harrington, Langston Hughes, Julian

Mayfield, Claude McKay, Charles White, and 40 other writers, artists, actors, sculptors, painters, doctors, lawyers, clergymen, photographers, philosophers. Edited, and with an introduction by John Henrik Clarke. Berlin: Seven Seas Publishers 1964. 361 pp. ill. (Seven Seas Books)

CONNELLY, Marc: The green pastures. New York 1930

CULLEN, Countee: Caroling dusk. New York 1927 (No. 2179)

DONOGHUE, Dennis: Legal murder. Original production: The Theatre Guild, New York, October 1933

GERSHWIN, George and Ira-HEYWARD, Du Bose: Porgy and Bess. Music by George Gershwin, libretto by Du Bose Heyward and Ira Gershwin. New York 1935 (piano score)

GREEN, Paul: In Abraham's bosom. In: Green: Lonesome road. New York 1926 (No. 2626)

-Roll sweet chariot: a symphonic play of Negro people. New York 1935

HICKS, Granville and others: Proletarian literature in the United States. New York: International Publishers 1935, vii, 384 pp. Anth.

HUGHES, Langston: I wonder as I wander. New York 1956 (Nos. 2836-7)

-Selected poems. New York 1959 (No. 2845)

HUGHES, Langston and BONTEMPS, Arna: The poetry of the Negro, 1746-1949. Garden City, N.Y. 1949 (No. 1189)

-The book of Negro folklore. New York 1959

JOHNSON, Hall: Run, little chillun. Original production: New York 1933

JOHNSON, James Weldon: The book of American Negro poetry. New York 1922 and 1931 (No. 2193)

KERLIN, Robert Thomas: Negro poets and their poems. Washington, D.C. 1923 and 1935 (No. 2194)

LINDSAY, Vachel: The Congo, and other poems. New York 1914

LOCKE, Alain Le Roy: The new Negro. New York 1925 (No. 2199)

-Four Negro poets. New York 1927 (No. 2200)

LOCKE, Alain Le Roy and GREGORY, Montgomery: Plays of Negro life. New York 1927 (No. 2201)

MCKAY, Claude: Selected poems. New York 1953 (No. 1697)

MOTLEY, Willard: Knock on any door. New York 1947 (No. 3049-3050)

MURPHY, Beatrice M.: Negro voices. New York 1938 (No. 2205)

O'NEILL, Eugene: The Emperor Jones. Cincinnati 1921

-All God's chillun got wings . . . London 1925

RICHARDSON, Willis: The deacon's awakening. Original production: St. Paul, Minn. 1921

–The chip woman's fortune. Original production: Ethiopian Art Players, New York, May 1923

–The broken banjo. Original production: The Krigwa Players, New York, 1. August 1925, contained in: Locke & Gregory: Plays of Negro life. New York 1927

–Plays and pageants from the life of the Negro. Washington 1930 (No. 2210)

RICHARDSON, Willis, and MILLER, May: Negro history in thirteen plays. Washington 1935 (No. 2211)

SHACKELFORD, Otis M.: Lillian Simmons, or, The conflict of sections. Kansas City, Mo. 1915 (No. 3156)

TORRENCE, Ridgely: Three plays for the Negro theatre. New York 1917 (Contains: Granny Maumee, The rider of dreams, Simon the Cyrenian)

VECHTEN, Carl Van: Nigger heaven. New York 1926

WARD, Theodore: Big white fog; a Negro tragedy. Original production: Great Northern Theatre, Chicago, 1938 (Act 3, Scene 1 in: Brown–Davis–Lee: The Negro caravan. New York 1941)

WHITE, Newman Ivey and JACKSON, Walter Clinton: An anthology of verse by American Negroes. Durham, N.C. 1924 (No. 2215)

WILSON, Frank: Sugar cane. In: Locke & Gregory: Plays of Negro life. New York 1927

–Brother Mose. Original production: Negro Division, Federal Theatre Project, New York 1928

–Walk together, children. Original production: Negro Division, New York Federal Theatre Project, Lafayette Theatre, New York, 4 February 1936

B. Secondary Literature

BOND, Frederick Weldon: The Negro and the drama. Washington 1940

BONE, Robert A.: The Negro novel in America. New Haven, Conn. 1958

BRAWLEY, Benjamin Griffith: The Negro in literature and art in the United States. New York 1934

–The Negro genius. New York 1937

BROWN, Sterling Allen: Negro poetry and drama. Washington 1937

–The Negro in American fiction. Washington 1937

DuBois, William Edward Burghardt: The souls of black folk. Chicago 1903 (No. 2504)

Gloster, Hugh Morris: Negro voices in American fiction. Chapel Hill, N.C. 1948

Jahn, Janheinz: Muntu. London/New York 1961

Johnson, James Weldon: Black Manhattan. New York 1930

Jones, LeRoi: Blues people–Negro music in white America. New York 1963

Mitchell, Loften: Black drama. New York 1967

Redding, Jay Saunders: To make a poet black. Chapel Hill, N.C. 1939

Schuyler, George S.: Carl Van Vechten. In: Phylon, vol. XI, Atlanta, Ga. 1950

Thorpe, Earl Endris: The mind of the Negro. Baton Rouge, La. 1961

Wagner, Jean: Les poètes nègres des États-Unis. Paris 1963

Washington, Booker Taliaferro: Up from slavery. New York: The Association Press, cop. 1900, 1901. xxiii, 330 pp. (Race relationships in the South. II.) A

Wright, Richard: How 'Bigger' was born. New York 1940

–La letteratura negra negli Stati Uniti. Milan 1961

20 important articles in Phylon, vol. XI, no. 4, Atlanta, Ga. 1950

TABLE 6

Literature of the Negro Renaissance and the Depression

AFROAMERICANISMS

~ artificial serio-comic 'Negro' dialect (*Dunbar*)

= realistic dialect (*Edmonds*)

+ 'preacher'-style (*J. W. Johnson*)

! afro-american stylistic forms: blues, work song, ballads, or rhythmic prose (*Hughes, Brown*)

THEMES

1. rural themes or folk realism (*Toomer*)

2. Christian themes or attitudes (*Cotter, jr.*)

3. historical themes (*O'Neill*)

5. war themes (*Daly*)

6. college themes (*Shaw*)

Numbers after titles refer to my *Bibliography*

8. emphasis on psychological problems (*Cullen*)

9. main characters are white (*Attaway*)

TENDENCIES

W ideology of social conformity and success in economic terms, c.f. B. T. Washington (*Micheaux*)

Idealistic protest:

a 'bourgeois': demanding privileges for the 'gifted tenth' (*DuBois*)

b 'passing', the colour line (*J. W. Johnson, Fauset, Larsen*)

c separatist (*Griggs*)

d militant protest: 'fighting back' irony and satire (*Schuyler*)

e

f race = class (*DuBois*)

Harlem-style

X anti-bourgeois primitivist exotic romanticisation of Africa (*Van Vechten*)

Proletarian protest:

Y proletarian realism, race = class (*Wright*)

Z historical realism (*Bontemps*)

O nihilism (*F. Johnson*)

Poetry

1899		
1909		
1911	= McKay: Songs of Jamaica
1912	= McKay: Constab ballads 1684

Prose

c Griggs: Imperium in imperio 2628

a Grant: Out of darkness 2624

af DuBois: The quest of the silver fleece 2507

a Jones, Y.: The climbers 2946

a Cotter, sr.: Negro tales 2428

b Johnson, J. W.: Autobiography of an ex-colored man 2911–2912

Plays

1913	~ Johnson, F.: A little dreaming 2896		
1914	X Lindsay: Congo		
1915	! Johnson, F.: Visions of the dusk 2897	W Micheaux: The conquest 3034	1d Torrence: The rider of dreams =1 Torrence: Grannie Maumee
1916	! Johnson F.: Songs of the soil 2898	b Ashby: Redder blood 2247 Wa Micheaux: The forged note 3035 b Gilmore: The problem 2602 b Walker, T. H. B.: J. Johnson 3247 W Shackelford: Lillian Simmons 3156	
1917	~ Johnson, J. W.: Fifty years 2914	c Adams: Ethiopia, the land of promise 2218 b Downing: The American cavalryman 2501	
1918	2 Cotter, jr.: The band of Gideon 2432 a Johnson, G. D.: The heart of a woman 2902	W Micheaux: The homesteader 3036 W Fleming: Hope's highway 2580	
1919		a Dreer: Immediate jewel of his soul 2502	a Grimké: Rachel 2634 3 O'Neill: Emperor Jones 1 Wilson: Sugar cane Richardson: The deacon's awakening
1920	d McKay: Spring in New Hampshire 1685	a Johnson, F.: Tales of darkest America 2899	
1921			
1922	d McKay: Harlem shadows 1686 9 Braithwaite: Sandy Star and Willie Gee	d Pickens: Vengeance of the gods 3096	
1923	1 Toomer: Cane 3225	1 Toomer: Cane 3225	
1924		a Fauset: There is confusion 2563 a1 White: The fire in the flint 3291 a Jones, J. H.: By sanction of law 2936	O'Neill: All God's chillun got wings Richardson: The chip woman's fortune Richardson: The broken banjo

	Poetry	Prose	Plays
1925	X8 Cullen: Color 2444	X Vechten: Nigger heaven	Green: In Abraham's bosom
1926	!X Hughes: Weary blues 2767–2768	d White: Flight 3293	Johnson, G. D.: Plumes 2904
1927	X8 Cullen: Copper sun 2446 !X Hughes: Fine clothes to the Jew 2769 +X Johnson, J. W.: God's trombones 2915		
1928		f DuBois: Dark princess 2509 a Larsen: Quicksand 2960 X McKay: Home to Harlem 1687–1690 Xe Fisher: The walls of Jericho 2573	3 Hill, L. P.: Toussaint Louverture 2708 W2 Wilson: Brother Mose
1929	2,8 Cullen: The black Christ 2447	b Fauset: Plum bun 2564 X McKay: Banjo 1691–1692 Xa Thurman: The blacker the berry 3214 b Larsen: Passing 2961 Xd Hughes: Not without laughter 2770–2778	X Thurman: Harlem 3215
1930		X1 Bontemps: God sends Sunday 2307 e Schuyler: Black no more 3149 b Fauset: The chinaberry tree 2565	Ya Edmonds: Shades and shadows 2551
1931	!Y Hughes: Dear lovely death 2779		~2 Connelly: The green pastures
1932	!Y1 Brown: Southern road 2354 !Y Hughes: The dream keeper 2781	e2 Cullen: One way to heaven 2448 5 Daly: Not only war 2457 Xe Thurman: Infants of the spring 3216 Xd McKay: Gingertown 1693	!X Hughes: Scottsboro limited 2782
1933		X1 McKay: Banana bottom 1694 b Fauset: Comedy American style 2566 3 Hill, J. H.: Princess Malah 2704 e Hughes: The ways of white folks 2784–2787	= Y Johnson, H.: Run, little chillun Y Donoghue: Legal murder
1934		X1 Lee: Beale Street 2963 +X Hurston: Jonah's gourd vine 2868	= Y Edmonds: 6 plays for a Negro theatre 2552

1935	eY Davis: Black man's verse 2467	=18 Henderson: Ollie Miss 2688	1 Heyward & Gershwin: Porgy and Bess d Hughes: Mulatto 2796–2799 X Hughes: Little Ham 2788 Cullen: Medea 2449 Green: Roll sweet chariot Hughes+Bontemps: When the Jack hollers 2789 X Wilson: Walk together children Hughes: Joy to my soul 2790 X Hughes: Don't you want to be free? 2792 Y
1936		YZ Bontemps: Black thunder 2312 6 Shaw: Greater need below 3161	3 Hughes: Emperor of Haiti 2793 Ward: Big white fog
1937	eY Davis: I am the American Negro 2468	=8 Hurston: Their eyes were watching God 2870–2872	Y Hughes: Front porch 2795
1938	Y Hughes: A new song 2794	a Turpin: These low grounds 3232 Y1 Lee: River George 2964 Y1 Wright: Uncle Tom's children 3330–3340	= Butcher: The seer
1939		1 Gilbert: Aunt Sara's wooden god 2600 Y9 Attaway: Let me breathe thunder 2254 Z Bontemps: Drums at dusk 2315 Y Turpin: O Canaan! 3233 Y Wright: Native son 3341–3354	Y Wright+Green: Native son 3356
1940	Hayden: Heart-shape in the dust 2666		
1941		!Y Attaway: Blood on the forge 2255	

Chapter 14

'INDIGENISM' AND 'NEGRISM'

1. Indigenism in Haiti

The waves of the 'Negro Renaissance' reached the shores of Haiti–travelling by way of Paris. For there the combination of jazz, Dada, 'Negro Art', cubism and Josephine Baker, had produced a self-confident and sophisticated enjoyment of the primitive; Tristan Tzara, indeed, declared all his life that he had invented 'Negro Poetry'. These Paris fashions gave rise to a partly exotic, partly ethnological 'Africa literature', including the novels of René Maran (1887–1959), which I shall be discussing later (pages 228–9).

Since 1915 Haiti had been occupied by United States marines, who had embittered the population by their arrogance and racial prejudice. The intellectuals who could afford it had moved to Paris, but meanwhile impotence and despondency were the precursors of a national revival. Writers of the older generation clung to their French culture, hoping it would confirm the old values. In the *Mercure de France* issue for New Year 1925 Louis Morpeau wrote: 'The occupation brings one benefit, that of forcing us to realize how much our Gallic-black heredity, our Afro-Latin affinities and our French culture differ from the crude North American pragmatism which is convinced that all civilization is primarily material.'[1]

In the same year Morpeau produced his *Cent-Ans* anthology including all the Haitian writers who would have considered a seat in the Académie Français as the crown of their poetic career. No revival could start from such as Morpeau. For the older generation repudiated all cultural ties with Africa, and tried to show that the unfortunate accident of having dark complexions did not stop them living and writing just like Frenchmen. The only attitude they could adopt under the Americans was one of resignation.

But there was also a group of Haitian students living in Paris who enthusiastically embraced the anti-bourgeois exoticist movements. Émile Roumer, for instance (born 1903), in his collection *Poèmes d'Haïti et de France*, produced jaunty and uninhibited studies of life among Haiti's lower class. The effect they make is all the more striking because he interlarded them with words from the vernacular, while pressing them into classical Alexandrines,[2] which are sometimes deliberately halting.

Philippe Thoby-Marcelin (born 1904) went a step further. In Paris in 1926 he became spokesman of the anti-civilization exoticist movement:

Ma joue appuyée contre la fraîcheur de l'aube,
Jurant un éternel dédain aux raffinements européens,
Je veux désormais vous chanter : révolutions, fusillades, tueries
Bruit de coco-macaque sur des épaules noires,
Mugissements du lambi, lubricité mystique de Vaudou ;
Vous chanter dans un délire trois fois lyrique et religieux,
Me dépouiller de tous oripeaux classiques
    et dresser nu, très sauvage
    et très descendant d'esclaves,
Pour entonner d'une voix nouvelle le
    de profundis des civilisations
    pourrissantes.[3]

'Leaning my cheek against the freshness of the dawn,
Swearing eternal scorn for European refinements,
I would sing you from now on : revolutions, shootings, killings,
Noise of coco-macaque on black shoulders,
Groans of the lambi,* mystic lust of Voodoo ;
I would sing you in an ecstasy thrice lyrical and religious,
Strip myself of all classical banners
    and stand up naked, very much the savage,
    very much the descendant of slaves,
To chant in a new voice the *de profundis* of rotting civilizations.'

In 1927 Thoby-Marcelin, Roumer, Normil Sylvain (1900–29), Carl Brouard (born 1902) and Jacques Roumain (1907–44) returned to Haiti. With Antonio Vieux (born 1904) and Daniel Heurtelou (born 1906) they founded the journal *La Revue Indigène* (July 1927–Feb. 1928), which was to become the mouthpiece of the revival and give it its name.

But the group of 'indigenists' did not merely extend a Paris vogue which stemmed from Harlem. It achieved more than that, thanks largely to Jean Price-Mars (born 1876), who in his long career was

* Lambi–an empty shell, the instrument which called the slaves in Haiti to rise against their masters.

doctor, ethnologist, minister, ambassador, senator and university chancellor; from 1918–30 he taught sociology at the Port-au-Prince Lycée. He had steeped himself in African history, taught his pupils a pride in their African heritage, investigated Voodoo, Haiti's folk religion, and taught that this was no contemptible relic of primitive backwardness but a living treasure of independent culture which nobody need be ashamed of, and – what is more – was to be found just outside their door. He recommended young writers to immerse themselves in Haiti's living native culture, instead of pursuing a romantic exoticism based on what they had merely read up about Africa. He took care, in fact, to keep their enthusiasm down to earth. He was an intellectual teacher such as North America's Negro Renaissance had lacked; a scholar who put the culture, not the race, in the foreground. His epoch-making book *Ainsi parla l'oncle* did not appear till 1928.

Under the influence of his doctrine the new group called itself 'indigenist'. This meant that they set out to defend, present and glorify the native Afro-Haitian folk culture which had been neglected till then. The young intellectuals no longer joined together, as their fathers had done, in the exclusive circles of big cities, to imitate Paris. They went into the country, studied the peasants' language and way of life, and took part in Voodoo ceremonies. In 1927 a collection of poetry by Carl Brouard called *Le Tam-Tam Angoissé* (which was not in fact published) gave its motto on the title-page: 'It is absurd to play the flute in a country where the national instrument is the mighty assotôr.'[4] Assotôr is the name for the big drum in a Voodoo orchestra.

The poetry Bouard was then writing represents a period of transition: in spite of the blatantly sexual exoticism to shock the bourgeoisie, it deals with figures from a living folk mythology, still falsely over-primitive in tone but pointing towards a new realism. In the last number of the *Revue Indigène* (February 1928), Brouard has a poem called 'Hymne à Erzulie' (the Voodoo goddess of fertility), which contains these lines:

> Déesse anthropophage de la volupté . . .
> qui dans le monde élastique et mol des rêves
> chaque nuit de jeudi
> ouvre à tes amants le secret de tes flancs. . . .[5]

> 'Man-eating goddess of pleasure . . .
> who in the soft elastic world of dreams
> each Thursday night
> reveal to your lovers the secret of your thighs. . . .'

The revue closed its last number with an 'Anthologie Indigène' summing up what had been achieved.

Its mission was taken over by the journals *Les Griots* and *La Relève* (1932–38). From the beginnings of the 'thirties, however, as in the United States, the race-class identification came into prominence. In the *Revue* Jacques Roumain had still been choosing folklorist themes for his poetry:

> C'est le lent chemin de Guinée;
> Tes pères t'attendent sans impatience. . . .[6]

> 'It is the slow road to Guinea;
> Your fathers wait for you without impatience. . . .'[7]

But in 'Bois d'Ebène', written in Brussels in 1938, he extolled the international solidarity of the working class:

> Nous proclamons l'unité de la souffrance
> et de la révolte
> de tous les peuples sur toute la surface de la terre
> et nous brassons le mortier des temps fraternels
> dans la poussière des idoles.[8]

> 'We proclaim the unity of suffering
> and of revolt
> by all the peoples on all the surface of the world
> and we mix the mortar for the days of fraternity
> in the dust of the idols.'

Dominque Hippolyte (1889–1967) introduced Countee Cullen, still in the *Revue*. In 1932, in the *Relève*, Price-Mars directed Haiti's attention to the North American 'Negro Renaissance'. Langston Hughes, James Weldon Johnson, Jessie Fauset, DuBois, Claude McKay and Dunbar were reviewed or translated. In his novel, *Récolte* (1946), Félix Morisseau-Leroy (born 1912) portrays student life in the early 'thirties at Port-au-Prince: 'The young men felt solidarity with the youth of Europe and Asia, of Africa and Latin America. They knew by heart the poetry of Langston Hughes translated by René Piquion.'[9]

But Indigenism was no mere echo and imitation of the Negro Renaissance. For one thing, it drew inspiration much more consciously from the life of the ordinary Afro-American people. To achieve a convincing tone for folk poetry, the indigenists would have had to rely on Creole, the Afro-Haitian vernacular, and the time was not yet ripe for that. Consequently they did their finest work in the novel, not in poetry. In the novel the world was divided into opposite sides. One side consisted of either the urban, Westernized, Christian middle class, or the alien White American capitalist exploiter. On the other side there was the native Haitian Voodoo-practising peasant, an exploited Black who clung fiercely to his African heritage. His role was to defend himself both through the religious strength of his Voodoo worship and through his *coumbite*–the neighbourhood aid or community work taken over from Africa, which the indigenists usually made into a 'collective' community.

So the novels of indigenism show a penetration into Afro-American ideas and values which is lacking in the novels stimulated by the Negro Renaissance. Jacques Roumain's world success, *Gouverneurs de la Rosée* (Masters of the Dew), which was influenced by Richard Wright, lays new stress on the social side, but does not disparage, ignore or distort the folklore elements. The social side is also prominent in *Les Horizons sans Ciel* by Jean Brierre (born 1909), the works of Anthony Lespès (born 1907) and Morisseau-Leroy, and the first novels of Jacques Stéphen Alexis (1922–62?). Folklore is emphasized even more by Milo Rigaud (born 1904), Pétion Savain (born 1906), Jean-Baptiste Cinéas (1895–1958), Edris Saint-Amand (born 1918) and Alexis's *Arbres Musiciens*. As an illustration of an indigenist novel, here is a summary of the novel *La bête de Musseau* (The Beast of the Haitian Hills) by the Marcelin brothers:

Morin Dutilleul, a small shopkeeper from Port-au-Prince, decides, after his wife has died in child-birth, to fulfil his boyhood dream and become a farmer. He buys himself an estate in the small village of Musseau in the hills of Haiti. There he turns into an arrogant know-all and makes an enemy of the rich and dreaded farmer Bossuet, who is in league with powerful spirits. Dutilleul builds a fence round a spring on his estate so that the villagers have to fetch their water from a long way away, and finally cuts down a sacred masontree near his spring (altar of the mighty fertility god, Legba) because he has found a food-offering at the foot of it. Now disaster breaks over him and the whole village. 'La Cigouave', an evil bush-spirit, appears in the guise of a savage monster, which howls at night, injures and kills people, drives others to suicide, scares and terrorizes all the villagers, so that they lock themselves into their houses. Dutilleul meets the beast several times, usually when he has drunk heavily. From then on he lives in fear of the powers which his adversary Bossuet has conjured up against him. He tries to rationalize his fears and explain away the villagers' belief in Voodoo as mere superstition, but he cannot help realizing that the farmer's religion haunts him. In despair at this he succumbs to alcoholism, neglecting his farm. He goes to the town for a cure, and plans to stay there. But one morning when he wakes up, he finds himself back in the attic of his estate at Musseau. In front of his bed stands 'La Cigouave', half man, half beast. He runs away, pursued by the monster, and plunges into the ravine near his spring. After that the howl of the monster is never heard again and the people of Musseau can sleep undisturbed and in peace once more.

The Marcelin brothers keep the elements of Christian and Haitian religion constantly in balance, giving motives from both for the characters' actions. That is the great strength of these novels, of which the above is a typical example.

In Indigenism, Haiti found a valid national form for the novel. Since the Second World War that form has been increasingly influenced and given depth by the Negritude movement.

2. Negrism in Cuba

In Cuba the development ran parallel to that of Haiti, but with small though crucial differences. Primitivism was the rage there too, but it was fostered by the White Cubans, who are in the majority, not the Afro-Cubans. The beginning was not so emotional, the writers were less influenced by the Harlem-and-Africa vogue in Paris than by the German prophets of decline. Oswald Spengler and Leo Frobenius were the godfathers of this cult of the primitive – although the Haitian, Price-Mars, was also well acquainted with these philosophers: he sent his main work directly after publication to the head of the Frobenius Institute at Frankfurt with a personal dedication.

Fernando Ortiz, however, the great intellectual leader in Cuba, was not, like Price-Mars, a politician and an educator. A pure scientist, ethno-musicologist, historian and linguist, he began studying the cultural phenomena of the Afro-Cuban lower class (*Hampa Afrocubana*) quite early in his career. In 1906 he published a work on the Negro Sorcerers (*Los negros brujos*), in 1916 a book on the Negro slaves (*Los negros esclavos*), and in 1923 his Afro-Negristic Dictionary (*Glosario de afronegrismos*), which was of even greater importance for the literature. Coulthard calls it 'a collection of African or African-sounding words in the popular speech of Cuba, and of words of Spanish origin with new Cuban meanings. Many of these words have a markedly African rhythmic sonority and are to be found some years later in the compositions of the Afro-Cuban writers.'[1]

The decisive point was that this vocabulary depended on the African sound, not on the etymology: *sandunga* (grace) and *mondongo* (tripe) are Spanish words, but they sound 'African' and form a bridge to Afro-Cuban words like *cumbancha* (orgy), *rebambaramba* (tumult), and to genuine African words which therefore sound 'Spanish' too. Examples of the latter are the names of Yoruba gods, Shango, Eshu, Obatala and Olorun, which in Cuba become Changó, Echú, Obatalá and Olorún; and the musical instruments *maraca* (gourd-rattle), *marimba* or *marimbula* (xylophone) and *bongó* (drum). Hundreds of other examples could be adduced. And so through the sound of words and language the marriage of African rhythm and Spanish *copla** took place, which gave its stamp to Afro-Cuban poetry.

Its forerunners were the White Cuban José Manuel Poveda (1888–1926) with his poem 'The Cry of the Ancestors' (El grito abuelo),[2] the Uruguayan Ildefonso Pereda Valdés (born 1899) with his 'The Negroes' Guitar' (La guitarra de los negros),[3] and Luis Palés Matos (1890–1959) from Puerto Rico. But they scarcely advanced beyond the usual descriptive exoticism, except perhaps for Matos's onomatopoeia in the poem 'Danza Negra' (Negro Dance):

> Calabó y bambú.
> Bambú y calabó.
> El Gran Cocoroco dice: tu-cu-tú.
> La Gran Cocoroca dice: to-co-tó.
> Es el sol de hierro que arde en Tombuctú.
> Es la danza negra de Fernando Pó.
> El cerdo en el fango gruffe: pru-pru-prú.
> El sapo en la charca sueña: cro-cro-cró.
> Calabó y bambú.
> Bambú y calabó.[4]

> 'Calabo and bamboo.
> Bamboo and calabo.
> The great Cocoroco says: Tu-cu-tu.
> The great Cocoroca says: to-co-to.
> The iron sun blazes in Timbuktoo.
> The negroes dance in Fernando Po.
> The pig grunts in the mud: pru-pru-pru.
> The toad croaks in the pond: cro-cro-cro.
> Calabo and bamboo.
> Bamboo and calabo.'

* Copla–a short verse used in Spanish folk-song.

The three authors who created the Afro-Cuban style in 1928 were also Cubans of European descent: José Zacarías Tallet (born 1893), Ramón Guirao (1908–49) and Alejo Carpentier (born 1904). Their poetry is likewise descriptive, aiming at the exotic and the primitive, but with Guirao's 'Girl Rumba Dancer' (Bailadora de Rumba), Tallet's 'Rumba' and two poems by Carpentier, Afro-Cuban folk poetry, as Guirao wrote, 'became united with the so-called new sensitivity (*nueva sensibilidad*).'[5] That was when rumba rhythm was first adopted in Spanish verse. Tallet's 'Rumba' begins:

> ¡Zumba, mamá, la rumba y tambó!
> ¡Mabimba, mabomba, mabomba y bombó![6]

approximately

> 'Thunder, mama, the rumba with drumbom!
> Mabimba, mabomba, mabomba and pompom!'

The stressed syllables, emphasized by position or rhyme, are stressed very sharply, the unstressed syllables–one, two or three in number–are fitted in rhythmically in such a way that each second stress comes into the musical off-beat. In the verse quoted above, there are first two, then one, then three 'theses' (unaccented syllables) between the stresses (x́ xx x́ x x́ xxx x́). If you try to scan this in terms of troche and iambics (x́x/xx́/xx́/xx́/xx́) or of dactyl and trochees (x́xx/x́x/x́x/x́x/x́), you get a verse of 5½ feet and cannot help stumbling–for you cannot count this verse in feet at all. Every second accent must come between the metre, i.e. off-beat, and this rumba rhythm, which can only be expressed by musical notation, is retained throughout the whole long poem:

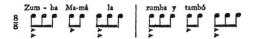

Carpentier blends descriptive exoticism with the religious folklore of the *Santería* and *Ñañiguismo*, which I have described in *Muntu*,[7] and thereby achieves the same effect as Haitian Indigenism. His 'Liturgy' begins:

> La Potencia rompió,
> ¡ yamba ó!
> Retumban las tombas
> en casa de Ecué.[8]

'The power broke out,
yamba ó!
The tombs are booming
in the house of Ecué.'

'Ecué-yamba-ó' is the title of his completely indigenist first novel. 'Yamba-ó' means 'be praised' in Afro-Cuban, and Ecué is in *Ñañiguismo* 'the great mysterious one', death or Jesus Christ. This is the only novel of Afro-Cubanism, and in it Carpentier describes the Santería with scrupulous ethnological accuracy, including the Afro-Cuban dialect and African religious formulas:

> −¿Jura usté decil la verdá?
> −¡Si senol!
> −¿Pa qué viene usté a esta Potencia?
> −¡Pa socorrel a mi'hemmanos!
> El Isué declaró con voz sorda, monótona:
>   Endoco, endiminoco. . . . etc.

' "You sweal to tell the tru'?"
"Yes, lold."
"Why do you come to this cult?"
"To help my blothers."
And Isue spoke with hollow monotonous voice:
"Endoco, Endiminico
Aracoroko, arabé suá.
Enkiko Bagarofia
Agusiké, El Bongó
Obón.
Iyamba." '[9]

Nicolás Guillén (born 1902) was the first Afro-Cuban to break through to Negrism, in 1930. He gave an inner life to the new achievements in form. 'He is the only poet of this school,' writes Vitier, 'for whom the Negro theme was neither a fashion nor simply a subject but the productive centre of his whole creative activity. In his first work, "Motivos de son" [Sound Motifs]–1930–he already revealed the quality which the other cultivators of the Afro-Cuban style lacked: he wrote from within.'[10] And again: 'His whole poetry revolves round the axis of rhythm, and his final pages, the starkest and most universal, are pure and exquisite *sounds*.'[11]

With Guillén the Afro-Cuban forms are no longer decorative costumes, but necessary stylistic means which relax the seriousness of

the class war, dissolving grievance and accusation in African cheerfulness, without diminishing the political effect. His forerunners were
only important because they created stylistic means for his authentic
voice. In his popular poetry for recitation to the drum Guillén combines rhythm and musical feeling, sensuality and humour, Afro-Cuban
closeness to nature and will to freedom, with the traditional forms
of Spanish poetry. His sultry tropical ballads, the scathing wit of his
freedom songs, are well known in most of the world, though few
(curiously enough) have been translated into English–so I give an
example below, in the poem 'Sensemayá' (English translation by
Akanji):

para matar una culebra

¡Mayombe–bombe–mayombé!
¡Mayombe–bombe–mayombé!
¡Mayombe–bombe–mayombé!

La culebra tiene los ojos de vidrio;
La culebra viene y se enreda en un palo;
con sus ojos de vidrio, en un palo;
con sus ojos de vidrio.
La culebra camina sin patas;
La culebra se esconde en la yerba;
caminando se esconde en la yerba,
caminando sin patas.

¡Mayombe–bombe–mayombé
¡Mayombe–bombe–mayombé!
¡Mayombe–bombe–mayombé!

Tu le das con el hacha, y se muere:
¡dale ya!
¡No les des con el pie, que te muerde,
no les des con el pie, que se va!

Sensemayá, la culebra,
sensemayá.
Sensemayá, con sus ojos,
sensemayá.
Sensemayá, con su lengua,
sensemayá.
Sensemayá, con su boca,
sensemayá. . . .

La culebra meurta no puede comer;
la culebra muerta no puede silbar;
no puede caminar,
no puede correr!
La culebra muerta no puede mirar;
la culebra muerta no puede beber;
no puede respirar,
no puede morder!

¡Mayombe-bombe-mayombé
Sensemayá, la culebra. . . .
¡Mayombe-bombe-mayombé!
Sensemayá, no se mueve. . . .
¡Mayombe-bombe-mayombé!
Sensemayá, la culebra. . . .
¡Mayombe-bombe-mayombé!
¡Sensemayá, se murio![12]

to kill a snake

'Mayombe-bombe-mayombé!
Mayombe-bombe-mayombé!
Mayombe-bombe-mayombé!

The snake has eyes of glass.
The snake appears and it winds round the post
With eyes of glass round the post,
With her eyes of glass.
The snake creeps without feet.
The snake hides in the grass,
Hides creeping in grass,
Creeps without feet.

Mayombe-bombe-mayombé!
Mayombe-bombe-mayombé!
Mayombe-bombe-mayombé!

Give her the axe and she dies:
Give it her now!
Don't give her the foot, for she bites,
Don't give her the foot, for she runs.

Sensemayá, the snake,
Sensemayá.

Sensemayá with the eyes,
Sensemayá.
Sensemayá with the tongue,
Sensemayá.
Sensemayá with the mouth,
Sensemayá.

The dead snake does not eat,
The dead snake does not hiss,
Does not creep,
Does not run.
The dead snake does not drink,
The dead snake does not look,
Does not breathe,
Does not bite.

Mayombe–bombe–mayombé!
Sensemayá, the snake. . . .
Mayombe–bombe–mayombé!
Sensemayá does not move. . . .
Mayombe–bombe–mayombé!
Sensemaya the snake. . . .
Mayombe–bombe–mayombé!
Sensemayá is dead. . . .'[13]

There were other Afro-Cuban writers, such as Alfonso Hernández Catá (born 1885), José Antonio Portuondo (born 1911), Vicente Gómez Kemp (born 1914), Rafael Esténger (born 1889), José Rodríguez Méndez (born 1914), and Teófilo Radillo (born 1895). They were all White Cubans, for whom Negrism was only a brief fashion, enduring no longer than the fame of Eusebia Cosme, whose celebrated recitals enhanced the poets' work by her brilliant renderings of it.

Other notable writers are Ignacio Villa (born 1902), who used dialect, Emilio Ballagas (1908–54), who produced highly accomplished onomatopoeic verse, and the Afro-Cuban Marcelino Arozarena (born 1912). The latter, in his greatest poem, 'Cubandalucia', compares Cuba and Andalusia, symbolized by combinations of sound and meaning like 'alsá' (Cuban exclamation) and 'olé' (Spanish exclamation), 'guanicán' (slang for 'money' in the Cuban dialect) and 'parné' (slang for 'money' in Andalusian dialect):

–Qué mides?
–Granadino García Lorca.
–Grano en la misma mazorca, camagüeyano Guillén.[14]
En mí
el guanicán se despalpita;
en tí
el parné:
pero somos milionarios de¡alsá! y ¡olé!

'What have you got?
García Lorca of Granada.
I can match that: I have Guillén of Camaguey.
In me
The guanicán died;
in you
the parné:
yet are we millionaires in alsá! and in olé!'

Arozarena used rhyme especially for heightening the rhythmical
effect, and provides an inside view of Afro-Cuban religion in many of
his poems. Here, for instance, is 'Caridá'; I have discussed in *Muntu*
the mythological allusions and significance of this poem:[15]

'Guasa, columbia, a conconcó mabó . . .'

La garganta de aguardiente raja en el eco rojizo
y en la fuga galopante del bongó
hay desorden de sonidos desertores del embriago
y rugiente tableteo del rabioso ¡pacata!

¿Por qué no viene a la bacha la hija de Yemayá,
la pulposa,
la sabrosa,
la rumbosa y majadera Caridá?

La mulata que maltrata la chancleta chacharosa
en el roce voluptuoso,
en el paso pesaroso,
de su grupa mordisqueante y temblorosa
tentadora del amor.

La epilepsia rimbombante que revuelve sus entrañas,
el sopor electrizante que le endulza la emoción,
resquebraja su cintura
y la exprime con locura

en la etiópica dulzura del sabroso guaguancó,
que es embrujo en el reflujo de su sangre azucarada
y en espasmo en el marasmo del trepidante bongó.

'Guasa, columbia, a conconcó mabó . . .'

¿Por qué no viene a la bacha la rumbera Caridá,
si su risa guarachera de mulata sandunguera,
quando la rumba delira,
llama, rabia, grita y gira,
percutiendo poderosa el parche del bongó?

En dulce sopor que embriaga de la magia del embó
–jeste diablo de mulata–resquebraja la cintura
y la exprime con locura en la dulzura del sabroso guaguancó.

'Guasa, columbia, a conconcó mabó . . .'

¿Por qué no viene a la bacha la hija de Yemayá,
la pulposa,
la sabrosa,
la rumbera, majadera y chancletera Caridá?[16]

'Guasa, columbia, a conconcó mabó . . .'

'The brandy-throat hoarse is rasping in the reddish echo,
and in the galloping course of the bongó
there's a glorious din of discord caterwauling at an orgy
and a clattering uproarious of the bawling tambourine.

Why doesn't she come to the dance, the daughter of Yemayá,
the nutritious
and delicious
and lubricious captivating Caridá?

The mulatto woman who with battering boots and floorboards
     threshes
now in fine voluptuous folly,
now in slow step's melancholy,
as her bottom wriggles, bites and swishes,
telling temptingly of love.

Ecstasy reverberating which will set her entrails heaving,
and the languor palpitating for the fever's swift relieving,
makes her girdle tear asunder
sense and reason squeezing under

in the sweet Ethiopian wonder of delicious guaguancó,
with her submerging into the surging of her blood that is sweet
  as sugar
through all the spasms from the orgasms of the quivering bongó.

'Guasa, columbia, a conconcó mabó . . .'

Why doesn't she come to the dance, the haunting Caridá,
the mulatto woman flaunting all her laughter gaily taunting,
when the great rumba goes reeling,
roaring, wheeling, raging and squealing,
hammering with frantic feeling on the skin of the bongó?

The sweetness of trance drunk and dishevelled in enchantment's
  magic throe,
That mulatto–true she-devil–tears her girdle right asunder
squeezing sense and reason under in the wild wonder of delicious
  guaguancó.

'Guasa, columbia, a conconcó mabó . . .'

Why doesn't she come to the dance, the daughter of Yemayá,
the nutritious,
and lubricious,
the pulsating, fascinating, captivating Caridá?'

3. Development of Style

Cuba's Negrism, which significantly produced nothing but poetry,
went a step further in achieving stylistic methods from Afro-American
folklore than did Haiti's Indigenism, which could find its full stature
only in the novel. Indigenism captured the real life of the Afro-
Haitian peasants and their Afro-American religions. Negrism succeeded for the first time in putting Afro-Caribbean rhythms into
European language, and these were nearer to African than to North
American rhythms. The Negrists, however, remained European in
their values and ideas, with everything African considered 'savage'
and 'primitive'.

Réne Maran too did not attack these values, so he is not a forerunner of Negritude either. From the works of the Parisian 'Africa
vogue' mentioned at the beginning of this chapter, notably those by
Cousturier, Tharaud, Leblond and Soupault, Maran's novels *Batouala*
and *Djouma* stand out, because he went beyond revelling in the exotic

and set out to describe the conditions in Ubangi-Shari with 'Indigenist' realism.

Anyhow, Indigenism and Negrism lead logically to Negritude. For when writers tried to reproduce in language not only the Afro-American peasants' social life but also their thoughts and feelings, the question was bound to arise whether this could be done at all with the conventional vocabulary of a European language; whether European words did not in themselves falsify thought and meaning, and so needed changing and renewing in the spirit of a different cultural consciousness. Léon Laleau (born 1892), a rather conventional poet, who came quite late to Indigenism, recognized the problem and gave it valid expression in the poem 'Trahison':

> Ce cœur obsédant, qui ne correspond
> Pas avec mon langage et mes costumes,
> Et sur lequel mordent, comme un crampon,
> Des sentiments d'emprunt et des coutumes
> D'Europe, sentez-vous cette souffrance
> Et ce désespoir à nul autre égal
> D'apprivoiser, avec des mots de France,
> Ce cœur qui m'est venu du Sénégal?[1]

> 'This heart importunate which does not fit
> The clothes I wear, the language that I own,
> Has got a clamp that's biting into it,
> The borrowed feelings, customs still on loan
> From Europe. Oh, how bitter is the smart,
> The hopelessness I feel, deeper than all,
> Of taming, with the words of France, this heart
> Which came to me from distant Senegal.'

The question implied takes us directly to the basic problem of Negritude.

REFERENCES AND BIBLIOGRAPHIES

1. Indigenism in Haiti

The works in the chronological table are not listed again except where they are quoted from.

[1] Morpeau (2), p. 256.
[2] cf. Garret, pp. 135 f.

[3] ibid., p. 94.
[4] ibid., p. 129.
[5] ibid., p. 124.
[6] Fitts, p. 278.
[7] Hughes/Bontemps, p. 366.
[8] Roumain 1945, p. 8.
[9] Morisseau-Leroy, p. 30.

ALEXIS, Jacques Stéphen: Les arbres musiciens. Paris 1957 (No. 1237)
ANTHOLOGIE de la poésie haïtienne 'indigène'. Préface de Paul Morand. Port-au-Prince, Haïti: Imprimerie Modèle 1928. II, 82 pp.
COULTHARD, George Robert: Race and colour in Caribbean literature. London 1962
FITTS, Dudley: Antología la poesía americana contemporánea. Anthology of contemporary Latin-American poetry. Norfolk, Conn. 1942; new ed., New York and London 1947 (No. 1188)
GARRET, Naomi M.: The renaissance of Haitian poetry. Paris 1963
GOURAIGE, Ghislain: Histoire de la littérature haïtienne. Port-au-Prince 1960
–Les meilleurs poètes et romanciers haïtiens. (Pages choisies). Port-au-Prince: Imp. La Phalange 1963. ix, 414 pp.
HUGHES, Langston and BONTEMPS, Arna: The poetry of the Negro, 1746–1949. Garden City, N.Y. 1949 (No. 1189)
LESPÈS, Anthony: Les semences de la colère. Port-au-Prince(?) 1949 (No. 1662)
LUBIN, Maurice Alcibiade: Poésies haïtiennes. Rio de Janeiro 1956 (No. 1211)
MORISSEAU-LEROY, Félix: Récolte. Port-au-Prince 1946 (No. 1815)
MORPEAU, Louis: (1) Anthologie d'un siècle de poésie haïtienne, 1817–1925. Paris 1925 (No. 1217)
–(2) Lettres haïtiennes. In: Mercure de France, année 36, tome 177, 1. 1. 1925
POMPILUS, Pradel & FRÈRES DE L'INSTRUCTION CHRÉTIENNE: Manuel illustré d'histoire de la littérature haïtienne. Port-au-Prince 1961
PRICE-MARS, Jean: Ainsi parla l'oncle; essais d'ethnographie. Paris 1928
ROUMAIN, Jacques: Gouverneurs de la rosée. Port-au-Prince 1944 and Paris 1961 (No. 1896–1907)
(Masters of the dew. Transl. by Langston Hughes and Mercer Cook. New York 1947 (No. 1900))
–Bois d'ébène. Port-au-Prince 1945 (No. 1908)

SAINT-AMAND, Edris: Bon Dieu rit. Paris 1952 (No. 1914)

SAINT-LOUIS, Carlos and LUBIN, Maurice A.: Panorama de la poésie haïtienne. Port-au-Prince 1950 (No. 1220)

THOBY-MARCELIN, Philippe and MARCELIN, Pierre: Canapé-vert. New York 1944 (No. 1955)

(Canapé-vert. Transl. by Edward Laroque Tinker. New York 1944. No. 1956)

–La bête de Musseau. New York 1946 (No. 1957)

(The beast of the Haitian hills. Transl. by Peter C. Rhodes. New York 1946 and London 1951. No. 1958)

UNDERWOOD, Edna Worthley: The poets of Haiti, 1782–1934, translated by Edna Worthley Underwood. Portland, Me. 1934 (No. 1224)

2. Negrism in Cuba

[1] Coulthard, p. 28.
[2] Vitier 1952, p. 76.
[3] Ballagas 1946, p. 236.
[4] Latino, p. 5.
[5] Guirao, p. 52.
[6] Vitier 1952, pp. 223–5.
[7] Jahn, pp. 62–78.
[8] Guirao, p. 77.
[9] Carpentier, p. 180.
[10] Vitier 1952, p. 229.
[11] Vitier 1958, p. 355.
[12] Guillén 1952, pp. 68–70.
[13] Guillén 1958, p. 39.
[14] Arozarena, p. 51.
[15] Jahn, p. 95.
[16] Arozarena, pp. 9–11.

AROZARENA, Marcelino: Canción negra sin color. La Habana: Ediciones Unión 1966. 71 pp. (Cuadernos Unión.) Lyr

BALLAGAS, Emilio: Antología de la poesía negra hispano-americana. Madrid 1935 (No. 1185)

–Mapa de la poesía negra americana. Buenos Aires 1946 (No. 1186)

CARPENTIER, Alejo: Ecué-yamba-ó! Madrid 1933 (No. 1352)

COULTHARD, George Robert: Race and colour in Caribbean literature. London 1962

GUILLÉN, Nicolás: Sóngoro cosongo. Motivos de son. West Indies Ltd. España. Buenos Aires 1952 (No. 1545)
–Ballad of the two ancestors–Sensemayà; two poems transl. by Sangodare Akanji. In: Black Orpheus, No. 3, Ibadan, May 1958
–All other works in Nos. 1532–64
GUIRAO, Ramón: Orbita de la poesía afrocubana, 1928–37. La Habana 1938 (No. 1207)
JAHN, Janheinz: Muntu. London/New York 1961
LATINO, Simon: Los mejores versos de la poesía negra. Buenos Aires 1956 (No. 1192)
PALÉS MATOS, Luis: Danza negra (poem). First published in 1926 in Puerto Rico, also in 'Heraldo de Cuba', La Habana 1927
–Poesía, 1915–56. Introd. by Federico de Onís. San Juan: Ediciones de la Universidad de Puerto Rico 1957. 305 pp.
PEREDA VALDÉS, Ildefonso: Antología de la poesía negra americana. Montevideo 1953 (No. 1195)
TALLET, José Zacarías: La rumba (poem). First published in the Cuban journal Atuei, August 1928
VITIER, Cintio: Cincuenta años de poesía cubana (1902–52). La Habana 1952 (No. 1225)
–Lo cubano en la poesía. La Habana 1958
WILLIAMS, Eric: Four poets of the greater Antilles. In: Caribbean Quarterly, vol. 2, No. 4, Port-of-Spain, Trinidad, 1952

3. Development of Style

[1] Saint-Louis/Lubin, p. 312.

CENDRARS, Blaise: Anthologie nègre. Paris 1921; new ed., 1928 (The African saga. Transl. by Margery Bianco. New York 1927)
COUSTURIER, Lucie: Mes inconnus chez moi. Paris 1920
–Mes inconnus chez eux. Paris 1925
DELAFOSSE, Maurice: Les noirs de l'Afrique. Paris 1922
–L'âme nègre. Paris 1923
GIDE, André: Voyage au Congo. Paris 1927
LEBLOND, Marius-Ary: Ulysse Cafre ou L'histoire dorée d'un noir. Paris 1924
MARAN, René: Batouala. Paris 1921 (No. 1716–24)
(Batouala. Transl. by Adele Szold Seltzer. New York 1922. No. 1718)
(Batouala, a negro novel from the French of René Maran. [Differ-

ent translation; no translator's name.] London: Cape 1922. 192 pp.)

Djouma, chien de brousse. Paris 1927 (Nos. 1727–30)

SOUPAULT, Philippe: Le nègre. Paris 1927

THARAUD, Jérôme and Jean: La randonnée de Samba Diouf. Paris 1922

TABLE 7

Indigenism and Negrism

Indigenism (Haïti): Roman
Negrism (Cuba): *Italic*
Anthologies: SMALL CAPS

+: written but not published in the year indicated

Number following title refers to my Bibliography

	Poetry	Prose
1925	Roumer: Poèmes d'Haïti et de France 1909	
1926	*Palés Matos: Danza negra*	
	Pereda Valdés: La guitarra de los negros 2143	
1927	Brouard: +Le tam-tam angoissé	
1928	ANTHOLOGIE INDIGÈNE	Price-Mars: Ainsi parla l'oncle
	Roumain & Roumer: Appel & La chanson des lambis 1892	
	Tallet: Rumba	
1930	Brierre: +Le drame de Marchaterre	Roumain: La proie et l'ombre 1893
	Brierre: +L'adieu à la Marseillaise	
	Guillén: Motivos de son 1532	
1931	Laleau: Musique nègre 1637	Roumain: La montagne ensorcelée 1895
	Brierre: Le drapeau de demain 1299	Roumain: Les fantoches 1894
	Guillén: Sóngoro cosongo 1533	
	Ballagas: Júbilo y fuga 1262	

1932
Brierre: Le petit soldat 1300
Rigaud: Rythmes et rites 1884
Thoby-Marcelin: La négresse adolescente 1952
Laleau: Le choc 1638

1933
Brierre: Chansons secrètes, 1301
Laleau: Ondes courtes 1639
Pressoir: Au rythme des coumbites 1875
Rigaud: Rites et rythmes 1886
Rigaud: Tassos 1887
Guillén: West Indies Ltd. 1534
Rigaud: Jésus ou Legba ou Les dieux se battent 1885
Cinéas: Le drame de la terre 1404
Cinéas: La vengeance de la terre 1405
Alexis, S.: Le nègre masqué 1244
Carpentier: Ecué-yamba-ó! 1352

1934
Ballagas: Cuaderno de poesía negra 1263
Gomez Kemp: Acento negro 1516
ONIS: ANTOLOGÍA ESPAÑOLA E HISPANO-AMERICANA 1193

1935
BALLAGAS: ANTOLOGÍA HISPANOAMERICANA 1185
Brierre: Les horizons sans ciel 1302
Casséus: Viejo 1369

1936
PEREDA VALDÉS: ANTOLOGÍA NEGRA AMERICANA 1194

1937
Bonhomme: L'âme du lambi 1292
Laleau: Orchestre 1640
Guillén: Cantos para soldados y sones para turistas 1535
Guillén: España 1536

1938
GUIRAO: ORBITA DE LA POESÍA AFROCUBANA 1207
Savain: La case de Damballah 1929

1939
Roumain: +Bois d'ébène 1908
Ballagas: Sabor eterno 1264
Pedroso: Más allá canta el mar 1844
Pedroso: Antología poética 1843

1940
Morisseau-Leroy: Plénitudes 1814
Bélance: Rythme de mon coeur 1273
Benoit: Chants sauvages 1279
Bernard: Le souvenir demeure 1282
Camille: Assaut à la nuit 1336

1941
Thoby-Marcelin: Dialogue avec la femme endormie 1953
Magloire Saint-Aude: Dialogue de mes lampes 1698
Magloire Saint-Aude: Tabou 1699
Bélance: Luminaires 1274

PART FOUR

The New Problems

Chapter 15

THE NEGRITUDE SCHOOL

1. Caliban and Prospero

Caliban and Prospero: as O. Mannoni and George Lamming (born 1927) have pointed out, the relationship between these two characters in *The Tempest* can be interpreted as similar to the relationship of the two opposing sides in a colonialist society. This is not, of course, to drag Shakespeare into modern controversies or credit him with ideas some way ahead of his time! But the parallel drawn strikes me as highly illuminating, and I believe can be followed up further than has been done by Mannoni and Lamming. Here, then, is a dialogue that takes place between the two characters:

Caliban   This island's mine, by Sycorax my mother,
Which thou takest from me. When thou camest first,
Thou strokedst me and madest much of me, wouldst
   give me
Water with berries in't, and teach me how
To name the bigger light, and how the less,
That burn by day and night: and then I loved thee
And show'd thee all the qualities o' the isle,
The fresh springs, brine-pits, barren place and fertile:
Cursed be I that did so! All the charms
Of Sycorax, toads, beetles, bats, light on you!
For I am all the subjects that you have,
Which first was mine own king: and here you sty me
In this hard rock, whiles you do keep from me
The rest o' the island.

Prospero   Thou most lying slave,
Whom stripes may move, not kindness! I have used thee,
Filth as thou art, with human care. . . .
                          I pitied thee,
Took pains to make thee speak, taught thee each hour
One thing or other: when thou didst not, savage,
Know thine own meaning, but wouldst gabble like

> A thing most brutish, I endow'd thy purposes
> With words which made them known. But thy vile face,
> Though thou didst learn, had that in't which good
>   natures
> Could not abide to be with; therefore wast thou
> Deservedly confined into this rock,
> Who hadst deserved more than a prison.

Caliban   You taught me language; and my profit on't
> Is, I know how to curse. The red plague rid you
> For learning me your language![1]

Lamming stresses the fact that both Prospero and Caliban are exiles, and has this to say on the question of language:

'Prospero has given Caliban Language; and with it an unstated history of consequences, an unknown history of future intentions. This gift of language meant not English, in particular, but speech and concept as a way, a method, a necessary avenue towards areas of the self which could not be reached in any other way. It is this way, entirely Prospero's enterprise, which makes Caliban aware of possibilities. Therefore, all of Caliban's future–for future is the very name for possibilities–must derive from Prospero's experiment, which is also his risk.

'Provided there is no extraordinary departure which explodes all of Prospero's premises, then Caliban and his future now belong to Prospero . . . Prospero lives in the absolute certainty that Language, which is his gift to Caliban, is the very prison in which Caliban's achievements will be realized and restricted.'[2]

Lamming puts down Caliban's limitations to his being a part of nature, which is no doubt the way Shakespeare conceived the character; the other possibility, the 'extraordinary departure', is not followed up. But I find it instructive to take a closer look at this aspect, so as to shed light on the phenomenon of Negritude.

Lamming is right: if Caliban is no more than a part of nature, he will never be able to break out of the prison of Prospero's language: all the culture he can obtain, as is Prospero's intention, must then derive from Prospero's language and mentality; and everything Caliban does will be derivative. But suppose Caliban is also part of a culture, a different culture unfamiliar to Prospero. Caliban remembers this but can grasp it only in images, not words; he is imprisoned in Prospero's language and his own servility. Shakespeare's text provides clues for this line of interpretation as well:

Caliban   Be not afeard; the isle is full of noises,
               Sounds and sweet airs, that give delight and hurt not.
               Sometimes a thousand twangling instruments
               Will hum about mine ears, and sometime voices
               That, if I had then waked after long sleep,
               Will make me sleep again: and then, in dreaming,
               The clouds methought would open and show riches
               Ready to drop upon me, that, when I waked,
               I cried to dream again.[3]

Like any other creature Caliban feels the urge for freedom, but he also knows the basis for his oppressor's power:

> . . . there thou mayst brain him,
> Having first seized his books . . .
>   Remember
> First to possess his books; for without them
> He's but a sot, as I am, nor hath not
> One spirit to command: they all do hate him
> As rootedly as I. Burn but his books.[4]

Let us now suppose that in an 'extraordinary departure' Caliban carries out the revolt suggested to him by his urge for freedom, no longer as the helpmate of foreign buffoons like Stephano and Trinculo but on his own initiative and with his own resources. Then he would have nothing to rely on but the riches dropping upon him from the clouds in dreams; such riches have always been his only source of strength. And to gain his freedom, he must consider the 'thousand twangling instruments' not as the voice of nature but as culture; and culture does not emerge out of nothing but always has a source. For his mother, Sycorax the sorceress, although conquered by Prospero, possessed magic powers, magic knowledge, mastery over 'toads, beetles, bats', i.e., over nature, and therefore culture.

Once Caliban has recognized the limits and roots of Prospero's power, he may try some further unsuccessful revolts, but if his urge to freedom remains unbroken, the idea is bound to occur to him in the end–helped by the education Prospero has given him, however defective–that his mother's powers, the voices, the instruments and the riches that drop in dreams, all belong together: that they form a culture, but one very different from Prospero's book culture, He, Caliban, must at last wrench this from dreams into reality, in other words consciously recognize it. He does this through language, Prospero's language, for he possesses no other.

So he captures, in his own and Prospero's language, a culture Prospero did not create and cannot control, which he, Caliban, has recognized as his own. But in the process the language is transformed, acquiring different meanings which Prospero never expected. Caliban becomes 'bilingual'. That language he shares with Prospero and the language he has minted from it are no longer identical. Caliban breaks out of the prison of Prospero's language. This provides a new point of departure.

Prospero's lessons cannot be unlearned, so Caliban will continue to understand Prospero's language. But Prospero will have only a partial grasp of the language which is now Caliban's own, so long as he retains his old attitudes. He is bound to miss essential parts, nuances and references, everything that relates to that different cultural background, and so he will misunderstand Caliban's new language.

But Prospero can have himself initiated into the new language, which has been extended by Caliban to take in new fields of experience. The condition for this, however, is that Prospero asks Caliban questions, that he is willing to be instructed, and is instructed. In fact he must abandon his colonialist arrogance, shed his claim to be the master race, and consort with Caliban on the same level. Thus Caliban's liberation gives Prospero too a great opportunity: the chance of turning from a tyrant into a humane person.

2. The Achievements of Negritude

The literary movement which produced its works between 1934 and 1948 and became known under the name of 'Negritude' may be described as the successful revolt in which Caliban broke out of the prison of Prospero's language, by converting that language to his own needs for self-expression.

The idea of the new movement began in Paris in 1934, when a few students founded the journal *L'Étudiant Noir*. They were Léopold Sédar Senghor (born 1906) from Senegal, Léon Damas (born 1912) from French Guiana, and Aimé Césaire (born 1913) from the West Indian island of Martinique.

This event was preceded by another, which Lilyan Kesteloot sees as the origin of Negritude and with which she starts her study: in 1932 Étienne Léro (1909–39), René Ménil and Jules Monnerot, all from Martinique, founded in Paris the journal *Légitime Défense*; there was only one issue, which contained a strident manifesto. In it these students from Martinique rejected the bourgeois conventions and humanitarian hypocrisy which imposed on them a 'borrowed personality'; they rejected the European literary models offered them at school, and vowed their allegiance to the proletariat and surrealism. They rejected Victor Hugo and Alexandre Dumas, but adopted new models which were just as European: Marx, Freud, Rimbaud and Breton.

So they did not even fully catch up with the successful revolt carried out some time before by the Harlem style and by Indigenism. Through accepting the thesis that the cultural revolution must be preceded by a political one, they blocked the way to the recognition of an African culture; and by slavishly copying surrealism, they remained imitators who had only changed their models. A poem by Léro, 'Sur la Prairie', will serve as an example:

> Sur la prairie trois arbres prennent le thé
> Tes mains sont cachées
> Mes mains sont cachées
> Une seule bouche et l'heure d'été
> Laisse-moi jouer au jeu de l'habitude
> Beau paquebot aux lignes de mes mains.[1]

> 'On the prairie three trees take tea
> Your hands are hidden
> My hands are hidden
> A single mouth and the hour of summer
> Let me play the game of habit
> Fine steamer on the lines of my hands.'

The group who founded *L'Étudiant Noir* took, from the outset, a more independent attitude to communism and surrealism. 'For us politics was only an aspect of culture,'[2] Senghor wrote in 1960 in a letter to Lilyan Kesteloot; and 'We accepted surrealism as a means but not as an end, as an ally not as a master. We were willing to find inspiration in surrealism, but solely because surrealist writing rediscovered the language of Negro Africa.'[3]

These writers knew the works of the Negro Renaissance, and also knew some of its authors personally–'Senghor the Senegalese'[4] is mentioned in Claude McKay's novel *Banjo*; they realized the movement's importance. Césaire stressed the fact that it was authentic: 'The ordinary Negro, whose grotesqueness or exoticism a whole literature sets out to emphasize, is made a hero, drawn seriously and passionately, and the limited power of his art is successful . . . To

create a world, is that a small thing? To make a world emerge where
only the junk-shop's exotic inhumanity rose before!'[5]

Senghor stressed the form of the Negro Renaissance: 'It remains
near to song, it is made to be sung or spoken, not to be read. Hence
the importance of the rhythm, Negro rhythm, so despotic beneath its
appearance of freedom. Hence the importance of the music, so difficult to render in translation ... In short, a poetry of flesh and earth,
to talk like Hughes, a poetry of the peasant who has not broken off
contact with the forces of the earth.'[6] Senghor saw the Negro Renaissance as more indigenist than it really was. In fact the expression
'forces of the earth' (*les forces telluriques*) projects on to it his personal
aspiration of 'back to the sources' (*retour aux sources*).

Coming from different parts of the world, Senghor, Damas and
Césaire inspired each other and succeeded in avoiding provincialism.
They caught up with Negro Renaissance, Indigenism and Negrism,
and in the process of introducing African elements into poetic art
took a decisive step forward. This was because they achieved a re-
versal of values, and saw Africa no longer as only exotic and 'primitive' but as a specific culture which they must search for and rediscover.

The process of getting closer to Africa became more and more a
conscious one, and eventually led Senghor to the study of African
style which he brought into his celebrated essay: 'The spirit of civilization or the laws of Negro-African culture' (*L'Ésprit de la civilisation
ou les lois de la culture négro-africaine*). The political consequences
of this psychological revolt helped a good deal towards the decolo-
nization of Africa; I have tried to show the cultural and spiritual sides
in my book *Muntu*. The literary harvest, Caliban's breakout from
the prison of Prospero's language, was reaped in three fields: seman-
tics, rhythm and subject matter.

Césaire must be given chief credit for the semantic achievements.
Words in the French poetic language gained extended meanings and
new associations not to be explained from the historical experience
of French literature. A European can easily confuse these with the
spontaneous images of European surrealism which are determined
by absurdities and coincidences. In Césaire's writing they have a firm
semantic and syntactical coherence. I have already given examples
from Césaire's work in *Muntu*.[7]

The rhythmic innovations were made mainly by Senghor and
Damas. French poetic language, which has quantitative metres with
no accentuation, was forced to scan and also made to 'dance' in an
Afro-American fashion by Damas, in a purely African fashion by

Senghor. Besides the techniques from music and dancing, formal means of producing rhythm in language include, as Senghor writes, 'alliterations, paranomasias, anaphoras, which are based on a repetition of similar phonemes* or sounds, and create secondary rhythms which reinforce the effect of the whole.'[8] But that is not all. The emphasis on rhythm leads logically to the demand: 'I persist in thinking that a poem is not completed unless it combines song, words and music.'[9]

Mrs. Kesteloot has given some fine examples of how Senghor's rhythmic techniques are revealed in his own poetry. I quote these below, marking by numbers where vowel phonemes are repeated, and adding a rough translation. Mrs. Kesteloot writes: '. . . even oftener he [Senghor] works himself up into a dance rhythm–specially that typically African dance which doubles its step by jumping, one-two on one foot, one-two on the other, Senghor recreates this step by doubling or hammering home the accentuated syllables.'[10]

A. Et quand sur son ombre elle se taisait, resonnait le tam-tam
   des tanns obsédés.[11]

'And when in his shadow it had come dumb, came the beat
   of tom-tom from throbbing deep creeks.'[12]

B. Nous n'avancerons plus dans le frémissement fervent de nos
   corps égaux épaules égales.[13]

'We shall swing along no longer the tingling thrill to feel of
   body frames the same and soldered the shoulders.'[14]

C. Ma tête bourdonnant au galop guerrier des dyoung-dyoungs,
   au grand galop de mon sang de pur sang.[15]

'My head's in a roar with the gallop of war of the dyoung-
   dyoungs,† the gallop and thud of my thoroughbred blood.'[16]

Numbers indicate similar or related sounds, whether vowel diphthong or consonant.

* Phonemes–group of sounds belonging to the same phonetic cluster.

† Dyoung-dyoung–royal tom-tom at the court of Sin (a kingdom in Senegal, Senghor's home).

These examples show that such features are not beyond translation into other languages, once the rhythmical technique is recognized, bearing in mind that the consonants count, of course, as well as the vowels.

Mrs. Kesteloot continues: 'We can also recreate this dance-step by repeating the consonants which mark the accents. The alveolars and bilabial plosives play the part of the hands beating the tom-tom.'[17]

(1 alveolar, 2 bilabial plosives)

    D. Des peaux précieuses, des barres de sel, de l'or du Bouré,

       de l'or du Boundou.[18]

    'The precious pelts and the bars of salt, the gold from Bureh,

       the gold from Boundou.'[19]

Mrs. Kesteloot offers yet another example:

'Senghor gave the longest poem in *Chants d'Ombre* the title "Que m'accompagnent kôras et balafong".'

In this title the names of the instruments give the verse its sonorous quality: repetition of the hard C (que m'acc . . . k . . .) and of the final 'ong, the nasal sound of which should be stressed ('agn and 'fong). So the line is accentuated thus:

Que m'*acc*ompa*gn*ent *kô*ras et bala*fong.*

This example, though in itself minimal, reveals to us a major difficulty for us Westerners! To 'grasp' the rhythm of a poem by Senghor, we must break away from the French way of accentuating words. In the line above we automatically put the accent on the syllables *pa, ras* and *fong,* that is on the final ones:[20]

Que m'accom*pa*gnent kô*ras* et bala*fong.*[21]

In many of his poems Senghor's cadence follows a pattern which we meet again in the African cultural field: the mainly falling speech melody of West African tone languages. There the high, low and medium tones of single words in a sentence may be incorporated into a falling tonal curve, so that the high tone of the last word in a sentence may be lower than a low tone at the beginning of the sentence. We often find such a falling intonation in the North American Blues, sung in English. And no less often in Senghor's poetry. I would illustrate this with the beginning of his 'Élégie de minuit', in which every verse begins with the highest of high tones and then goes down in an undulating curve. The alliterations and sequences of vowels here are again denoted by figures, showing that this whole verse sequence has a consonant alternation of bilabial plosives (1) with alveolar semi-vowels (2), and a vowel alternation of the sound *ä* (3) with nasalized *a* (4). At the beginning of the lines, in the 'high tone' region, the *ä* is sharpened to *e* (3), the nasalized *a* to *oá* or *áh* (4), and the labial plosive is heightened by *s* (1) or by combining two consonants. It shows also that not only the line structure but the structure of the whole poem follows the falling tonal curve. *The emphatic sounds* (12) are most numerous at the beginning of the first lines, becoming fewer in the beginnings of lines that follow:

Eté splendide Été qui nourris le Poète du lait de ta lumière

Moi qui poussais comme ble de Printemps, qui m'enivrais de la

verdeur de l'eau du ruissellement vert dans l'or du temps

Ah! Plus ne peux supporter ta lumière, la lumière de tes lampes,

ta lumière atomique qui disintègre tout mon être

Plus ne peux supporter la lumière de minuit.[22]

The English approximation has to make do with fewer bilabial plosives, helped out with velar compounds and nasals; and there are internal vowel harmonies in each of the four lines:

'Ah summer splendid summer, suckling the Poet with milk of
   your light's brightness,
I who once grew like corn in the spring, drunk with delight at
   the water all green, at the glitter of green in the season's gold,
Now I can't bear any more garishly bright the glare of the light
   from your shining, glare of your brightness atomic, breaking
   in pieces my being,
I can't bear any more the glare of the brightness of midnight.'[23]

Léon Damas, who is usually underrated in the shadow of Senghor and Césaire, had already adopted dance rhythms in his poetry before them. In his collection *Pigments* (1937) he adopted for the first time the African stylistic technique so characteristic of the poets of Negritude, of heightening the effect by repetition and the setting of poems like 'Hoquet' (hiccup) 'Bientôt' and 'Obsession',[24] to racy Afro-Caribbean dance rhythms, which he uses functionally, not descriptively as in Negrism. In *Graffiti* (1952) he brought the dance principle of duplication into short poems like the following:

> D'avoir un instant cru
> à la main dégantée
> à la main dégantée au printemps
> dégantée au printemps né
> au printemps né de la magie
> de la magie du rythme
>
> la meute édentée
> scrofuleuse
> et borgne
> a crié sus
> à mon cœur de fou sans haine[25]

The English translation cannot hope to produce the sound values as well as the repetition technique:

> 'When I for a moment believed
> in the gloveless hand
> in the gloveless hand in the spring
> gloveless in the spring that's born
> in the spring that's born of a magic
> born of a magic rhythm
>
> the toothless mob
> scurvy
> and one-eyed
> cried havoc on
> my madman's hateless heart.'

In his most recent volume *Black-Label* (1956) he 'composed' the whole four-part poem of eighty-four pages like a piece of music, with each part held together by a *leitmotiv* verse like:

> BLACK-LABEL À BOIRE
> pour ne pas changer
> Black-Label à boire
> à quoi bon changer

Within this framework he connects simple images to form a train of thought, which, however, does not, and is not meant to, produce any logical sequence in the European sense. An idea is never pursued to its conclusion, but is taken up periodically and repeatedly. Grouping, paragraphing and connection within the sequences of images, are done by keeping to the same sound values, which also carry the message of the image:

> BAMAYE DO BRAZIL
> BAMAYE DO BRAZIL
> montrant la voie aux gueux
> montrant la voie aux peu
> montrant la voie aux rien
> montrant la voie aux chiens
> montrant la voie aux maigres
> montrant la voie aux nègres.[26]

Césaire has never deliberately produced specific rhythmic formulas, but his whole poetry is propelled forward through rhythm. Senghor writes of him: 'What is surprising about his using his pen like Louis Armstrong his trumpet? Or more accurately perhaps, like the devotees of Voodoo their tom-toms? He needs to lose himself in the dance of words, the tom-tom rhythm, to rediscover himself in the Universe.'[27]

In theme, Senghor was the first to introduce into French poetry African customs and manners, myths and celebrations personally experienced, also hero figures, chiefs, kings, priests, shrines, spirits, springs and animals–his 'Royaume d'Enfance' which he was constantly invoking. Birago Diop (born 1906) set a model for prose with his recreation of African stories and myths in the oral style of a professional narrator: 'Les Contes d'Amadou Koumba' (1947). Césaire was the first to bring alive in his poetry the cosmic connection of all powers and living things, the existential unity of man and nature and the magic of the word.

The aim of the subject matter is to capture the African reality; the semantic shifts of meaning bring about the magic of words and rhythm; the 'architecture of being'[28] (in Senghor's phrase) is the heart-beat of the universe, evoking ecstasy, giving the poetry sound and weight. So the semantic, rhythmical and thematic achievements of Negritude have a fruitful connection with each other as characteristics of a specific philosophy and attitude to the world, the conception of an African style and the unity of an African culture. These ideas, which I have described in *Muntu*, are proclaimed as part of the Negritude movement's programme by Senghor in his essays and have been propagated in the magazine *Présence Africaine* edited by Alioune Diop (born 1910). In 1948 Jean-Paul Sartre tried to give them an existentialist interpretation. The theoretical foundation, which rests on the philosophical works of Placied Tempels and Alexis Kagame (born 1912), is still disputed however.

But it is essential to be familiar with these ideas for a deeper understanding of the writing of Negritude. In connection with this view of the world, the African writer has a very important function: he is word-magician and announcer, Africa's spokesman, sponsor and interpreter to the outside world, Africa's educator within. His rhythmical word produces the images which when put together become poetry and prose. Reality offers dormant subject matter, which his word awakens, turns into images and projects towards the future. The function of this kind of writing is not to describe things as they are for the sake of description, but to create prototypes: visions of what ought to be. Therefore the style is 'in the imperative'. When the writer transposes his visions of the future into the present, or even back into the past, as if what he commanded were taking place before his eyes or as if the new reality invoked had already come into being, his imperative achieves its highest force:

> Paysan frappe le sol de ta daba. . . .
> je me souviens de la fameuse peste qui aura lieu en l'an 3000
> il n'y avait pas eu d'étoile annoncière . . .
> le premier jour les oiseaux mourront
> le second jour les poissons échouèrent
> le troisième jour les animaux sortirent des bois
> et faisaient aux villes une grande ceinture chaude très forte
> frappe le sol de ta daba. . . .[29]

> 'Farmer strike the soil with your daba. . . .*
> I remember the famous plague which will happen in the year 3000
> there was no prophetic star . . .
> the first day the birds will die
> the second day the fishes were grounded
> the third day the animals came out of the woods
> and made for the towns a great hot mighty belt
> strike the soil with your daba. . . .'

* A *daba* is a double-bladed hoe.

3. The Meaning of Negritude

According to Senghor, he and Césaire 'launched' the word 'negritude' in the years 1933–35.[30] The first time it appeared in one of their works, however, was in Césaire's poem, written in 1938, 'Cahier d'un retour au pays natal'. Since then it has come to bear many different shades of meaning, which have been put together by Mrs. Kesteloot:[31] I have added some more and put them in a systematic order. I give below, with categories in the margin, and the significant words in italics, examples of some of the ways in which the word has been used, varying from an instrument, a style, a particular form or feature of style, a quality or an attitude, to 'being', 'way of being', race, skin-colour, or the sum of all values:

Instrument	(1)	'. . . so that our negritude should be the effective *instrument* for a liberation.'[32] (Senghor)
Style form	(2)	'The monotony of tone, which is what distinguishes poetry from prose, is the seal of negritude, the *incantation* which allows access to the truth of essentials.'[33] (Senghor)
Style	(3)	'The thing which makes up a poem's negritude is less the subject than the *style*.'[34] (Senghor)
Stylistic feature	(4)	'. . . . the *rhythm* born of emotion . . .'
Quality	(5)	'. . . produces emotion in its turn. And also produces *humour*, the other side of negritude.'[35] (Senghor)
Attitude	(6)	'Negritude, in contrast, is *understanding* through sympathy.'[36] (Sartre)
Attitude	(7)	'I shout hurrah! *The old negritude* is progressively turning into a corpse.'[37] (Césaire)
Attitude	(8)	'It is the same with independence as with negritude. This is first of all a *negation* . . . rejection of the Other, refusal to assimilate . . . rejection of the Other is *self-affirmation*.'[38] (Senghor)
Being	(9)	'. . . the affirmation of our *being*, our negritude . . .'[39] (Senghor)
A Way of Being	(10)	'My negritude is not a stone hurled against the clamour of the day my negritude is not a speck of dead water on the dead eye of the earth my negritude is no tower and no dome.'[40] (Césaire)

A Way of	(11)	'We could not return to the negritude of the past,
Being		the negritude of the sources.'[41] (Senghor)
A Way of	(12)	'Night, you dissolve all my contradictions, all con-
Being		tradictions in the *primeval unity* of your negri-
		tude.'[42] (Senghor)
Being-in-	(13)	'Negritude, to use Heidegger's language, is the
the-World		Negro's *Being-in-the-world*.'[43] (Sartre)
Race	(14)	'Haiti, where negritude emerged for the first time.'[44]
		(Césaire)
Oppressed	(15)	'You do not know the restaurants and swimming
Race		pools,
		and nobility forbidden to black blood,
		And Science and Humanity, setting up their police
		cordons
		at the frontiers of negritude.'[45] (Senghor)
Skin-Colour	(16)	'His very negritude was losing its colour.'[46] (Césaire)
Sum of all	(17)	'Negritude is the cultural heritage, the values, and
Values		above all the *spirit* of Negro-African civilization.'[47]
		(Senghor)
Sum of all	(18)	'Negritude, the *sum of* black Africa's *cultural*
Values		*values* . . .'[48] (Senghor)

To help explain the relationship of these different meanings and shades of meaning, setting them against the background of African thought, I would like to quote from an essay of mine on 'Value Concepts in Sub-Saharan Africa':

'In African thinking, the universe consists of a network of living forces. The universe is a field of forces. Man and woman, dog and stone, even yesterday and east, beauty and laughter—all these are forces related to each other and in continuous interaction. The universe is a unity, in which each part depends on the others, and no part is changeless. If you take possession of part of a thing, you thereby participate in its life force. If you tear a leaf from a tree, not only does the tree quiver, but the whole universe is affected, since nothing stands alone. For Europeans, force is an attribute: a being *has* force. In African thinking, force *is* being, being *is* force, a physical-spiritual energy and potency. The totality of all these living forces is NTU, Being . . . which, however, is never conceived of as separable from its manifestations. In NTU, the cosmic universal force, all single forces are tied together. The individual forces fall into four groups, within each of which there is a hierarchical ordering: *Muntu, Kintu, Hantu* and *Kuntu*.

'... the *Kuntu* group contains all the forces of relationship, of acting on and of manipulating, of way and manner of acting. They answer questions about the *how* of a culture–that is, about its *style*. Kuntu-forces are function-forces (forces-modalité) . . .'[49]

Style, qualities, attitudes, 'way of being' are all *Kuntu* forces; so are stylistic forms, features and 'instruments', if considered dynamically, in action; and so are specific external factors like race and skin colour, which are the African's way of 'being in the world'. The *Kuntu*-forces, in a world of forces, produce specific values and are in themselves the sum of such values. If we bear in mind this structure, the apparent contradictions in the above statements are resolved: every 'Being'-force, and the qualities and methods resulting from it–which are forces in their own right–make up both the whole and all its parts: i.e., according to these writers' statements, *negritude*.

Admittedly the negritude writers did not establish their special structure beforehand, but developed it as they went along or retrospectively, This was to the poetry's advantage, for it was hardly ever written merely to make it fit into a programme.

Because they claimed to feel and represent their own dynamic 'being-in-the-world', these writers looked on all Afro-American writers before them as their forerunners and discovered negritude in the earlier writers' works.

They were quite justified in this, seeing that all the literary schools of an era are, of course, the 'legitimate heirs' of their predecessors, and that in their predecessors' works, as I have tried to show, there really were African or Afro-American stylistic features and forms. Being very much on the look-out for these, the negritude writers were bound to notice them. So their own writings, besides developing new qualities, contain a good deal that is traditional, which has only been put into a wider and more comprehensive context. Indeed the whole history of neo-African literature can be recapitulated, as it were, in these writers' works.

Here are memories, as if from their own experience, of the days of slavery, its suffering and revolts. We read in Senghor:

> Car il faut bien que tu oublies ceux qui ont exporté dix
> millions de mes fils dans les maladreries de leurs navires
> Qui en ont supprimé deux cent millions.[50]

> 'For you must surely forget those who exported ten millions
> of my sons in the leper-houses of their ships,
> Who enslaved two hundred million of them.'[51]

And in Césaire:

> Et l'on nous vendait comme des bêtes,
> et l'on nous comptait les dents . . .
> et l'on nous tâtait les bourses
> et l'on examinait le cati ou décati de notre peau
> et l'on nous palpait et pesait et soupesait
> et l'on passait à notre cou de bête domptée le collier de la
> servitude et du sobriquet.[52]

> 'And they sold us like beasts,
> and they counted our teeth . . .
> and they felt our testicles
> and they tested the lustre or dullness of our skin
> and they felt over us and weighed us and weighed us up
> and round our tamed-beast necks they put the collar of
> slavery and of nickname.'

And in Damas:

> . . . sous le fouet qui se déchaîne
> sous le fouet qui fait marcher la plantation
> et s'abreuver de sang de mon sang de sang la sucrerie.[53]

> '. . . beneath the whip which rages
> beneath the whip which keeps the plantation going
> and bathes in the blood of my blood from the blood of the
> sugar works.'

Here are the themes, the stylistic forms and features of the Negro Renaissance, the Harlem atmosphere:

. . . où de bar en bar	'. . . where from bar to bar
où de verre en verre	where from glass to glass
j'ai saoulé ma peine	I drowned my pain
(à même) la piste enduite	right to the dance-floor
et patinée de steps	trodden and worn with steps
de stomps	with stomps
de slows	with slows
de songs	with songs
de sons	with sons
de blues[54]	with blues' (Damas)

Here is the Harlem anti-civilization primitivism in Senghor and Damas as well as Césaire. The symbols of civilization are worthless:

Vieille France, vieille Université et tout le chapelet déroulé[55]
(Senghor)

(the last words by a modernism might be translated as 'all that jazz')

The clothes are all wrong:

J'ai l'impression d'être ridicule	'I feel I am absurd
dans leurs souliers	in their shoes
dans leur smoking	in their dinner-jacket
dans leur plastron	in their stuffed shirt
dans leur faux-col.[56] (Damas)	in their stiff collar.'[57]

One must behave as a 'savage':

Et je boirai long longuement le sang fauve qui remonte à son
cœur
Le sang lait qui flue à sa bouche, les senteurs de terre
mouillée.[58] (Senghor)

'And I'll linger long drinking in the strong blood bubbling back
into her heart
The milk blood which spills into her mouth with the smells of
the sodden soil.'

for:

Pourquoi arracher mes sens païens qui crient?[59]

'Why try to tear out my pagan senses that shout?'

Eia pour ceux qui n'ont jamais rien inventé
pour ceux qui n'ont jamais rien exploré
pour ceux qui n'ont jamais rien dompté. . . .[60] (Césaire)

'Hurray for those who have never invented anything
for those who have never explored anything
for those who have never tamed anything.'[61]

So far these famous lines are merely repeating the old primitivism
in a louder voice. But then the poem soars directly to the heights of a
new negritude concept:

mais ils s'abandonnent, saisis, à l'essence de toute chose
ignorants des surfaces mais saisis par le mouvement de toute chose
insoucieux de dompter mais jouant le jeu du monde.

'but they give themselves up, possessed, to the essence of things,
ignoring the shells but possessed by the rhythm of things,
not caring to tame but working in well with the world.'

Naturally negritude also contains the exoticism of the Negro
Renaissance, and the longing for an imaginary Africa:

L'Afrique saigne, ma mère.[62] (Césaire)
'Africa, my mother, bleeds.'
Déjá me poignent le flanc les cents regrets du Pays noir[63]
  (Senghor)
'My side already burns with yearning hundredfold for the dark
  land'

> Rendez-les moi mes poupées noires
> mes poupées noires
> poupées noires
> noires.[64] (Damas)

> 'Give me back my black dolls
> my black dolls
> black dolls
> black.'[65]

Et nous baignerons mon amie dans une présence africaine
Des meubles de Guinée et du Congo, graves et polis, sombres et
  sereins.
Des masques primordiaux et purs aux murs, distants mais si
  présents![66] (Senghor)

'And we'll steep ourselves, sweet, in feelings deep of our Africa
  round about us,
With Guinea furniture and Congo too, heavy and smooth,
  sombre and serene.
With pure and primordial masks upon the walls, so far yet ever
  near.'[67]

A force de penser au Congo
je suis devenu un Congo bruissant de forêts et de fleuves.[68]
  (Césaire)

'From thinking of the Congo
I've turned into a Congo murmuring with forests and rivers.'

Then there is the voluptuous sensuality and flaunted vitality:

Femme nue, femme obscure
Fruit mûr à la chair ferme, sombres extases du vin noir.[69]
  (Senghor)

'Dark woman, naked woman,
Ripe fruit with flesh so firm, darkling delights of black wine.'[70]

Je charrie dans mon sang un fleuve de semences à feconder
  toutes les plaines de Byzance.[71] (Senghor)

'I carry in my blood a stream of fertile seed to impregnate all
  the wide plains of great Byzantium.'[72]

As in the writing of the Depression period, we find also an identification of race with class and the idea of a proletarian revolution:

Pour le dernier assaut contre les Conseils d'administration qui
  gouvernent les gouverneurs des colonies.[73] (Senghor)

'For the last assault against the councils of administration which
  govern the governors of colonies.'

La Marseillaise catholique.
Car nous sommes là tous réunis, divers le teint . . .
Divers de traits de costume de coutumes de langue; mais au fond
  des yeux la même mélopée de souffrances à l'ombre des longs
  cils fiévreux
Le Cafre le Kabyle le Somali le Maure, le Fân le Fôn le
  Bambara le Bobo le Mandiago
Le nomade le mineur le prestataire, le paysan et l'artisan le
  boursier et le tirailleur
Et tous les travailleurs blancs dans la lutte fraternelle.
Voici le mineur des Asturias le docker de Liverpool le juif
  chassé de l'Allemagne, et Dupont et Dupuis et tous les gars
  de Saint-Denis.[74] (Senghor)

'The true catholic Marseillaise.
For here we are all met as one, varied in hue . . .
Varied in features and costume and custom and tongue; but
  deep in the eyes the same sad chant of distress beneath the
  long feverish lashes
Kaffer Kabyle Somali and Moor, Fan Fon Bambara Bobo and
  Mandiago
Nomad and miner and slave, peasant and artisan, poor student
  and gunner

And all the white workers in the great fraternal struggle.
Here is the miner from Asturias the docker from Liverpool the
     Jew out of Germany driven, and Dupont and Dupuis and all
     the lads from Saint-Denis.'[75]

Significantly, however, the Negritude writers do not show any
trace of indigenism. They are too committed for that, identifying too
fervently with their subject. Césaire's portrayal of the Martinique
peasants in the first part of 'Retour au pays natal' is a document of
ecstatic compassion, a brilliant display of images soaring to a climax,
a volcano of exploding indignation. And Senghor is not describing
the funeral rites of other people, he is consorting with his own ancestors, is always on the most confidential terms with his dead, talks to
them, prays to the masks and puts himself under their protection:

Je songe dans la pénombre d'une après-midi.
Me visitent les fatigues de la journée
Les defunts de l'année, les souvenirs de la décade
Comme la procession des morts du village à l'horizon des tanns.*

C'est le même soleil mouillé de mirages
Le même ciel qu'énervent les presences cachées
Le même ciel redouté de ceux qui ont des comptes avec les
     morts
Voici que s'avancent mes mortes à moi.[76]

'I dream in the dim dusk-light of an afternoon
I am called on by the toils of all the day,
By the dead of the year, by the memories of the decade,
Like the long march of village dead right to the wide horizon
     of tanns.

It's the same sweet sun steeped in mirages,
The same sky perturbed by the beings concealed,
The same sky of dread for those who risk a reckoning with the
     dead
And here are my dead moving forward to me.'[77]

'All these references to the dead in Senghor's poetry,' Ulli Beier
writes, 'are not conscious statements or pronouncements of belief.
These are, on the contrary, images that rise in his mind not because
he is asserting his "negritude", but because he is an African and
allows himself to be one.'[78]

* Tanns—a Serer word for the extensive creek-like estuaries of Salum, Senghor's
home.

Herein lies the greatest achievement of negritude, that a genuine African feeling for life, and attitude to life, could be and was expressed in a European language. As shown above, this is just what the *philosophical* concept of negritude means; and here the term is used to denote a *literary* era. Here it attained the goal of a century's laborious searching by all Africa's exiles. Only an African could have attained this goal, an African, of course, who was assimilated enough to master a European language right to its last refinements.

This achievement was necessary before negritude could cross the ocean to Africa and help to free other Africans, threatened by the call for assimilation, who felt themselves trapped in Prospero's language. Birago Diop, also a Senegalese, immediately took the cue:

> Dans un des trois canaris
> des trois canaris où reviennent certain soirs
> les âmes satisfaites et sereines
> les souffles des ancêtres
> des ancêtres qui furent des hommes,
> des aïeux qui furent des sages,
> Mère a trempé trois doigts. . .[79]

> 'In one of the three pots
> the three pots to which some evenings there return
> the souls satisfied and serene
> the breath of the ancestors,
> of the ancestors who were men
> the grandsires who were sages,
> Mother dipped three fingers. . . .'[80]

Indigenism, on the other hand, with its folkloric realism, which aims at sympathetic description, is found only in negritude writers of the second rank, such as Paul Niger (1917-62) from Guadaloupe, who after studying in Paris became administrator in Katiola on the Ivory Coast. He wrote typical indigenist poetry like:

Mamadou, apprends-moi le chant pur de l'Afrique. . . .
Sous la blessure du Soleil
Sous le kapok de la lune courbe parfaite aux sens de géomètre
Le corps de Mamadou m'apprend le rythme de la brousse
Fuyance et devenir puissant chute
Source
Le corps d'Amadou n'est pas le corps sans parfum. . . .[81]

'Mamadou, teach me Africa's pure song. . . .'
Under the wound of the Sun
Under the kapok of the moon's curve so perfect in the
    geometrician's sense
Mamadou's body teaches me the rhythm of the bush
Flight and becoming powerful fall
Source
Mamadou's body is no body without a scent.'

The novel *Karim* by Ousmane Socé (born 1911) is also indigenist.
The deeds of the hero of the title, who tries to imitate his heroic
ancestors by daring his rivals to contests of extravagance, is described
without any complexities. It is the story of a good black Moslem told
in immaculate French, set in a Senegal accurately portrayed from a
folkloric angle. In his other novel, *Mirages de Paris*, Socé showed that
the theme of Paris was more in tune with the elegance of his pen.

Although indigenism is completely missing in the great negritude
writers, there are occasional passages reminiscent of negrism:

Et de la terre sourd le rythme, sève et sueur, une onde odeur de
    sol mouillé
Qui trémule les jambes de statue, les cuisses ouvertes au secret
Déferle sur la croupe, creuse les reins tend ventre gorges et
    collines
Proues de tam-tams. . . .[82] (Senghor)

'And rhythm springs from out the earth, its sap and its sweat,
    a wave with the scent of sodden soil,
Which will shiver the legs of a statue, the thighs to the open
    secret.
It breaks upon the rump, and hollows loins, and tenses belly,
    throat and breasts,
Prows of tom-toms.'

or

voum rooh oh
voum rooh oh
à charmer les serpents à conjurer les morts
voum rooh oh[83] (Césaire)

'To charm snakes, to conjure up the dead'

Whatever the negritude writers may owe to their predecessors, they
brought it into the great complex of their own conception. Even

when borrowing or taking over, they often excelled those earlier writers in inspiration and poetic power. Their self-confidence was firmly based on a real achievement.

One result of this self-confidence was that laughter could break in again, and was allowed free play. It is saying something that neo-African writing had not entirely lost its sense of humour, in spite of its history; but its laughter was the laughter of escapism, as with Langston Hughes and his famous book-title (and slogan) *Laughing to Keep from Crying*. The negritude writers could laugh from their hearts, because they believed in an African future. Many of their poems end, too, on a note of jubilant, self-confident optimism:

Car qui apprendrait le rythme au monde défunt des machines
    et des canons?
Qui pousserait le cri de joie pour réveiller morts et orphelins à
    l'aurore?
Dîtes, qui rendrait la mémoire de vie à l'homme aux espoirs
    éventrés?
Ils nous disent les hommes du coton, du café, de l'huile
Ils nous disent les hommes de la mort.
Nous sommes les hommes de la danse, dont les pieds reprennent
    vigueur en frappent le sol dur.[84] (Senghor)

'For who will be teachers of rhythm to a withered world, to a
    world of machines and guns?
Who will shout aloud for joy to waken the dead and orphans
    to the morning?
Who is to restore a new memory of life to a man with his hopes
    slit to bits?
Still they call us the men of cotton and oil and coffee,
Still they call us the men of death.
We are the men of the dance, with feet that find new strength
    again in stamping the hard soil.'[85]

La faiblesse de beaucoup d'hommes est qu'ils ne savent devenir
    ni une pierre ni un arbre
Pour moi j'installe parfois des mèches entre les doigts pour
    l'unique plaisir de m'enflammer en feuilles neuves de
    poinsettias tout le soir
rouges et verts tremblants au vent
comme dans ma gorge notre aurore.[86] (Césaire)

'The weakness of many men is that they don't know how to
    become a stone or a tree
As for me I sometimes stick tinder between my fingers sheerly
    for the pleasure of blazing up in new poinsettia leaves all
    evening
red and green trembling in the wind
as in my throat our dawn.'

4. Negritude and its Critics

'I think that negritude is dangerous,' writes David Rubadiri (born
1930) from Malawi, 'because its final result is to press down the
creative spirit, to tie it, sometimes so tight that a work of art becomes
meaningless.'[1]

Does he mean the sterile tying down of the mind by an ideology?
But the true poet does not let himself be tied, even when there is a
political power behind the ideology. When Césaire belonged to the
Communist Party, he was incapable of producing 'Party' poetry, his
work remained negritude poetry. No doubt Rubadiri means that the
poetry of negritude is anyhow insignificant, and he tries to prove this
by quoting Damas's primitivist lines, published in 1937:

> J'ai l'impression d'être ridicule
> avec mes orteils qui ne sont pas faits
> pour transpirer du matin jusqu'au soir qui déshabille
> avec l'emmaillotage qui m'affaiblit les membres
> et enlevent à mon corps sa beauté de cache-sexe.[2]

> 'I feel I am absurd
> with my toes which are not made
> for sweating from morning till evening's undressing
> with the swaddling which weakens my limbs
> and takes from my body its loin-cloth beauty.'[3]

Rubadiri comments: 'When you come to think of it, any self-
respecting nudist of any race could declare this.[4] Doesn't he know
what a poetic simile is?'

In fact Rubadiri is only sharpening the attack which Ezekiel
Mphahlele (born 1919) began in his book *The African Image*.
Mphahlele rejected Senghor's statement that emotion was 'Negro'
and advocated a poetic realism to be based on the poet's personal
experience. But this rejection was of negritude's ideology, which need

not affect one's judgement on negritude poetry; a non-Christian who asserted that Christian poetry must be bad would simply be showing that he knew nothing about poetry. The course Mphahlele recommended, on the other hand, merely indicated his personal preferences.

In his book Mphahlele's attitude was still relatively moderate, but in many conferences of recent years it has hardened to dogmatic and categorical assertions. For instance, he said in Berlin in 1964: 'There have even been attempts to read Senghor's poetry to the accompaniment of drums – poetry in French. I have heard this and I frankly must say I felt it was phoney. Because the rhythm of drums is just not the rhythm of French poetry.'[5]

This is a personal opinion, which can be countered by another personal opinion, that of Lilyan Kesteloot: 'Recently also, during a recital of Negro poetry at the Congolese University of Lovanium, the poem "Chaka" was delivered by a black student to a tom-tom accompaniment. It was astonishingly successful, and the whole of Leopoldville was talking about the "Senghor recital". Clear proof that this writer's poetry loses its apparent tonelessness when it is recited as it should be.'[6] Between these two contradictory opinions I shall express no further judgement until careful investigations of the Serers' musical rhythm have been completed, in reference to the obvious vowel and consonant patterns in Senghor's poetry. The question cannot be settled without comparing his poetical rhythms to the rhythms of his specific musical background.

Such investigation, which alone can resolve the dispute, would be futile, however, if one were to believe Mphahlele. According to him, the rhythms that each language employs because of its own inherent qualities as a language, whether French or English, are incapable of accommodating the rhythms of an African language. 'You write French, so you use French rhythms. You write an African language, you use the rhythms inherent to that language.'[7]

Yet European poetry has continually been influenced by classical rhythms. I am deliberately talking of poetry, not of language in general, as this would include not only prose but even everyday speech. The Afro-American rumba rhythm successfully penetrated into the Spanish poetry of Cuban negrism; there is Arabic metre and rhythm in Swahili; and Vilakazi tried hard to enhance his Zulu poetry with English rhymes, verse-forms and rhythms. One may justifiably ask in each case whether the attempt succeeded or failed, but one cannot exclude the very possibility of success. Many poems by Guillén, for instance, obviously succeeded.

Mphahlele did admit that idioms and symbols can indeed be carried over into another language 'with exciting results very often'.[8] But he then gave as contrary examples some translations from sentences in Bantu languages, where 'taste', 'feel' and 'smell' are expressed by 'hear' : 'Do you hear how it smells?'–'Take it, hear it, it's sweet.'[9] In the language of poetry, however, such usages are quite permissible. Édouard Maunick (born 1931) from Mauritius has a line which says : 'La lumière sentait l'iode'–the light smelt (or felt–here also a double meaning of 'sentir') of iodine (or the sea).

Gerald Moore too finds negritude poetry 'rhetorical' and sentimental. He stigmatizes as 'typographical tricks'[10] the attempts Damas made to clarify the rhythm by arranging his lines for visual effect; and declares that Césaire's technique is 'unmistakably surrealist'.[11] As evidence he quotes a passage where only the breaking of the lines in the English translation is absurd. They are long lines, and the narrow type-face of the original edition of 1947 could accommodate only 35 letters (including spaces). This number of letters was taken over in a later edition with a type-face not much wider. The lines were separated and broken up like prose just for the purpose of showing that two lines following each other always belong together :

> '(TOUSSAINT, TOUSSAINT
> L'OUVERTURE)
> is a man who fascin-
> ates the white hawk of white death
> is a man alone in the ster-
> ile sea of white sand
> is an ole darky braced against
> the waters of the sky.'[12]

Compare the original :

> (TOUSSAINT, TOUSSAINT L'OUVERTURE)
> c'est un homme qui fascine l'épervier blanc de la mort blanche
> c'est un homme seul dans la mer inféconde de sable blanc
> c'est un moricaud vieux dressé contre les eaux du ciel

Moreover, these critics cite only passages where the Negritude writers' new achievements recede from view; where the foreground is clearly occupied by the heritage which, as I showed in the previous section, they took over from the previous eras. This kind of presentation is unfair. It would be equally unfair to cite Rubadiri's poem 'A Negro Labourer in Liverpool',[13] parts of which are over-sentimental, but in line with Afro-American poetry at the beginning of this century; or to remind Mphahlele of his poetic conversation with the north wind,

> 'now lisping
> dead prophecies
> collected from ruins of lost empires'.[14]

Such quotations do not characterize the whole work of these writers.

Again, the critics in question are writing in English. Their criticism is based on what is often an inadequate translation, in which the rhythms and melodies of the negritude writers are lost. Thus the examples of Senghor's rhythms which I gave in Section 3 (pp. 245–6) go like this in the translation by John Reed and Clive Wake (only in the case of D is there something like a phonetic equivalent to Senghor's internal harmonies):

A. And when in his shadow it fell silent, the drums sounded from the insistent *tanns*[15]
B. No more advance in the eager trembling of equal bodies equal shoulders[16]
C. My heart pounding with the warrior gallop of the *dyoung-dyoungs*, great gallop of my blood my pure blood.[17]
D. Precious pelts bars of salt and gold from Bouré, of gold from Boundou.[18]

There is a saying by Wole Soyinka (born 1934): 'I don't think a tiger has to go around proclaiming his tigritude.'[19] Referring to this in his two books Gerald Moore remarks that 'this attitude is a trifle unfair'.[20] Moore would have us think that Africa's authors writing in English, especially the younger Nigerian school, reject negritude, and that this school simply accept the individualist stream recommended by Mphahlele–the idea that there is no such thing as a negritude, a 'being African'. The result has been violent arguments between French-writing and English-writing African authors, on the 'motion', as it were, of 'Tigritude versus Negritude'.

Soyinka put the record straight at the Berlin conference in 1964: 'As Aimé Césaire said, it is quite common for things to be quoted out of context and for portraits to be issued by foreign critics and even by African interviewers which end up by a little bit of distorting the real image. The point is this that, to quote what I said fully, I said: "A tiger does not proclaim his tigritude, he pounces." In other words: a tiger does not stand in the forest and say: "I am a tiger." When you pass where the tiger has walked before, you see the skeleton of the duiker, you know that some tigritude has been emanated there. In other words: the distinction which I was making at this conference (in Kampala, Uganda, 1962) was a purely literary one : I was trying to distinguish between propaganda and true poetic creativity. I was saying in other words that what one expected from poetry was an intrinsic poetic quality, not a mere name-dropping.'[21]

So a tiger's tigritude or tigerishness must be expressed in his work. This is just what the theorists of negritude have claimed, so the critic may legitimately look for and define the quality of 'tigerishness' in the 'tiger's' work.

Nigeria's young neo-African writers, except for Gabriel Gbaing-bain Okara (born 1921), were all born between 1931 and 1935. Their attitude to the negritude writers born between 1906 and 1913 is like that of sons to fathers–which might explain a certain animosity. They have become writers in the conditions of political and cultural independence which the older writers had to fight hard for. They did not have to resist assimilation or work out decades of exile. They could take advantage of the freedom which negritude had won them: freedom from the tyranny of the European model as the sole standard of all poetic values; freedom to write as an African in European languages without having having to 'proclaim' that they were Africans; freedom, therefore, to write just as prompted by their environment, upbringing and talent. Since then, in consequence, it has depended only on the quality of their work whether they produce the effect which negritude had always demanded; that the African image, the African rhythm, should be authentic, that the 'tiger' should be recognizable as such by his activities, and should not be mistaken for a polar bear.

These Nigerian writers are the legitimate heirs of negritude, and they know it. Caliban's victory and break-out from the prison of Prospero's language is now a thing taken for granted. Chinua Achebe (born 1931) writes: 'The English language will be able to carry the weight of my African experience. But it will have to be a new English, still in full communion with its ancestral home but altered to suit its new African surroundings.'[22] Yet they are not the heirs of negritude alone: by their own choice they are also the heirs to all the poetic experiences of Europe and America as well as to their native African traditions. Their windows are open all round, so open that they recognize also the differences within the African traditions.

The best compact survey of Africa's English-speaking literature is probably an essay by John Pepper Clark (born 1935), who writes:

'The truth is that these differences do exist among the numerous peoples of Africa, forming for each that special cultural make-up and sensibility of which any artist anywhere must partake . . . before he can bring forth any work of meaning to his people and mankind in general.'[23] And then: 'A person can be African by birth or race and yet be unable to produce work in either English or French that is of the African experience, with due respect, of course, to his particular portion of the continent. . . .[24] The West African . . . swims in a stream of double currents, one traditional, the other modern.'[25] He is ' "modern" and "traditional" at the same time, making him a citizen of two worlds.'[26]

Clark speaks only for the West African. Obiajunwa Wali (born 1932) adds: '. . . traditional African society on the one hand, and the colonial experience on the other, constitute some uniformity in their own ways for the African, irrespective of geography and theory.'[27] The only further remark I would make here is that there is probably an additional point of unity, connected with a specific rhythm. So far I can only formulate negatively this inner unity of African culture: rhythm and dancing can be found all over the world, but Africa is the place where you cannot live without dancing, where life without dancing would cease to be life.

The young Nigerian writers are the heirs to several traditions and they are therefore also heirs to negritude. They are closer than they perhaps suppose to the young French-speaking African writers like Tchicaya U Tam'si (born 1931) from the Congo, Édouard Maunick from Mauritius (an African by his own choice), Lamine Diakhaté (born 1929) and Sembène Ousmane (born 1923) from Senegal–to name only the most important. Like these, the Nigerians also show influences from negritude. Verses 2 and 4 in Clark's poem 'Agbor Dancer' are surely not far removed from negritude poetry:

> See how entangled in the magic
> Maze of music
> In trance she treads the intricate
> Pattern rippling crest after crest
> To meet the green clouds of the forest
>
> Could I, early sequester'd from my tribe
> Free a lead-tether'd scribe
> I should answer her communal call
> Lose myself in her warm caress
> Intervolving earth, sky and flesh.[28]

And many lines in the poetry of Christopher Okigbo (1932–67)
could almost come from Senghor:

> MASKS and beggar-masks
> without age or shadow
> Broken tin-gods whose
> vision is dissolved. . . .[29]

or:

> They say
> They will come and take away
> Our drumheads
> They say
> They will take our drumheads
> Into exile
>
> And mangle our tendons
> Puncture our membranes
>
> They say
> They will come and strip us
> Of our thunder. . . .
>
> If they should come today
> And ask for a praise song
>
> Tell them
> We have tuned our raw hides
> For a waking.[30]

Here is an authenticity of image and rhythm such as Damas set
out before to achieve. Achebe finds that 'you cannot cram African
literature into a small, neat definition. . . . I do not see African literature as one unit but as a group of associated units—in fact the sum
total of all the *national* and *ethnic* literatures of Africa.'[31]

To a large extent I agree with this, and that is why my history of
neo-African literature draws to a close with the radiations of negritude affecting a few present-day writers. In another volume, to be
organized less historically and more according to regional styles, I
shall deal with the neo-African literature of the present, i.e. the
literature of all African and Afro-American writers who have become
known since 1950.

I have deliberately refrained from mentioning the European influences on present-day African writers—from Chaucer to Eliot and
Pound, from Chrétien de Troyes to Saint-John Perse and Claudel—

because almost all European critics stress such influences exclusively wherever they spot them. No doubt they are not equipped to discover the non-European influences; or so one may charitably assume. So my book should be considered as complementary to the works of these critics, serving in some small way to redress the balance.

But for those who would put down any influence from European literature as a triumph of Europe over another culture, I would remind them of Caliban and Prospero. Through his arrogance Prospero was just as much a prisoner as Caliban. By continually harping on his own 'noble nature' and on the lowliness of Caliban the 'savage', Prospero reveals only his weakness, insecurity, guilty conscience and the fact that he is confined within the four walls of his 'biological' ideology. Caliban's emancipation, his break-out from the prison of Prospero's language, gives Prospero too a chance of freedom, I would repeat. But of course it does not set him free automatically.

He can ignore Caliban's free and expanded language. He can try to persuade himself that he has still got Caliban trapped in the 'Prospero' language and attitudes. He can go on taking Caliban's new free language for the 'gabble' which he once taught Caliban. In this way he can go on being the language instructor, and consider language (in Lamming's words) as his way of 'measuring the distance which separates him from Caliban.'[32] Prospero can preserve his arrogance so long as he closes his ears and gives up his own rights to a world of freedom and humanity. The writers of Negritude were indeed vehement and often strident. They were trying to break through Prospero's deafness.

REFERENCES AND BIBLIOGRAPHIES

1. Caliban and Prospero

[1] Act I, Scene 2, lines 331–47, 353–65.
[2] Lamming, pp. 109 f.
[3] Act III, Scene 2, lines 144–52.
[4] Act III, Scene 2, lines 96–7, 99–103.

LAMMING, George: The pleasures of exile. London 1960 (No. 1650)
MANNONI, O.: Psychologie de la colonisation. Paris 1950
  (Prospero and Caliban; the psychology of colonization. New York 1956)

2. The Achievements of Negritude
3. The Meaning of Negritude

[1] Senghor 1948, p. 51.
[2] Kesteloot, p. 92.
[3] ibid., p. 94.
[4] McKay, p. 267.
[5] Césaire 1941, p. 41 f.
[6] Senghor 1945, p. 33.
[7] Jahn 1961, pp. 144 f.
[8] Senghor, L'ésprit. . . ., p. 62.
[9] Senghor, Éthiopiques, p. 123; cf. 1965, p. 96
[10] Kesteloot, p. 194 f.
[11] Senghor, Poèmes, p. 29.
[12] cf. Senghor, Selected poems, p. 12.
[13] Senghor, Poèmes, p. 69.
[14] cf. Senghor, Selected poems, p. 36.
[15] Senghor, Poèmes, p. 58.
[16] cf. Senghor, Selected poems, p. 30.
[17] Kesteloot, p. 195.
[18] Senghor, Poèmes, p. 32.
[19] cf. Senghor, Selected poems, p. 15.
[20] Kesteloot, p. 196.
[21] Senghor, Poèmes, p. 28.
[22] Senghor 1961, p. 59.
[23] cf. Senghor, Selected poems, p. 89.
[24] Damas 1962, p. 17; 1964, p. 54.
[25] Damas 1952, p. 16.
[26] Damas 1956, p. 50.
[27] Senghor, Éthiopiques, p. 118; cf. 1965, p. 94.
[28] Senghor, L'esprit. . . ., p. 60; 1965, p. 87.
[29] Césaire 1948, p. 72.
[30] Senghor 1959, p. 14.
[31] Kesteloot, pp. 110–14.
[32] Senghor 1959, p. 14.
[33] Senghor, Éthiopiques, p. 120; cf. 1965, p. 94.
[34] Senghor 1948, p. 173.
[35] Senghor, Éthiopiques, p. 116.
[36] Sartre 1948, p. xxxi.
[37] Césaire 1960, p. 89.
[38] Senghor 1959, p. 25.

[39] ibid., p. 14.
[40] Césaire 1960, p. 73; cf. 1958, p. 40.
[41] Senghor 1959, p. 14.
[42] Senghor, Poèmes, p. 37; cf. Selected poems, p. 19.
[43] Sartre 1948, p. xxix.
[44] Césaire 1960, p. 46.
[45] Senghor, Poèmes, p. 83; 1965, pp. 132 f.
[46] Césaire 1960, p. 65.
[47] Senghor to Kesteloot, op. cit., p. 110.
[48] Senghor 1959, p. 14.
[49] Jan 1964, pp. 56, 58.
[50] Senghor, Poèmes, p. 93.
[51] cf. Senghor, Selected poems, p. 49.
[52] Césaire 1946, p. 165.
[53] Damas 1962, p. 45.
[54] Damas 1956, pp. 14, 57.
[55] Senghor, Poèmes, p. 31; cf. Selected poems, p. 14.
[56] Damas 1962, p. 39.
[57] cf. Damas 1958, p. 25.
[58] Senghor, Poèmes, p. 196.
[59] ibid., p. 189; cf. Selected poems, p. 59.
[60] Césaire 1960, pp. 73 f.
[61] cf. Césaire 1958, p. 40.
[62] Césaire 1946, p. 123.
[63] Senghor, Poèmes, p. 137.
[64] Damas 1962, p. 43.
[65] Damas 1958, p. 24.
[66] Senghor, Poèmes, p. 177.
[67] cf. Senghor, Selected poems, p. 57.
[68] Césaire 1960, p. 50.
[69] Senghor, Poèmes, p. 16.
[70] cf. Senghor, Selected poems, p. 6.
[71] Senghor, Poèmes, p. 199.
[72] cf. Senghor, Selected poems, p. 89.
[73] Senghor, Poèmes, p. 60; cf. 1965, p. 126.
[74] Senghor, Poèmes, p. 61.
[75] Senghor 1965, pp. 126 f.
[76] Senghor, Poèmes, pp. 45 f.
[77] cf. Moore/Beier, p. 50.
[78] Beier, p. 17.
[79] Senghor 1948, p. 143; Diop 1960, p. 71.

[80] cf. Moore/Beier, pp. 64 f.
[81] Niger, p. 31.
[82] Senghor, Poèmes, p. 144.
[83] Césaire 1960, p. 52.
[84] Senghor, Poèmes, pp. 23 f.
[85] cf. Senghor, Selected poems, p. 9; cf. Moore/Beier, pp. 49 f.
[86] Césaire 1948, p. 88.

A. Literary Works and Anthologies

CÉSAIRE, Aimé: Les armes miraculeuses. Paris 1946 (No. 1375)
–Soleil cou-coupé. Paris 1948 (No. 1376)
–Four poems, translated by Miriam Koshland: Since Akkad, since
　Elam, since Sumer; Word; Africa; from: 'Notes on a return to
　the native country.' In: Black Orpheus, No. 2, Ibadan, January
　1958
–Cahier d'un retour au pays natal. Éd. définitive. 2nd ed. Paris 1960
　(Nos. 1372-4)
　(Bilingual edition, French and English on opposite pages: Cahier
　d'un retour au pays natal, précédé par Un grand poète noir, par
　André Breton, with translations by Lionel Abel and Ivan Goll.
　New York: Brentano's 1947. No pagination (158 pp.)–Half title:
　Memorandum on my Martinique.)
DAMAS, Léon-Gontran: Graffiti. Paris 1952 (No. 1435)
–Black-Label. Paris 1956 (No. 1436)
–Two poems, translated by Miriam Koshland: Black dolls–Balance
　sheet. In: Black Orpheus, No. 2, Ibadan, January 1958
–African songs of love, war, grief and abuse. Translated by Miriam
　Koshland and Ulli Beier. Ibadan 1961 (No. 1437)
–Pigments. Éd. définitive. Paris 1962 (No. 1431)
–Four poems: Obsession–For sure–According to my legend–Good
　breeding (from 'Pigments'). In: Black Orpheus, No. 14, Ikeja,
　February 1964
–Névralgies. Paris: Présence Africaine 1966. 79 pp. Lyr
DIOP, Birago: Les contes d'Amadou Koumba. Paris 1947 and 1961
　(Nos. 234–5)
　(Tales of Amadou Koumba. Translated by Dorothy Blair. London:
　Oxford University Press 1966. 158 pp.)
–Leurres et lueurs. Paris 1960 (No. 237)
MCKAY, Claude: Banjo. New York 1929 (Nos. 1691–2)

MOORE, Gerald and BEIER, Ulli: Modern poetry from Africa. Harmondsworth, Middlesex 1963 (No. 37)

NIGER, Paul: Initiation. Paris 1954 (No. 1828)

SENGHOR, Léopold Sédar: Anthologie de la nouvelle poésie nègre et malgache de langue française. Paris 1948 (No. 15)

–Éthiopiques. Paris 1956 (No. 557)

–Nocturnes. Paris 1961 (No. 560)

–Poèmes. Paris 1964 (No. 548)

–Selected poems; translated by John Reed and Clive Wake. London/ New York 1964 (No. 564)

–Prose and poetry. Selected and translated by John Reed and Clive Wake. London: Oxford University Press 1965. vi, 181 pp. (A three crowns book.) Es+Lyr

SOCÉ, Ousmane: Karim. Paris 1935 and 1948 (No. 574)

–Mirages de Paris. Paris 1937 and 1956 (No. 575)

B. Secondary Literature

ALLEN, Samuel W.: Negritude: agreement and disagreement. Pp. 310–23 in: Pan-Africanism reconsidered. Ed. by the American Society of African Culture. Berkeley and Los Angeles 1962

BEIER, Ulli: The theme of the ancestors in Senghor's poetry. In: Black Orpheus, No. 5, Ibadan 1959

CÉSAIRE, Aimé: in the journal Tropiques, No. 2, Fort-de-France, Martinique, July 1941

DAMAS, Léon-Gontran: The birth of negritude. (Extract from a talk given in New York on 14th Jan. 1965.) In: AMSAC Newsletter, vol. 7, No. 5, New York 1965

FRANKLIN, Albert: La négritude: réalité ou mystification? Réflexions sur 'Orphée noir'. In: Les étudiants noirs parlent . . . Présence Africaine, No. 14, Paris 1953

GRUNEBAUM, G. E. von: French African literature: some cultural implications. The Hague 1964

GUIBERT, Armand: Léopold Sédar Senghor, l'homme et l'œuvre. Paris 1962

JAHN, Janheinz: Muntu. London/New York 1961

–Value conceptions in sub-Saharan Africa. Pp. 55–69 in: Cross-cultural understanding, arranged and edited by F. S. C. Northrop and Helen H. Livingston. New York 1964

JUIN, Hubert: Aimé Césaire, poète noir. Paris 1956

KAGAME, Alexis: La philosophie băntu-rwandaise de l'être. Brussels 1956

KESTELOOT, Lilyan: Les écrivains noirs de langue française: naissance d'une littérature. Brussels 1963

MAINBERGER, Gonsalv: Eschatologie évangélique et idéologies néo-africaines. In: L'Afrique et le monde en transformation. 7e séminaire annuel d'étudiants africains chrétiens. Geneva, from 3 to 10 April 1964 (mimeographed)

MELONE, Thomas: De la négritude dans la littérature africaine. Paris 1962

MOORE, Gerald: Seven African writers. London 1962

PIQUION, René: Négritude. Port-au-Prince 1961

SARTRE, Jean-Paul: Orphée noir. Foreword in Senghor: Anthologie de la nouvelle poésie nègre et malgache de langue française. Paris 1948 (No. 15)
(Black Orpheus. Translated by S. W. Allen. Paris: Eds. Présence Africaine 1963)

SENGHOR, Léopold Sédar: Trois poètes négro-américains. In: Poésie 45, No. 23, Paris 1945

–L'esprit de la civilisation ou les lois de la culture négro-africaine. In: Présence Africaine, No. VIII–X, Paris 1956

–Rapport sur la doctrine et la propagande du parti. Speech at the 'Congrès constitutif du Parti du Rassemblement Africain', 1959, mimeographed MS.

–Liberté I: Négritude et humanisme. Paris 1964 (No. 566)

TEMPELS, Placied: Bantoe-filosofie. Antwerp 1946
(Bantu philosophy. Translated into English from La philosophie bantoe, the French version by A. Rubbens of Fr. Temples' original work. Colin King, translator. Paris: Éds. Présence Africaine 1959)

THOMAS, Louis-Vincent: Les idéologies négro-africaines d'aujourd'-hui. Dakar 1965

–Panorama de la négritude. In: Actes du colloque sur la littérature africaine d'expression française, Dakar, 26–9 Mars 1963. Dakar 1965

–Senghor à la recherche de l'homme nègre. In: Présence fAricaine, No. 54, Paris, 2e trimestre 1965

WAUTHIER, Claude: L'Afrique des Africains. Paris 1964
(The literature and thought of modern Africa. Translated by Shirley Kay. London 1966)

4. Negritude and its Critics

[1] Rubadiri, p. 41.
[2] Damas 1962, p. 39.
[3] cf. Damas 1958, p. 25.
[4] Rubadiri, p. 41.
[5] My tape.
[6] Kesteloot, p. 197.
[7] My tape.
[8] ibid.
[9] ibid.
[10] Moore, p. 4.
[11] Moore/Beier, pp. 16 f.
[12] Césaire, p. 47.
[13] in Reed/Wake, pp. 70 f.
[14] Mphahlele 1959, p. 24.
[15] Senghor, p. 12.
[16] ibid., p. 36.
[17] ibid., p. 30.
[18] ibid., p. 15.
[19] Moore, p. xvi; Moore/Beier, p. 18.
[20] Moore/Beier, p. 18.
[21] My tape.
[22] Achebe, p. 30.
[23] Clark 1965, p. 21.
[24] ibid.
[25] ibid., p. 24.
[26] ibid.
[27] Wali, p. 33.
[28] Clark 1962, p. 12.
[29] Okigbo, p. 17.
[30] ibid., p. 16.
[31] Achebe, p. 27.
[32] Lamming, p. 110.

ACHEBE, Chinua: English and the African writer. In: Transition, vol. 4, NO. 18, Kampala, Uganda, 1965

CÉSAIRE, Aimé: Cahier d'un retour au pays natal. Éd. définitive. Paris 1956 (Nos. 1372–4); bilingual ed., French and English, see page 272

CLARK, John Pepper: Poems. Ibadan 1962 (No. 185)

–Poetry in Africa today. In: Transition, vol. 4, No. 18, Kampala 1965

DAMAS, Léon-Gontran: Two poems, translated by Miriam Koshland: Black dolls–Balance sheet. In: Black Orpheus, No. 2, Ibadan, January 1958,

–Pigments. Éd. définitive. Paris 1962 (No. 1431)

IRELE, Abiola: A defence of negritude. À propos of 'Black Orpheus' by Jean-Paul Sartre. In: Transition, vol. 3, No. 13, Kampala, March/April 1964.

JAHN, Janheinz: Senghor without propeller: an English translation that does not get off the ground. In: Black Orpheus, No. 19, Ikeja, March 1966

JEANPIERRE, W.: Négritude and its enemies (with a reply by Ezekiel Mphahlele). In: African literature and the universities, ed. Gerald Moore. Ibadan 1965

KESTELOOT, Lilyan: Les écrivains noirs de langue française: naissance d'une littérature. Brussels 1963

LAMMING, George: The pleasures of exile. London 1960 (No. 1650)

MAUNICK, Édouard: Les manèges de la mer. Paris 1964 (No. 675)

MOORE, Gerald: Seven African writers. London 1962

MOORE, Gerald and BEIER, Ulli: Modern poetry from Africa. Harmondsworth 1963 (No. 37)

MPHAHLELE, Ezekiel: The immigrant. In: Black Orpheus, No. 6, Ibadan 1959

–The African image. London/New York 1962 (No. 1035)

–The fabric of African cultures. In: Foreign Affairs, vol. 42, No. 4, Lancaster, Pa., July 1964

OKIGBO, Christopher: Lament of the drums. In: Transition, vol. 4, No. 18, Kampala 1965

PIQUION, René: Manuel de négritude. Port-au-Prince 1966

REED, John and WAKE, Clive: A book of African verse. London 1964 (No. 42)

RUBADIRI, David: Why African literature? In: Transition, vol. 4, No. 15, Kampala 1964

SENGHOR, Léopold Sédar: Selected poems. London 1964 (No. 564)

SOYINKA, Wole: And after the narcissist? In: African Forum, vol. 1, No. 4, New York, Spring 1966

WALI, Obiajunwa: The individual and the novel in Africa. In: Transition, vol. 4, No. 18, Kampala 1965

Chapter 16

CONCLUSION: TOWARDS MODERN
AFRICAN LITERATURE

The doctor and essayist Frantz Fanon (1925–61) from Martinique, an outstanding social and literary critic, who took an active part in the Algerian fight for freedom, saw the whole literature of the 'colonized peoples' as a direct line from assimilation to the fight for freedom, i.e. from conformism to protest. He expresses it as follows:

'If we wished to recapitulate through the works of colonized writers the different phases which characterize that evolution, we should see a panorama unfolding before our eyes in three phases. In the first, the colonized intellectual proves that he has assimilated the occupier's culture. His works correspond point by point with those of his metropolitan equivalents. The inspiration is European, and these works can easily be grouped with a well-defined movement in the metropolitan literature. This is the completely assimilationist period. In this literature of the colonized you will find "parnassians", symbolists, surrealists.

'In a second period the colonized writer becomes uncertain and decides to go back into his past. . . . But as he is not integrated with his people, as his relations with them are from outside, he confines himself to remembering. Old episodes of childhood will be brought up from deep down in his memory, old legends will be reinterpreted according to "borrowed" aesthetics and a conception of the world discovered beneath different skies. Sometimes this pre-struggle literature will be dominated by humour and by allegory. A period of anguish, of uneasiness, experience of death and also of disgust. He is sickened with himself; but already, from below, laughter is breaking through.

'Finally, in the third period, called the struggle, the colonized writer, after trying to lose himself in the people and with the people, sets out, on the contrary, to shake them out of their lethargy. . . . Here is protest literature, revolutionary literature, national literature. During this phase there are a large number of men and women who

277

before would never have thought of producing literary work; but now that they find themselves placed in exceptional circumstances – e.g. in prison, in the resistance, or on the eve of their execution – they feel the need to tell their country, to compose the sentence which expresses the people's will, to make themselves the mouthpiece of a new reality of action.'[1]

Fanon wrote as a fighter. In his situation, in the bloody and dirty war for freedom or annihilation, literature was no more than just another weapon. This is where we can see a parallel between Fanon and Mphahlele. In South Africa, as previously in Algeria, the battle is what matters. Who cares whether a partisan's sword-hilt is made of silver or alloy? This is no time for stylistics: literature, like a blade, is judged by its power to cut.

In such a situation literature is reduced to three alternatives: assimilation, escapism or rebellion; exoticism has always been close to escapism. In a context like this literature as a weapon is either blunt, jagged or serviceable; and when the battle is won, the weapon is no longer needed. Fanon's analysis leaves no room for a free literature of independent writers, such as has grown up in the last few years in many parts of Africa. His literary-history-in-three-phases does not include freedom.

But perhaps Fanon only meant that *colonial* literature ends when freedom begins, and that liberation makes it possible for a free, national or – as the case may be – international literature to arise. But if that is all he meant, it seems rather a 'glimpse of the obvious', expressed in a roundabout way.

If we first consider Fanon's three phases according to subject matter, they did not really form a chronological sequence of consent, confusion and struggle, in their relation to colonialism. For struggle or protest was there from the beginning. Revolt is inherent in slavery, and so is protest in 'apprentice literature'. The literature of struggle was born almost as soon as the alphabet was there. Mphahlele justifiably quotes a poem by an Xhosa writer, who called himself Hadi Waseluhlangeni (the people's harp), from 1884:

> 'I turn my back on the many shams
> That I see from day to day;
> It seems we march to our very grave
> Encircled by a smiling Gospel.
>
> For what is this Gospel?
> And what is salvation?

> The shade of a fabulous hili [ghost]
> That we try to embrace in vain.'[2]

Nor can protest and struggle be abstracted from exoticism, Fanon's second phase. The exotic elements in 'Negro Renaissance' indigenism and negrism are already more than a mere escape from reality; they are also defence weapons against prejudice. And the negritude writers did not hunt up childhood memories because they felt confused or sentimental; they looked for Africa, wrote about it and glorified it, to contrast it with Europe. They did not cry 'Back to the Sources' because they wanted to opt out of the struggle and retreat to Frobenius's 'Island of the Blest' or some other Paradise Lost, but to find a source of spiritual power for the struggle. They were demonstrating that they were different, as a protest against assimilation; so literature was a weapon in the struggle. In South Africa, where the enemy was too strong and the fighter needed a breathing-space, a glorification of the simple traditional life was sometimes escapism; but only there. Concern with the past is not itself escapism, of course; but in this case assessment of the past conformed all too often with the assessment of the oppressor, who accordingly favoured such writings.

So the phase of struggle, with the writer rousing the people, which Fanon saw as the third phase chronologically, was there right from the start. There are very few African or Afro-American writers who did *not* wish to rouse their people, their fellow victims of oppression.

If we now consider Fanon's three phases at stylistic level, the first phase does partly fit. African writers were obliged, in their struggle against foreign prejudice and tutelage, to use the style and language of Europeans as taught in European capitals. But this is not the whole story. For there were quite a number of African writers who used predominantly African stylistic forms. One of the early writers, Mqhayi (see p. 104), even expressed his protest against colonialism in the style of a typically African praise- and mocking-song. Here is an extract (in A. C. Jordan's translation) from his poem recited in 1925 when the Prince of Wales was touring South Africa:

> 'Ah, Britain! Great Britain!
> Great Britain of the endless sunshine!
> She hath conquered the oceans and laid them low;
> She hath drained the little rivers and lapped them dry;
> She hath swept the little nations and wiped them away;
> And now she is making for the open skies.

> She sent us the preacher: she sent us the bottle,
> She sent us the Bible, and barrels of brandy;
> She sent us the breechloader, she sent us cannon;
> O Roaring Britain! Which must we embrace?
> You sent us the truth, denied us the truth;
> You sent us the life, deprived us of life;
> You sent us the light, we sit in the dark,
> Shivering, benighted in the bright noonday sun.'[3]

Nor did such protest in traditional forms occur only in South Africa. Ephraim Amu in Ghana, in the first quarter of this century, was already composing his songs from African motifs and with African rhythms. They are in the Twi language and there is no alienation from the people: they are still sung today. But even then Amu was not only on the look-out for specific African forms of the Christian hymn, he was also just what Fanon called a 'rouser'. His song 'Hearken, you Africans!' contains these lines:

> 'We've seen it all before,
> We hear and we see,
> What happens makes us sore.
> The rest are all ahead!
> The rest are all ahead!
> But now we take our chance,
> We too must now advance.'[4]

The style of the 'second phase', according to Fanon, rests on a psychological reaction: 'The colonized intellectual has thrown himself eagerly into Western culture. But just when the nationalist parties are mobilizing the people in the name of national independence, he may sometimes throw off these acquisitions which suddenly strike him as alien. Yet it is easier to proclaim your rejection than to go through with it. . . .'[5]

According to Fanon, the African intellectual who has gained a foothold in Western civilization and adapted his whole outlook to fit his new role, soon finds he is no match for those who have grown up in the dazzling cultural tradition he is trying so hard to acquire, which is displayed in a glorious panorama by the dominating power. Hence he feels rejected and is compelled to look elsewhere for cultural support. Unable to find anything to compare with that panorama he has glimpsed, he is forced to withdraw into himself. But being endowed with unusual sensibility, as well as a hypersensitive reaction to his environment, he now develops typical symptoms, first of withdrawal and then of frustrated protest.

Fanon, however, has unconsciously accepted European standards of value, in questioning whether Africa can provide the inspiration a writer needs. The ideas and reactions described by Fanon may, no doubt, represent the personal experience of particular writers, but how general is such a picture? Are there really no qualities to be found in the African tradition which might satisfy a writer, stimulate his mind, enrich his style? Has the writer no other function but to pour out on to paper his own emotions? Fanon's attitude here is quite close to that of Jean Wagner (see pp. 188–91).

Fanon has generalized from a very limited sample of writers, and even derives a whole style from his generalization: 'This offers sufficient explanation for the style of the colonized intellectuals who decide to express such a phase of awareness in the process of self-emancipation. A jerky style full of images. A nervy style vitalized by rhythm, thoroughly imbued with explosive life. Highly coloured too, bronzed, sunlit, violent.'[6]

Césaire's style may be partly explained along these lines, but they will not even work with Senghor, whose style is not jerky or nervy. It is not surprising that Fanon's conclusions are at best only partly correct, because the methods he uses are inadequate: he tries to interpret literature purely psychologically, completely overlooking the historical aspect of particular literatures. Human reactions to similar situations will no doubt always resemble each other. A rejected lover, for instance, will have similar feelings, and will behave in the same sort of way, in all ages and among all peoples. But the style of the literary works originating from these reactions is not only different from writer to writer but also from one stylistic era to another. Certain stylistic modes and *genres*, after all, are not equally available to everyone in every age; they will appear, be developed and passed on, at particular times.

Two centuries before Petrarch no lover was writing sonnets, because the sonnet only made its appearance in the thirteenth century. And ten years before Guillén no poet would have produced poetry in rumba rhythms, even if he had been psychologically in the same situation as Guillén. Yet the sonnet originated in the thirteenth century, because it corresponded to a particular need, a historically specific pattern of thought, a historically explicable mental attitude.

Similarly, in the course of the history of neo-African literature, new literary forms and stylistic features grew up, with European and

African stylistic elements mixed in varying degree. They grew up in a process of laborious searching and striving, between advances and setbacks, in a process which is mainly characterized by the continuous adoption of African stylistic elements into a written literature. This happened at first hesitantly and gropingly, then more and more consciously, deliberately, intensively, successfully and rapidly – because every writer who pressed ahead on a path already taken, could rely on the experience and success of his predecessors. It is the task of those who write literary history to describe this process, this historical chain of stylistic changes and innovations.

All purely psychological, political or sociological interpretations, therefore, must always remain inadequate, for they neglect the aspect which makes literature what it is. Psychology, however, can explain why particular literary critics adopt towards literary phenomena the attitudes that they do.

Any idea once given a literary form, any image once brought into a poem, any rhythm once adopted, is a heritage at the disposal of the current generation of writers. The present generation of African writers has a choice, therefore, of a great many traditions from which to create new traditions of their own. There is the heritage of assimilationism, which embodies all the trends from Western literature. There is the heritage of African protest, which played a big part in all the historical trends of neo-African culture. There is the heritage of the long laborious road taken by the Afro-Americans in search of their identity and their African roots, to which negritude gave direct access for the first time. And there is the rich heritage, still not exhausted, of Africa's oral literature. In another volume I shall be investigating how the African and Afro-American writers in the last two decades have reacted and are reacting to these manifold traditions. Thus History will shed its light on the present.

REFERENCES AND BIBLIOGRAPHIES

[1] Fanon, pp. 166 f.
[2] Mphahlele, p. 168.
[3] Drachler, p. 84.
[4] Wiegräbe, p. 21.
[5] Fanon 1961, pp. 164f .
[6] ibid., p. 165.

ABRAHAMS, Peter: The path of thunder. New York 1948; London 1952 (Nos. 779–801)

–Tell freedom. London/New York 1954 (Nos. 809–16)

AMU, Ephraim: 25 songs in the Twi language. London 1932

DHLOMO, Herbert I. E.: Valley of a thousand hills. Durban 1941 (No. 860)

DRACHLER, Jacob: African heritage. Intimate views of the black Africans from life, lore, and literature. Selected and edited, with an introduction, by Jacob Drachler. Preface by Melville J. Herskovits. New York: Collier Books 1964. 286 pp. Anth.

FANON, Frantz: Les damnés de la terre. Paris 1961 (No. 1487)

(The wretched of the earth. Preface by Jean-Paul Sartre. Transl. from the French by Constance Farrington. New York: Grove Press 1965. 255 pp.)

MAINBERGER, Gonsalv: Mythe et réalité de l'homme noir (À la mémoire de Frantz Fanon). In: Présence Africaine, No. 46, Paris, 2ᵉ trimestre 1963

MPHAHLELE, Ezekiel: The African image. London 1952 (No. 1035)

WAUTHIER, Claude: L'Afrique des Africains. Paris 1964

(The literature and thought of modern Africa. Translated by Shirley Kay. London 1966)

WIEGRÄBE, Paul: Das alte und das neue Lied im Ewelande 2nd edn. Bremen 1938

APPENDIX

SURVEY OF THE MATERIAL

1. Some Statistics for Sub-Saharan Africa ('Agisymba')

In 1964 I completed a *Bibliography of Neo-African Literature*, which was published in 1965–in English, under that title, by André Deutsch, London, and Frederick Praeger, New York. Its purpose was to indicate the writers who must be studied in order to decide whether they belong to neo-African literature. It included only creative literature in the form of published books–collections of poetry, collections of stories, novels, autobiographies, anthologies–and plays that have been produced. I did not include single poems and stories to be found in anthologies, newspapers and magazines.

This bibliography contained 3,566 titles altogether. If I add the titles up to 1st January 1967, the figure is 4,100. I have counted only complete works. For the sixteenth- to eighteenth-century writers I have counted all their works, including essays and treatises; with other writers these shorter works were only included if they had special literary importance and not merely importance *qua* subject matter.

Naturally the Bibliography could not be comprehensive in the light of our present knowledge, so the following figures are still necessarily tentative and incomplete, but refer to my files of 1st January 1967.

In Africa south of the Sahara (the area I have called Agisymba in the German and French editions) there are 805 writers. Just over half of these (425) write in European, the remainder (380) in African languages. There are about 900 works written in European, about 560 in African languages.

There are altogether some 700 African languages. The written works in African languages, however, are distributed over only 41 of these. Most of these works appeared in Southern Africa: 394 works by 265 writers in 18 different languages. The languages here with most works are Southern Sotho in Lesotho with 98, Xhosa and Zulu in South Africa with 72 and 41 respectively, Nyanja in Malawi with

26, Northern Sotho in the Transvaal with 41, Bemba in Zambia with 22. The other languages—I add the number of works in brackets—are Shona in Rhodesia (16), Tswana in Botswana (16), Venda in the Transvaal (13), Lozi in Zambia (10), Tsonga in the Transvaal (10), Ndebele in Rhodesia (9), Tumbuka in Malawi (7), Tonga in Zambia (5), Luvale in Zambia (5), Tswa in the Transvaal (1), Chewa in Malawi (1) and Lenje in Zambia (1).

In West Africa 79 writers produced 106 works in 13 languages. The most important languages here are Twi in Ghana with 40 works and Yoruba in Nigeria with 27 works. Other languages in Ghana, with the number of works produced in brackets again, are Ewe (8), Ga (6), Akuapem (5), Fanti (2) and Nzema (2); in Nigeria, Hausa (9), Ibo (1) and Edo (1). In Cameroun there are 3 works in Bulu and 1 in Duala; in Mauretania, 1 work in Fulani.

In East Africa including Madagascar 35 writers produced 59 works in 9 languages, the most important being Swahili with 29, then Ganda in Uganda with 11 works. The others are Malagasy (7), Rwanda in Ruanda (3), Nyoro-Toro (4) and Acholi (2) in Uganda, Kamba in Kenya, Kikuyu in Kenya and Chaha in Ethiopia with 1 each. (Literature in Amharic is not included. I do not consider it 'Agisymbian'.)

Of the 1,460 works from Sub-Saharan Africa 900 were written in European languages, about half (nearly 500) in English, about a third (over 300) in French; 60 in Portuguese, 5 in Latin, 7 in Cape-Dutch ('Afrikaans'), 6 in German, 1 in Dutch, 1 in Spanish. There are over 200 collections of poetry in European languages, about 150 novels, about 250 collections of stories, over 200 plays, 50 autobiographies; the remainder is distributed between biographies, sermons, speeches and treatises.

Of the 200-odd collections of poetry, over 100 are in French, 60 in English, 30 in Portuguese, 5 in Cape-Dutch ('Afrikaans'), and 1 in Latin. Of the 250-odd collections of stories nearly 185 are in English, 40 in French, 20 in Portuguese, 3 in German. Of the 150 novels 70 are in French, 65 in English, 10 in Portuguese, 2 in Cape-Dutch ('Afrikaans'), 1 in Spanish. Of the 200-odd plays 135 are in English, 75 in French, 1 in Portuguese. There are 40 autobiographies in English, only 7 in French and 3 in German. The difference between the number in English and in French can be explained by the fact that the Africans writing in French preferred to write autobiographical novels (counted among the novels) rather than straight autobiography.

There are 133 anthologies of modern African literature: 1 multilingual, 32 English, 22 French, 17 German, 10 Portuguese, 8 Russian,

4 Italian, Hebrew, 3 Xhosa, Zulu, Danish, 2 Czech, Serbo-Croat, Swedish, Norwegian, Hungarian, Uzbek, 1 Southern Sotho, Northern Sotho, Shona, Dutch, Spanish, Rumanian, Moldavian, Bulgarian, Ukrainian, Finnish, Estonian, Volga Tartar, Ossetic, Azerbaijani.

The population of Sub-Saharan Africa (Agisymba) is reckoned at 209 million people. 805 writers means one writer to every 260,000 people. As there are 425 writers writing in European languages, there is one of these to every 492,000 people.

Fifty-eight per cent of Sub-Saharan Africans live in English-speaking areas, 31 per cent in French-speaking areas, and 6 per cent in Portuguese areas. Of all 805 writers 620 (77 per cent) live in English-speaking areas, 140 (17½ per cent) in French-speaking areas and 35 (4½ per cent) in Portuguese-speaking areas. If we count only the 415 writers who write in European languages–250 in English, 130 in French, and 35 (25) in Portuguese–the ratio in the English-speaking areas is 1 : 485,000 inhabitants, in the French-speaking areas 1 : 500,000, and 1 : 370,000 in the Portuguese-speaking areas. Portugal would seem to come out best in this, but at least 10 of the 35 writers writing in Portuguese are Portuguese nationals. If we exclude *them*–for we have also excluded, of course, the European population of South Africa and their writers from the figures for English-speaking areas–there is one writer to 520,000 inhabitants. If we count all writers together, including those who write in African languages, there is one writer in the English-speaking areas to 198,000 inhabitants, in the French-speaking areas one to 465,000; and in the Portuguese areas the ratio of one to 520,000 remains the same, as there is not a single author who writes in an African language. These statistics reflect the forming of élites, since writers are part of the élite. In French-speaking Africa the élite with a European education is larger, whereas in the English-speaking areas education and literacy are more widespread. The total number of writers would, of course, be far higher if we count also those who have not had any books published but are represented in anthologies and magazines.

2. Statistics for Afro-America

The Afro-Caribbean cultural areas consist of the West Indies and the Guianas. There are the following literary languages there: English, French, Spanish, Dutch, Creole, Papiamento and Surinaams. No book has yet appeared in Surinaams, only single works in anthologies and magazines. Among the Afro-Caribbeans I have included for the statistics below those 'Euro-Caribbeans' who use an Afro-Caribbean style and so clearly belong to neo-African literature.

In round figures, which are probably on the low side, 290 writers produced 850 works, so that with 50 anthologies added there are 900 works altogether. 490 of these were produced by 166 writers in French, 240 by 90 writers in English, 110 by 27 writers in Spanish, 6 by 4 writers in Dutch, 2 by 2 writers in Papiamento, 2 by 1 writer in Creole. There are also 20 anthologies in English, 16 in French, 8 in Spanish, 3 in Dutch and 3 in German.

Of the 850 works there are 440 collections of poetry, 190 novels, 140 plays, 50 collections of stories, 10 autobiographies, and 20 miscellaneous.

In South America 33 writers produced 172 works. 23 writers produced 145 works in Portuguese, and 10 produced 27 in Spanish. There are 104 collections of poetry, 33 novels, 23 collections of stories, 10 plays, 2 autobiographies and 3 anthologies.

In North America I have certainly not been able to find all the Afro-American writers. I did find 600, who produced 1,175 works, all in English except for 3 writers with 26 works and 2 anthologies in French. Altogether there are 520 collections of poetry, 250 novels, 140 plays, 135 autobiographies, 85 anthologies, 65 collections of stories, and 65 miscellaneous. All writers who have not had any books published are again excluded from these statistics.

3. Translations

So far as I could discover there are 645 translations up to the end of 1964. From Sub-Saharan Africa, 178 works have been translated into other languages, from the Caribbean area 134, from South America 14, from North America 320. African and Afro-American literature has been translated into 44 languages. It would be too wearisome to list here the number of translations into the various languages, so I append a table below (Table 8).

4. Magazines

There are a number of magazines devoted to Africa's culture and Afro-American literature. The most important of these is *Présence Africaine, Revue Culturelle du Monde Noir*, founded and edited by Alioune Diop, which has appeared since October 1947 in Paris and Dakar. The first series, Nos. 1 to 14, spans the period from 1947 to

1953. It was then turned into a bi-monthly, which appeared as a new series from April 1955 till January 1961 with Nos. 1 to 35. Since No. 36 (1st quarter 1961) it has appeared as a quarterly, which had reached No. 59 by September 1966. Since No. 32/33 the magazine has also appeared in English. The thinnest issue has 140 pages, special issues have had up to 450, and the average is 250. The editorial address is 42, rue Descartes, Paris.

In Ibadan in Nigeria *Black Orpheus* appears, 'A Journal of African and Afro-American Literature'. This was founded by Ulli Beier and myself in 1957, and we edited Nos. 1 to 6 (November 1959). From No. 7 (June 1960) to No. 13 (November 1964) the editors were Ezekiel Mphahlele, Wole Soyinka and Ulli Beier. Till No. 11 it was published by the General Publications Section of West Nigeria's Ministry of Education in Ibadan. No. 12 appeared in the Mbari Publishing House in Ibadan, and since No. 13 it has been published by Longmans of Nigeria for the Mbari Club in Ibadan. Since No. 17 the editors have been Ulli Beier, Abiola Irele and Ronald Dathorne. At the end of 1966 it had reached No. 20. The size is fifty-two to seventy-two pages, plus eight to twelve pages of pictures on art paper. The publisher's address is P.M.B. 1036, Ikeja, Nigeria.

Since November 1961 the bi-monthly *Transition*, a Journal of the Arts, Culture and Society, has appeared in Kampala, Uganda, founded and edited by Rajat Neogy. Up till the end of 1966 twenty-seven issues had been published, each with fifty-six large pages. The address of publishers and editorial is P.O. Box 20026, Kampala, Uganda.

In Yaoundé, Cameroun, the bilingual quarterly *Abbia*, 'Revue Culturelle Camerounaise, Cameroon Cultural Review', has appeared since February 1963, edited by Bernard Fonlon. In February 1963 the editors were Andrew Maimo and Marcien Towa, in May Towa was joined by Francis Mbassi Manga and Peter Mukoko-Mokeba, while Maimo left. In December Félix Loung came in to replace Towa and also Raphaël Onambele, who was replaced in October 1964 by Jacques-Muriel Nzouankeu. Since August 1965 the editors have been Loung, Nzouankeu and Mfone Moutchia. By the middle of 1966 thirteen numbers had appeared, their size varying between 132 and 308 pages. The editorial address is B.P. 808, Yaoundé, Cameroun.

The Johannesburg quarterly *The Classic* appeared in 1963, having been announced some time before, edited by Nathaniel Nakasa for the Classic Foundation in New York. A literary magazine in South Africa edited by an African, which included emigrants among its contributors, and was 'as non-political as the life of a domestic servant, the life of a Dutch Reformed Church predikant or that of an opulent Johannesburg business-man' (*Classic*, No. 1, page 4), obviously faced considerable difficulties. By December 1964 three numbers had appeared, when it became known that the editor had left South Africa. In 1965 No. 4 appeared, edited by Barney Simon and Casey Motsisi, followed by Nos. 1–3 of vol. 2 in 1966.

In January 1961 the Ghana Society of Writers published the first issue of *Ikyeame*, announced as a quarterly, edited by E. A. Winful, Geormbeeyi Adali-Mortty and Cecile McHardy. The second number did not appear till July 1962, only half as big and described as a half-yearly magazine, edited by Neville Dawes, George Awoonor Williams, Efua Sutherland and MacNeille Steward. Two more issues appeared, one in 1964 and one in 1965. Editorial address is P.O. Box M.15, Accra, Ghana.

In spring 1966 *The Journal of the New African Literature* was started in Stanford, California, mimeographed, and edited by Joseph O. O. Okpaku, a Nigerian, to appear twice a year. At the end of 1966 two numbers had appeared. Editorial address: Box 4392, Stanford University, Stanford, California, U.S.A.

On the West Indian island of Barbados in the Caribbean the literary magazine *Bim* has appeared since 1942 in December and June; it is extremely important for the development of English-speaking writers in the Caribbean area. Founded by E. L. Cozier and W. Therold Barnes, it was edited from 1943 to 1949 (Nos. 3–28) by Barnes and Frank A. Collymore. From 1959 (No. 29) A. N. Forde joined the editorial staff. Since No. 41 (1965) the editors have been Collymore, Forde, L. Edward Brathwaite and Harold Marshall. Up to June 1966 forty-three issues have appeared, containing on average 70 pages. Address is Woodville, Chelsea Road, St. Michael, Barbados.

A similar half-yearly, *Kyk-Over-Al*, had appeared since 1945 in Georgetown, British Guiana, edited by A. J. Seymour for the Society of Writers there; but it ceased publication after No. 28 in 1962.

There are many magazines all over the world which periodically concern themselves with modern African and Afro-American literature and sometimes devote special issues to it; but it would lead too far to list them here. The most important of them are: in Africa, *Drum* (up to 1960 in South Africa, then in London) with other issues in Nigeria and Ghana; *Nigeria Magazine, La Vie Africaine*, followed by *L'Afrique Actuelle* (Paris); *Bingo* (Dakar), *The New African* (London), *Awa* (Dakar); in America, *Crisis* (New York), *Negro*

Digest (Chicago), *Freedomways* (New York), *Africa Report* (Washington), *African Forum* (New York).

From the short-lived magazines which often introduce a new literary conception, mention should be made here of the *Revue Indigène*, which was edited by a group of writers in Port-au-Prince (see page 215) from July 1927 till February 1928; and *Tropiques*, 'Revue Culturelle', which appeared from April 1941 till October 1943 in Fort-de-France on the island of Martinique, edited by René Menil, Aristide Maugée and Aimé Césaire.

There is no magazine in North or South America which concerns itself exclusively with Afro-American literature. The quarterly *Phylon*, a magazine for 'Race and Culture', which appears at the University of Atlanta, Georgia, founded by W. E. B. DuBois and until 1944 also edited by him, is devoted to literature as well, particularly book reviews. Since 1944 the editors have been: De A. Reid till 1949, Mozell Hill till 1958, and Tilman C. Cothran since 1960.

TABLE 8

Translated works from African and Afro-American Literature (sub-Saharan)

Translated into	SUB-SAHARAN AFRICA					W. Indies Guianas	AMERICA		Full Total
	West	Central	East	South	Total		South	North	
German	22	1	3	14	40	31	3	59	133
French	3		1	9	13	16	3	47	79
Russian	13			6	19	16			35
Italian	5			3	8	9		23	40
Spanish	1			1	2	4		33	39
English	9		4	6	19	16			35
Danish	2			4	6	4		25	35
Dutch	4			5	9	4	1	19	33
Swedish	1			4	5	2	1	17	27
Norwegian	2			3	5	1		20	23
Japanese	2				2			6	22
Czech	3			4	7	4	2	12	19
Portuguese				1	1	1		3	14
Hungarian	3			1	4	4		1	11
Polish	1			3	4	5	1	4	11
Serbo-Croat	1			1	2	2	1		9
Rumanian	3			1	4	4	1	3	9
Bulgarian	2				3	2		5	8
Hebrew	1		1	1	2	1		5	8
Finnish								5	5
Turkish								5	5

Translated into	West	SUB-SAHARAN AFRICA			Total	AMERICA			Full Total
		Central	East	South		W. Indies Guianas	South	North	
Estonian	1			1	2	2			4
Slovak	1			1	2	2			4
Slovene				1	1			3	4
Lithuanian	1			1	2	1			3
Latvian				1	1	1		1	3
Ukrainian	1			1	2		1		3
Georgian				1	1	2			3
Uzbek	1			1	2				2
Welsh	1				1				1
Macedonian	1				1				1
Moldavian				1	1				1
Byelorussian				1	1				1
Chuvash				1	1				1
Yoruba	1				1				1
Nyanja				1	1				1
Xhosa								1	1
Arabic	1				1				1
Azerbaijan				1	1				1
Tajik				1	1				1
Bengali								1	1
Gujurati				1	1				1
Korean								1	1
Chinese	?	?	?	?	?	?	?	?	?

INDEX

Page numbers set in italics refer to tables and bibliographies